The War  and

This book is part of the European Science Foundation (ESF) programme 'Occupation in Europe: The Impact of National Socialist and Fascist Rule'.

ISSN: 1753-7894

The European Science Foundation (ESF) is an independent, non-governmental organisation of national research organisations.

Our strength lies in the membership and in our ability to bring together the different domains of European science in order to meet the scientific challenges of the future. ESF's membership currently includes 77 influential national funding agencies, research-performing agencies and academies from 30 nations as its contributing members.

Since its establishment in 1974, ESF, which has its headquarters in Strasbourg with offices in Brussels and Ostend, has assembled a host of research organisations that span all disciplines of science in Europe, to create a common platform for cross-border cooperation.

We are dedicated to supporting our members in promoting science, scientific research and science policy across Europe. Through its activities and instruments ESF has made major contributions to science in a global context. The ESF covers the following scientific domains:

- Humanities
- Life, Earth and Environmental Sciences
- Medical Sciences
- Physical and Engineering Sciences
- Social Sciences
- Marine Sciences
- Nuclear Physics
- Polar Sciences
- Radio Astronomy Frequencies
- Space Sciences

This series includes:

Vol. 1
Surviving Hitler and Mussolini: Daily Life in Occupied Europe
Edited by Robert Gildea, Olivier Wieviorka and Anette Warring

Vol. 2
The War for Legitimacy in Politics and Culture 1936–1946
Edited by Martin Conway and Peter Romijn

Vol. 3
People on the Move: Forced Population Movements in Europe in the Second World War and its Aftermath
Pertti Ahonen, Gustavo Corni, Jerzy Kochanowski, Rainer Schulze, Tamás Stark and Barbara Stelzl-Marx

The War on Legitimacy in Politics and Culture 1936–1946

Edited by
Martin Conway and Peter Romijn

With contributions by:

Erica Carter
Martin Conway
Hans Fredrik Dahl
Benjamin Frommer
Denis Peschanski
Mark Pittaway
Peter Romijn
Mary Vincent
Nico Wouters
Niels Wium Olesen

⊛BERG

Oxford • New York

First published in 2008 by
Berg
Editorial offices:
1st Floor, Angel Court, 81 St Clements Street, Oxford, OX4 1AW, UK
175 Fifth Avenue, New York, NY 10010, USA

Berg is the imprint of Oxford International Publishers Ltd.

Library of Congress Cataloguing-in-Publication Data

The war on legitimacy in politics and culture 1936–1946 / edited by Martin
Conway and Peter Romijn ; with contributions by Erica Carter … [et al.].
    p. cm.—(Occupation in Europe, ISSN 1753-7894)
    Includes bibliographical references and index.
    ISBN-13: 978-1-84520-481-5 (cloth)
    ISBN-10: 1-84520-481-6 (cloth)
    ISBN-13: 978-1-84520-821-9 (pbk.)
    ISBN-10: 1-84520-821-8 (pbk.)
    1. Legitimacy of governments—Europe. 2. Political culture—Europe.
3. Europe—Politics and government—1918–1945. I. Conway, Martin,
1960– II. Romijn, Peter. III. Carter, Erica.

    JN30.W39 2008
    320.9401'1—dc22

                                                           2008017352

British Library Cataloguing-in-Publication Data

A catalogue record for this book is available from the British Library.

ISBN 978 1 84520 481 5 (Cloth)
ISBN 978 1 84520 821 9 (Paper)

Typeset by JS Typesetting Ltd, Porthcawl, Mid Glamorgan
Printed in the United Kingdom by Biddles Ltd, King's Lynn

www.bergpublishers.com

Contents

Illustrations

Contributors

Erica Carter is Professor of German Studies at the University of Warwick. Her publications on German cinema and cultural history include *How German is She? Postwar West German Reconstruction and the Consuming Woman* (1997), *The German Cinema Book* (co-edited 2002) and *Dietrich's Ghosts. The Sublime and the Beautiful in Third Reich Film* (2004).

Martin Conway is Fellow in History at Balliol College, University of Oxford. He has written on various aspects of mid-twentieth-century European history and is the author of *Collaboration in Belgium: Léon Degrelle and the Rexist Movement 1940–44* (1993) and *Catholic Politics in Europe 1918–45* (1997).

Hans Fredrik Dahl is Professor of Media Studies at the University of Oslo. Norway. Among his works are a three-volume history of broadcasting in Norway and the biography of *Vídkun Quisling* (English paperback edition 2007).

Benjamin Frommer is Associate Professor of History at Northwestern University. He specializes in the history of modern East-Central Europe, with a focus on the periods of Nazi and Communist rule, and is the author of *National Cleansing: Retribution against Nazi Collaborators in Postwar Czechoslovakia* (2005).

Niels Wium Olesen is Associate Professor in Twentieth-Century Danish and European History at the University of Aarhus. He has written several articles and books on Danish and European mid-twentieth-century history. His latest book is *Danmark besat. Krig og hverdag 1940–45* (2005).

Denis Peschanski is Director of Research in the Centre National de la Recherche Scientifique (CNRS) as well as a member of the Centre for the Social History of the Twentieth Century at the University of Paris I. He is the author of a number of books including *Vichy 1940–1944. Contrôle et exclusion* (1997) and *La France des camps: l'internement 1938–1946* (2002).

Mark Pittaway is Senior Lecturer in European Studies at the Open University, United Kingdom. He has written on various aspects of the history of twentieth-century Central and Eastern Europe, and is the author of *Eastern Europe, 1939–2000* (2004)

Peter Romijn is the Head of the Research Department of the Netherlands Institute for War Documentation in Amsterdam and Professor of Twentieth-Century History at the University of Amsterdam. He has written on the politics of occupation and regime transition in the Netherlands and Europe in the Second World War, on the persecution of Jews in the Netherlands, and was co-responsible (with Hans Blom) for the report commissioned by the Dutch Government on the 'safe area' of Srebrenica (1995).

Mary Vincent is Professor of History at the University of Sheffield. She has published widely on religion and Right-wing politics in mid-twentieth-century Spain and also has an interest in the history of gender. Her most recent book is *Modern Spain 1833–2002: People and State* (2007).

Nico Wouters has a doctorate in history from the University of Gent. He has published many articles and several books (in Dutch and English) on local government, administrative collaboration and the persecution of the Jews during the Second World War, in Belgium as well as in an international perspective. His current scientific focus lies with the public treatment of war, occupation and collective trauma in post-1945 north-western Europe. He currently works for the city of Mechelen as the coordinator of the city's heritage policy. He is also a guest lecturer at the University of Antwerp.

Foreword

This book is intended as a collective volume that reflects the work of all of the members of the research team of the European Science Foundation (ESF) Programme on the Impact of National-Socialist and Fascist Occupation in Europe, 2000–2005. Chapters 1, 2 and 3 were principally written by the editors, Martin Conway and Peter Romijn. Benjamin Frommer was the co-author of Chapter 2, and Denis Peschanski assisted with the preparation of Chapter 3. Chapter 4 was written by Nico Wouters with Niels Wium Olesen and Martin Conway as co-authors. Chapter 5 was written jointly by Mary Vincent and Erica Carter. Chapter 6 was written by Mark Pittaway with Hans-Fredrik Dahl as co-author. We would, however, like to express the collective nature of the volume and in particular our debt to the other members of the team who participated in the workshops on which it is based: its initial co-director Pierre Ayçoberry, Stefania Bernini, Gianmarco Bresadola, Luigi Ganapini, Wichert ten Have, and Anna Maria Vinci. We are also grateful to Conny Kristel and Hans Blom for their support and encouragement as well as to Madelise Blumenroeder for her guidance through the complexities of a European research project. We are also indebted to Dara Price for her expert work in compiling the Index. As an exploration of what we regard as a new subject, we recognize that the conclusions presented here can only be provisional and we hope that they will act as a stimulus to work by others.

Martin Conway and Peter Romijn

–1–

Political Legitimacy in Mid-Twentieth-Century Europe
An Introduction*

I

This book is intended as an exploration of the role that the phenomenon of legitimacy played in the history of mid-twentieth-century Europe from the crises of the 1930s to the forms of political settlement that had emerged in Europe, both East and West, by the end of the 1940s. By undertaking this collective task, we are keenly aware of the necessarily tentative nature of the arguments we advance and the conclusions we reach. The concept of legitimacy (however one chooses to define it) has not featured prominently in the historiography of twentieth-century Europe and the major preoccupation that led us to launch the project from which this volume has emerged was to discover how valid it was to consider the highly familiar history of Europe during this period through the prism of legitimacy.[1] In doing so, we hope that our work may act as a stimulus to further research and may also contribute, albeit modestly, to a reshaping of the ways in which historians approach the political history of Europe's evolution from the rich and chaotic fluidity of the 1930s to the more fixed landscape of the decades that followed the Second World War. As historians working on different states and themes in twentieth-century European history, we were initially drawn together by the shared sense that there is a need for a more integrated approach to the political history of this era. The considerable outpouring of works over the last three decades on political movements and regimes of the 1930s and, more recently, on the experience of occupation rule in wartime Europe is now being supplemented by substantial work on the immediate post-war period.[2] This historiographical effort has brought considerable rewards in terms of a much more sophisticated understanding of the dynamics of the various authoritarian and fascist regimes of the era as well as a recognition of the deep complexity that characterized relations between occupiers, liberators and populations in wartime Europe. What has, however, perhaps tended to be absent from these works has been a consideration of the more durable evolutions in political culture that took place in

*This chapter was written by Martin Conway, with Peter Romijn as co-author.

the era of the 'long Second World War' from the economic and political upheavals of the early 1930s to the terminus that was reached at the end of the 1940s. Within that roughly fifteen-year period, the frontiers between the pre-war, the wartime and the post-war, though often recognized to be in many respects arbitrary and misleading,[3] have nevertheless tended to serve as obstacles to a broader perception of the political transitions that took place across the mid-century era as a whole.

Central to the approach adopted in this volume is therefore a concern to read *through* the history of the 1930s and 1940s by concentrating less on the fast-moving changes in political regime that took place in many areas of Europe than on the manifold ways in which those changes influenced, and in turn were influenced by, more long-term evolutions in political culture. This need for a more unitary approach to the political history of the era carries with it a need to recognize that the political cannot be divorced from the social and cultural realities within which it was embedded. This is not a novel point. Much of the best writing on pre-war and wartime Europe has long recognized that, although changes in regime were often provoked by the fortunes of war or the manoeuvrings of political elites, the success and, above all, the durability of these regimes depended to a considerable extent on their ability to combine the conquest of the summits of power with viable forms of interaction with social institutions and local communities.[4] This was not easy, either for externally imposed regimes of occupation (whatever their origin) or for those internally generated regimes (be they of the Left or Right) that in the name of revolution sought to bring about a reordering of political and social relations. The sinews of bureaucratic and military power had to be supplemented by predictable forms of give and take with the panoply of local notables, priests, trade-union officials and others who had carved out influential intermediate roles in Europe's modern political cultures. Such social negotiation, moreover, could not be separated from the need to integrate the exercise of political power within recognizable cultural frames of reference. The modern instruments of propaganda could of course manufacture perceptions of regimes, and regimes such as those in Nazi Germany, Fascist Italy and Nationalist Spain strove mightily to do so. But the limited and hard-won success of these propaganda campaigns indicated that the cultural sphere was not simply the malleable tool of Europe's political rulers.[5] Here again the imposing edifice of modern state power depended at least in part upon its ability to act, and to be seen to act, in ways which accorded with less immediately visible notions of how and in whose name political power should be exercised.

Building on these insights, the contention of this book is that the phenomenon of legitimacy provides a valuable means of approaching the complex and multilateral forms of interaction between rulers and ruled in mid-twentieth-century Europe. Problems of definition can hardly be avoided in a project of this kind and will be considered at greater length later in this chapter.[6] For now, however, it is necessary to state that in using the term legitimacy we are concerned not so much with formal or legal realities as with an informal set of values that existed within Europe's different political cultures and which acted on rulers and ruled alike. These values were neither uniform nor unchanging but, rather like the flexible tissue that holds together two bones, stretched in different directions (and on occasions broke) under the impact of different pressures. It follows from this perception of legitimacy that we are interested less in using legitimacy as an external measure by which to judge how far a particular regime was 'legitimate' or 'illegitimate' as with examining how notions of what constituted legitimate government influenced the political actors and populations of Europe. Thus, to take a highly familiar example, we are not concerned to establish whether the Third Republic, the Vichy regime, De Gaulle's *Gouvernement provisoire de la République Française* and the Fourth Republic were the legitimate French regimes of the era but with how far notions of what constituted legitimate government acted as an influence on the actions of the successive French rulers (and indeed German, Italian and Allied occupation authorities) and the responses of the population.

This approach, which might be termed 'legitimacy-in-action', does, we believe, provide a point of confluence for a number of the more fruitful trends in the recent historiography of Europe during the 1930s and 1940s. By reorienting attention away from the declarations of rulers to their interactions with the societies they ruled, it reflects the recognition that the pretensions of even the most aggrandising of state authorities were dependent on the willingness of the formal and informal agents of local power to implement their commands. This was particularly so in the context of wartime, when the demands imposed by rulers escalated and when the consequences of military campaigns led to the imposition of regimes of occupation on many European states. In these improvised circumstances, rulers and ruled interacted with each other on the basis of unwritten rules of engagement. German officials in France in 1940 or French officials in Germany in 1945 were operating in largely unknown territory in which the paralegal conventions governing the rules of modern war were less important than the urgent need to impose effective authority. The strategies they adopted varied greatly from the razed-earth terror of Nazi rule in some of the Eastern Territories to the very deliberate policy adopted by German officials in much of Western Europe in 1940 and by British and American officials in post-war Germany of working through pre-existing elites and institutions. Common to all of the myriad variations in local circumstance was, however, the disappearance of the routinized structures of modern government. As invaders, liberators, state officials, mayors and resisters co-existed or confronted each other across the largely destructed political landscape of Europe in the final war years, so the norms of what constituted legitimate government came to acquire both a new urgency and prominence.

At the same time, legitimacy is not, we would stress, some form of magic key that can be used to unlock the political history of the era. The relative importance of legitimacy varied considerably in different areas of Europe. Events in many areas of western and northern Europe were in this respect very different from the experience of some areas of central and eastern Europe. In the brutal and multilateral wars that occurred in the Balkans and the eastern borderlands of Poland within and beyond the Second World War, undiluted force trampled underfoot any notion of what constituted legitimate government.[7] Everywhere, moreover, the regimes that emerged after 1945 rested primarily (and often all too explicitly) on the outcome of military conflicts and the material sinews of bureaucratic state power. This was perhaps most visible in eastern Europe, where the Soviet occupation authorities defined what could, and could not, happen in the post-war era. But it was also true in much of western Europe where the constraining framework of the American-led military and security structures imposed a 'limited sovereignty' on individual states.[8] Power, in this sense, was very much a 'top-down' phenomenon in Cold War Europe, exercised through a state authority that in most areas of Europe was considerably stronger than had been the case in the pre-war era, but which also operated under the protective aegis of wider political, military and economic alliances.

The differing degrees of success with which the state authorities of the wartime and post-war eras succeeded in making themselves appear acceptable to their subjects or citizens do, however, indicate that legitimacy was more complex than a consequence of the possession of the intimidating instruments of governmental authority. Power might, in the all-too-familiar truism, have rested ultimately on the barrel of a gun, or on the more subtle instruments of modern state bureaucracies, but the processes by which Europeans came to accept such power as legitimate were on the whole distinctly more complex. The diverse legacies of monarchical and religious authority, as well as the more recent mobilizing forces of democracy, nationalism and class identity, ensured that there was no single definition of what constituted legitimate power. Regimes of different political and ideological hues, therefore, seized upon different facets of these cultures of legitimacy in order to buttress their pretensions to rule. The differences between success and failure in this process tended to be more relative than absolute. There was no clear dividing line between regimes that were and were not regarded as legitimate in Europe during the 1930s and 1940s. Much depended both on the wider political and military context in which they acted but also on the much more micro context of the actions of the local agents of distant and often rather hypothetical authorities and on their ability to adapt to the needs and expectations of the communities in which they acted.[9]

Such local diversity serves as a reminder of the divergent trajectories of Europe's states, regions and communities through the upheavals of the 1930s and 1940s. The war experiences of, say, the cities of Turin, Toulouse and Tallinn were very different, just as were those of the two similarly rural but in almost every other respect very different regions both known confusingly in English as Galicia. These differences were ones of wartime circumstance but also of political culture. The particular bundles of beliefs about the sources and practice of legitimate rule present in these societies reflected the diverse legacies of history as well as the more recent impact of different state regimes and political movements. Consequently, not merely the languages they used but also, more profoundly, the very ways in which Europeans thought about their rulers and imagined their political communities differed considerably. Nor were attitudes uniform within particular societies or regions. The pillars of social class, confessional or ethnic identity and political ideology, which were such a prominent element of the process of political modernization from the mid-nineteenth century onwards, generated diverse and sometimes antagonistic conceptions of legitimate government. These could, as in Spain in 1936 or in Greece in the mid-1940s, contribute to the explicit violence of civil war. Almost everywhere, however, the issue of what constituted political legitimacy formed an important focus for the ways in which European citizens disagreed with each other in parliaments, on the streets, in their workplaces or around tables in cafes.

In the light of these caveats, this book will eschew any artificial attempt to suggest a standard model of legitimacy. The role and nature of legitimacy varied greatly across the almost infinitely complex map of mid-century Europe. What it does seek to argue, however, is that notions of the origins of political power and the ways in which that power should be rightly exercised constituted an important element of the less visible substratum of Europe's political cultures. During times of constitutional rupture or national crisis, notably in the aftermath of military defeat or during the chaos of the final war years, the issue of where legitimate political authority lay often acquired a burning urgency. But in other more 'normal' times it also formed an influential if less immediately apparent component of the norms of political debate. Seen in this way, as a set of values which influenced the actions of political elites and the responses of the ruled alike, the concept of legitimacy does, we argue, help to explain the political history of Europe during this time of often abrupt transitions in political regime. Though those changes were dictated by the fortunes of war and the manoeuvrings, both local and national, of rival pretenders to power, they took place within a continuity of political cultures. Europe, in that sense, was by the middle of the twentieth century predominantly an 'old continent', where the political, ideological and social conflicts of the preceding decades had left a rich accretion of assumptions about the rules, procedures and forms that should govern the exercise of political power. It was by using those norms to their own ends but also by being seen to work within them that political rulers came to acquire legitimacy in their own eyes and, more importantly, in the eyes of those whom they sought to rule.

II

Analyses of political legitimacy have hitherto tended to be notable mainly for their absence from the historiography of twentieth-century Europe. Historians of earlier periods in European history as well as of non-European societies have long been attentive to the way in which the exercise of power by all rulers, be they sacred or secular, putative or actual, has to be located in a complex matrix of beliefs, rituals and practices.[10] In contrast, few works on the twentieth century address directly the issue of legitimacy. There are undoubtedly several reasons for this relative neglect. At its heart, however, would seem to lie a deeply rooted perception of the way in which modernity transformed the nature of political power. From the era of the French Revolution onwards, Europe was dominated by the rapid growth of secular state apparatuses, which extended their authority remorselessly over the social institutions, local communities and populations that fell within the boundaries of new or radically transformed nation-states. Whether perceived in a Marxist sense as the agent of dominant class interests or as an institution floating above the society it ruled, the state possessed massively increased material resources as well as new ideological justifications of its authority. Indeed, the political history of Europe in the later nineteenth and twentieth centuries became in many respects the history of states. Acting variously in the name of the nation or the *Volk*, the people or the proletariat, and the emperor, the *Duce* or the Republic, the states and their regimented armies of officials brought a new culture of bureaucratic uniformity to Europe flattening much of the pre-existing undergrowth of *ancien régime* convention, local autonomy and pre-industrial tradition.[11]

Such an approach has, of course, many strengths. In particular, when applied to the era of international, national and political crises inaugurated by the First World War, it rightly focuses attention on the material scaffolding of power which underpinned the determined efforts of rulers to conscript, tax and mobilize (or lull into quiescence) their citizens. Confronted by the manifold challenges of total warfare, economic change and revolutionary subversion, many of the rulers of Europe in what Eric Hobsbawm has termed 'The Age of Catastrophe' were effectively engaged in a grim process of 'regime struggle' in which the success of the various pretenders to power was measured more in terms of their ability to extract sacrifices from their populations than any more equal social contract.[12] For the many millions of Europeans who experienced the *Diktats* of total warfare, the chaos of revolutionary upheaval or the suffering of forced ethnic migration or genocide, political power had a grim but uncomplicated character. In these cases, legitimacy had little meaning. Power was the stark imposition of will on populations who had the choice to submit, to evade its reach or to try to manipulate it to their own ends. Seen at its most extreme in the killing fields of eastern Europe during the Second World War, this 'earth-shattering explosion of immense state-sponsored violence' was, as Ian Kershaw has argued, the dominant force in European history in the first half of the twentieth century – and one that extended its destructive power well beyond the European continent.[13]

At the same time, however, the modern explosion of European state power should not be allowed to disguise the extent to which even the most imposing, or oppressive, state apparatuses were embedded in complex grids of social relations. In particular, the tendency to focus on what one might term the self-made history of the state can distract attention from the social and cultural values in Europe's political cultures from which the state derived its authority but which also constrained it.[14] This is especially so in the case of the multitude of non-democratic regimes that emerged in Europe from the 1920s to the 1940s. Given their lack (in most cases) of a convincing electoral mandate, historians of these regimes have turned instead to studying public opinion in order to address the vexed question of how far the populations supported the actions carried out in their names. Starting with the fundamental work of Ian Kershaw on Nazi Germany, but subsequently extending to the study of Vichy France and the post-war Communist regimes of central and eastern Europe, such studies have done much to enrich our understanding of the interaction of non-democratic regimes with their populations.[15] But, as the authors of a number of these studies have been quick to recognize, the study of public opinion presents several methodological problems.[16] To the obvious difficulty of interpreting the subjective reports of partisan observers, police officials and civilian bureaucrats are added the problem of reducing the complex and often contradictory attitudes held by populations about their rulers to a daily opinion poll. In the cases of both the Third Reich and Vichy France, for example, historians have long recognised that the pervasive unpopularity of many of the regimes' measures and personnel went together with a pervasive acceptance of their existence and a resilient confidence in Hitler and Pétain.[17] In part, the explanation of such apparently divergent attitudes lies in the impact of mass propaganda. Using to the full the modern panoply of radio, cinema and education, regimes of the mid-twentieth century did much to frame the way in which their citizens perceived their rulers and the world in general. Propaganda, however, as historians now recognise, was often a blunt or even ineffectual tool, which at most could encourage populations to bend towards the ideological ambitions of their rulers.[18] The politically experienced citizens of mid-twentieth-century Europe were not passive tools of the pseudo-scientists of mass propaganda, and their responses to regimes were an amalgam of prior beliefs, present perceptions and quiet calculations of self-interest.

It is in this more complex understanding of the frameworks within which popular attitudes take shape that concepts such as legitimacy have a role to play. The 'organization of consent', to employ the fruitful term of Victoria de Grazia, was an integral element of the form of government developed not only by Italian Fascism but by a wide panoply of authoritarian regimes.[19] The almost three million women enrolled in Mussolini's *Massaie Rurali* by 1943 or the 950,000 members of the *Freie Deutsche Jugend* in the German Democratic Republic in 1949 were indicative of the way in which the ambitions of these regimes were not limited to ruling over society but also to ruling through it.[20] This redrawing, or effacement, of the frontiers between the public and the private brought the state much more intimately into the domestic sphere; but it simultaneously ensured that public responses owed much to the private interests of individuals, families and communities. *Eigensinn*, or the sense of self-interest that influenced forms of accommodation with authoritarian, fascist or communist regimes, provides one means of exploring what Alan McDougall has termed 'the often blurred frontiers between state and society' in mid-twentieth-century Europe.[21] But it would be misleading to trace the behaviour of individuals and groups under such regimes solely in terms of a calculus of their self-interest. The Nazi dictatorship, Peukert reminds us, 'was unable to abolish the reality of industrial society, but it did, through propaganda, impede the perception of that reality.'[22] Moreover, socially rooted notions of what constituted right, proper or legitimate government continued to mediate the ways in which individuals responded to regimes, even as those regimes were engaged in oppression of them. As Luisa Passerini well demonstrates in her study of Turin during the Fascist era, working-class Italians often combined a dismissive attitude to the symbols and rhetoric of the regime with a mediated acceptance of its existence.[23] In that case, as indeed in Germany after 1933, popularity was a less important measure than the extent to which the new regime succeeded through its manner of operation in coming to be regarded as legitimate. Thus, whatever many Germans may have felt about the actions and ideology of the regime, it is clear that the sense that the Nazi rulers were the legitimate rulers of Germany acted as a constraint on individual and collective acts of disobedience. Conversely, the failure of the Vichy rulers in France to neutralize the alternative poles of legitimacy represented by its internal and external opponents emboldened elites and individuals in their disengagement from Pétain's regime.[24] The contest for legitimacy that developed in France at both the national and local level was replicated in many other areas of Europe during the middle years of the 1940s. A variety of pretenders to power each claimed for themselves this elusive but powerful quality, drawing on the disparate resources of legality, history, patriotism and revolutionary rectitude. The success with which they did so owed much to the means at their disposal and the skill with which they manipulated the political circumstances of the moment. But in the subsequent process of settling out from which the post-war order gradually emerged, legitimacy was once again a significant factor. It was by rooting their possession of the levers of political, military and administrative power within a broader culture of legitimacy that the circumstantial rulers of the immediate post-war era provided their regimes of occupation or liberation, of continuity or revolution, with a more profound basis for their subsequent rule.

III

The relative neglect of the concept of legitimacy in the field of contemporary European history has had the consequence that much of the writing on the subject has emanated from political theorists. The works of Juan Linz, Rodney Barker and others have done much to illuminate the various resources exploited by regimes of the contemporary era in order to build and reinforce their legitimacy.[25] For many of these writers, the famous threefold distinction of the sources of legitimacy in tradition, charisma and bureaucratic state organization elucidated by Max Weber remains the essential point of departure.[26] One effect of this Weberian influence is the considerable emphasis placed on the changes in state power and organization that were taking place around the time that Weber himself was writing. According to this account, up until the mid-nineteenth century, legitimacy lay predominantly in the warp and weft of traditional world views, in which rulers and ruled alike aligned their behaviour according to precepts based on precedence and custom. Thereafter, however, the dominant determinant of legitimacy passed to the modern state structures. Due process, predictability, legality and equity were the essential qualities of the new culture of state power by which the elected rulers and, more especially, the state bureaucrats invested their exercise of power with the aura of legitimacy. Cutting across this process, and also destabilizing it, however, was the impact not only of twentieth-century forms of personal rule but more pervasively of charismatic political ideologies of collective liberation, such as nationalism, fascism and communism. Consequently, much political-science writing on legitimacy has emphasized the transience and instability of legitimacy during the twentieth century. In some fortunate territories, most commonly associated with a 'Western' liberalism, the transition to modernity has created a 'deep' legitimacy based around constitutional rule, democratic accountability and respect for legality. Elsewhere, however, notably in the post-colonial world, the chaotic impacts of warfare, economic change and political instability have prevented the emergence of more than a 'thin' veneer of legitimacy.[27]

At the same time, however, Barker and others have been at pains to stress that the subject of their enquiry is not so much reality as the perception of reality. Again following Weber, they emphasize that legitimacy was located not in legal or historical fact but in the *belief* of the ruled in the legitimacy of their rulers. Hence, writers such as Barker and François Bourricaud have followed Weber's lead in demonstrating the futility of normative approaches that seek to arrive at judgements about the legitimacy of regimes on the basis of a checklist of the attributes of 'good government'.[28] Given the inevitable heterogeneity and cultural specificity of any such list, they have pleaded for a reorientation of attention away from what Barker terms the 'metaphor' of legitimacy to the more tangible processes of legitimation. All rulers, they argue, engage to a greater or lesser degree in a continuous process of self-legitimation, drawing on a wide variety of legal, historical and ideological props to justify their rule to others and perhaps more especially to themselves.[29]

The Weberian emphasis on legitimation has an obvious appeal to historians. From Napoleon to Hitler and beyond, historians have been drawn towards studying the ways in which dominant rulers sought to 'sell' their possession of power to their people. Indeed, much of the recent historiographical preoccupation with phenomena such as myth, memory and cults of personality has been based implicitly on the assumption that all political forces seek more or less consciously to manipulate the legacies of past history to their own ends.[30] However, as the sternest recent critic of the Weberian framework, David Beetham, has energetically argued, the privileging of legitimation over legitimacy can be unduly self-limiting. When applied to a particular historical context, it tends to focus almost exclusively on the actions of the rulers at the expense of the reception of their actions, gestures and words within the population. Thus, if studies of legitimation are to avoid becoming the analysis of 'one hand clapping', they must also confront the larger and more historically and culturally challenging question as to how far the perception of a ruler within a particular society is determined by the values current within that society.[31]

This, in turn, Beetham argues, requires a return to the concept of legitimacy, approached not as an ideal-type but as a historically relative concept in which the degree of legitimacy possessed by a particular regime can be measured in terms of its practice of power, the evidence of consent and, perhaps most importantly, the extent to which its actions can be justified in terms of the values current within society.[32] Whatever the arbitrariness of certain of his categories, there is much in Beetham's concept of 'legitimacy-in-context' with which historians of twentieth-century Europe can readily empathize. By recognizing what one might term the specific genetic make-up of societies, Beetham rightly acknowledges that analyses of legitimacy require the simultaneous study of the actions and values of rulers and ruled alike. Catapulted into power by elections, revolution, military victory (or defeat) or social conflict, rulers and regimes throughout the twentieth century set about legitimizing their occupation of power by plundering indiscriminately and somewhat opportunistically the tombolas of legality, historical precedence, national identity and ideology. But the success or failure of such ventures depended on the degree of convergence between the regime they were seeking to create and the expectations and norms of the society within which it operated. This rendered certain political projects more viable than others. Or, as Stalin is alleged to have remarked to the post-war Polish prime minister, Stanislaw Mikolajczyk, 'Communism on a German is like a saddle on a cow.'[33]

Building on the work of Beetham as a well as of historians of other societies and periods, it therefore seems possible to construct an historical approach to the phenomenon of legitimacy which perceives it as a dynamic and fluid reality that existed in the critical space between rulers and ruled. The actions of regimes helped to contribute to their legitimation (or its inverse) by constructing legal rituals, forms of popular endorsement and propagandistic accounts of their origins and ideology. At the same time, however, concepts of what constituted legitimate political power existed within European societies beyond the direct control of rulers. These concepts evolved in response to events; but in the mature political landscapes of mid-twentieth-century Europe they were also and primarily the legacies of past history. Like the accretions of successive geological periods, they lay somewhat imperfectly on top of each other. Some of these were essentially historical in nature: legitimate government was that which was (or could plausibly claim to be) the heir to an unbroken process of succession and adaptation. Some, in contrast, were more legal or contract-based: legitimate government was that which derived from a founding constitution ratified by the assent of the people or their duly constituted representatives. Others, again, drew their strength from less formal but no less tangible realities: legitimate government was that which derived from the will of the nation, the people, the *Volk* or a universal or more particular God. But some, too, were focused less on origins than on performance: legitimate government was that which behaved according to recognizable standards of predictability and equity and which was seen to meet the collective and individual needs of the populace. Common to all of these notions of legitimacy was, however, an inescapable element of overlap and inconsistency. The textual clarity of law and the rhetorical simplicity of declarations by political leaders gave way to the much more murky textures of socially rooted norms and assumptions in which the traditional and the modern, the democratic and the anti-democratic and the secular and the religious were intertwined.

Such a historical analysis of the phenomenon of legitimacy within European societies over the twentieth century will therefore differ in two important respects from the approaches privileged by political theorists. Firstly, it offers a broader approach to power than a strictly political definition. By focusing on the long-term factors that determined what constituted legitimate rule within particular societies, it re-orientates attention away from a preoccupation with the actions of rulers. Rulers could, and in a number of prominent cases emphatically did, influence the way in which twentieth-century Europeans thought about the political communities to which they belonged. But the evolution of concepts of legitimacy within European societies tended to take the form of a steadily flowing river in which changes of direction were more gradual than abrupt. Secondly, by stressing the historical specificity of societies, it militates against any overarching model of legitimacy that neglects the differences between political cultures and their evolution over time. This also warns against approaching legitimacy with the assumptions of the present. The convergence of European regimes, north and south and latterly east and west, towards a particular form of democratic rule in the final decades of the twentieth century might suggest that liberal-democratic regimes *must* have possessed greater legitimacy earlier in the century than alternative forms of government. Though that might have been the case in some states and regions of Europe, it was far from being universally so. Democratic values were neither universal nor capable of a single interpretation.[34] A wide range of political ideologies of both Left and Right laid claim to the democratic label, and one of the virtues of a historical study of legitimacy is to demonstrate the plurality of political values that existed within twentieth-century Europe.

IV

If these points suggest the particular contribution which historians can make to the study of legitimacy, it must also be emphasized that inserting legitimacy into the political history of mid-twentieth-century Europe changes, if only modestly, the nature of the questions which historians are accustomed to ask about the political evolutions of the period. First and foremost, it encourages historians to take a step back from the actions and discourses of rulers. Rather as, for example, the work of Quentin Skinner has been concerned to analyse the 'social and intellectual matrix' from which the concept of the state emerged in Renaissance Europe, so there is perhaps a need for historians of contemporary Europe to look beyond the ideological constructs of political forces to the commonplace assumptions about the nature of just power that were rooted in European political culture.[35] Secondly, and concomitantly, legitimacy leads us to examine the political history of Europe in the 1930s and 1940s in ways other than an assessment of winners and losers. The political and subsequently military victories of fascism, their reversal in the final years of the Second World War and the consequent ascendancy of liberal-democratic and Soviet-communist models of government in western and eastern Europe have understandably focused attention on the rise and fall of regimes. The study of legitimacy, however, reorientates attention towards the broader operation of political power and to continuities that transcended the changes of regimes. Finally, it also implies directing our attention away from national events to the fabric of local life. The priority of local reality in wartime life has become a prominent theme of much of the recent historiography.[36] The realities of foreign occupation destroyed or marginalized national authorities and established new boundaries, even severing contacts between closely neighbouring towns.[37] The war simultaneously widened and narrowed horizons. Soldiers departed communities for distant lands, or arrived as exotic visitors, while the evolution of the global military conflict led Europeans to discover through maps in newspapers or pinned up on their walls the geography of the Caucasus or North Africa.[38] But, perhaps especially for women, the war gave a new importance to the local *Heimat* defined by the visible communities of family and neighbourhood. In this arena, the war was often profoundly disruptive. In the words used by the inhabitants of Montefegatesi, a village in the Tuscan Apennines, it was the *rastrellamento*, the rake that turns over all of the particles in the soil.[39] But alongside its disruptive impact, the war also served to reveal the assumptions and beliefs within local societies and which became particularly visible in their interaction with the succession of invading, occupying and liberating forces.

The radical diversity of these local experiences as well as of national circumstance must render redundant any attempt to write a unitary narrative of the 'struggle for legitimacy' in Europe during the 1930s and 1940s. To the pre-existing differences of political culture were added the very different and unequal impacts of the war years. Nevertheless, as this chapter has already tried to suggest, there are a number of themes that in our view emerge from the study of the history of Europe in this period through the prism of legitimacy. The first of these must be the complexity of the assumptions about the origins and nature of legitimate government current in Europe in the 1930s. The transitions in many European states over the previous fifty years towards a mass basis to political life had invested governmental power with a new and potent source of legitimacy, the will of the people, be that expressed formally through the rituals of elections, parliamentary or presidential, or less formally through the mobilization of crowds. This, however, had not effaced earlier values. Indeed, one of the most evident features of the disruptions in the exercise of governmental power that occurred through the war years was the way in which such disruptions revealed the strength of what one might regard as outmoded assumptions about the nature of governmental power. The legitimacy attached to the person of the monarch was, for example, highly visible in the history of the Low Countries or of Denmark during the war years; while Franco expropriated to his own ends the symbolism and imagery of a monarchical and Catholic 'True Spain'.[40] At a local level, too, the absence or dismissal in many areas of Europe of the democratically invested authorities created a space that was occupied, often with remarkable ease, by local committees or notables. Aristocrats, men of substance by virtue of wealth or family name and priests and bishops are figures who emerge prominently from many local histories of the war years. As the intermediaries between the communities and the external world, they acquired a pre-eminence that in many respects appeared to mark a return to the habits of an earlier age.[41]

The co-existence of different sources of legitimacy reveals the difficulty of speaking of any decisive moment of transition to an age of democratic modernity within twentieth-century Europe. Democracy, in its various contested definitions, was not a hegemonic principle in European political culture in this period. The practice of democratic participation, at least among adult males, had by the inter-war years a lineage stretching back over several decades at the national and more especially the local level in many states of northern and western Europe.[42] In these regions, Europeans had become accustomed to the anonymized rituals of elections and had come to value the opportunity that they provided to reject those who had failed to represent their interests adequately.[43] As the numerous inter-war electoral successes of movements of the extreme Left and Right well demonstrated, such participation, however, did not necessarily imply an acceptance of the norms of pluralist politics. Indeed, by the 1930s those politics had given way in much of Europe to regimes based on very different principles. The heterogeneous movements and regimes often misleadingly described as 'fascist' did at least have in common a wish to break with the model of parliamentary and 'responsible' government that had developed since the late nineteenth century. In place of the pretence by which corrupt parties and incompetent politicians claimed to rule in the name of the people, they offered a new political order based variously on the principles of Nation, People, Faith and Revolution.[44] The difficulties they experienced in translating what Paxton has termed these 'mobilizing passions'[45] into constitutional reality suggests that, regardless of the diplomatic and military choices that they made during the Second World War, the duration of many of the authoritarian regimes of the 1930s and 1940s would anyway have been finite. Their institutional failure did not, however, imply the demise of the forms of legitimacy on which they had built. As historians of fascism have long recognized, the anti-democratic revolt drew on the aspiration for a more united community.[46] At the most obvious level, appeals to the bonds of national or racial identity possessed the ability to mobilize millions of Europeans in the inter-national and inter-ethnic conflicts of the Second World War. The willingness of millions of Europeans (on all of the many sides of the conflict) to sacrifice their lives for their nation, as well as to murder those within and without who were perceived as the enemies of that nation, stands as an incontestable monument to the emotional forces that transcended the conventional politics of more quotidian times. Nor were these non-democratic forms of legitimacy solely secular in origin. The engagement of the churches, and their clergy and laity, with certain of the authoritarian regimes of the era demonstrated how Christian notions of 'just rule', be they Catholic, Protestant or Orthodox, provided an important further well-spring of assumptions about the nature of legitimate political power very different from those of democratic liberalism.[47]

Given the strength of these various traditions, the second theme therefore to emerge from this study is the limited ability of rulers to shape assumptions about legitimacy current in European societies. That dominant figures such as Mussolini, Atatürk or, of course, Hitler succeeded to some extent in making their citizens think differently about the political communities of which they were members is of course beyond dispute. Nevertheless, the study of legitimacy in this period must also to some extent be a study in anti-propaganda. The efforts of rulers and their agents to mould public attitudes tended to have consequences that were more immediate than profound. Unattractive policies could be rendered palatable and the images of unprepossessing rulers enhanced[48] but the central ways in which Europeans perceived the nature of their governments changed only slowly. The disabused manner in which citizens of all convictions tended to judge those who ruled over them was indicative not merely of a certain cynicism but also of how political attitudes were formed by influences of family, community and social class that were often stronger than those of regimes. Rulers remained, as Lawrence Wylie stressed in his pioneering anthropological study of a southern French village, 'them' rather than 'us', and the standards by which they were judged were similarly distant from the control of rulers.[49]

By emphasizing the relative independence of public attitudes, the study of legitimacy serves to highlight the limits of state power. This was especially apparent during the hiatuses in national government that occurred in many European states during the war years. Citizens, at least in much of north-western Europe, had become accustomed over the previous decades to the dictates and regulations emanating from public authorities. Obedience, or at least broad conformity, in matters of education, public health, taxation and even conscription had become, at least for the majority, a matter of routine. That remained the case for many Europeans, notably those in neutral states such as Sweden and Switzerland, throughout the war years. But in those many areas that experienced the dislocations of foreign rule Europeans were 'liberated' from these received assumptions. Axis or Allied occupation authorities, the emissaries of *émigré* governments or the representatives of self-proclaimed collaborationist regimes or resistance committees could not assume compliance with their dictates. Such acceptance had to be earned. One means by which rulers could do so was by providing demonstrably fair and efficient government; another was to root their forms of rule within the languages, rituals and forms of behaviour customary to the state, region or community. All wartime rulers were in this sense imperialist, and like all such exercises in imperial rule their success depended on a judicious mixture of force, persuasion and incentives to conform. That, broadly speaking, American and British regimes of occupation were more skilful in achieving this goal than were those of the Soviet Union or of Nazi Germany owed much to their more restrained use of force but also to their willingness to draw local intermediaries into their exercise of power. The German occupiers, and more especially the *Wehrmacht*, well understood this principle, which they implemented in many areas of Western (though not Eastern) Europe during the early years of the war.[50] Subsequently, however, the internal radicalization of power within the Third Reich as well as the more determined forms of opposition they encountered largely destroyed the tentative forms of *modus vivendi* that had developed. Rather than working with the norms and institutions of the societies that they occupied, the German forces became drawn into a crude and increasingly ineffectual attempt to impose their will on them.[51] The New Order regimes established in many areas of Europe during the early war years followed much the same trajectory. The forms of legitimacy that they possessed at the moment of their creation were dissipated, as their revolutionary pretensions and their dependence on Nazi sponsorship obliged them to wage war on the societies they claimed to represent.[52] Conversely, the success with which some, though certainly not all, resistance movements made the transition from heretical outsiders in 1940 to the symbols of national liberation in 1944–5 depended to a large extent on their ability to draw the wider community into support for their actions. The legitimacy that derived from patriotic opposition to oppressive and alien rule had to be supplemented by a more profound integration of the structures of resistance within the social hierarchies and forms of behaviour acceptable to local communities.[53]

The third theme that we believe emerges from this study is the ways in which the events of the 1930s and 1940s brought about changes in the ways in what constituted legitimate government. Once again, diversity is an irreducible reality. There was no common experience of the loosely connected series of conflicts that took place within the 'envelope' of the Second World War. In Denmark, for example, the survival until 1943 of a primarily diplomatic relationship between the Danish government and the German Foreign Office reinforced the legitimacy of the monarchy and pre-war political order.[54] At an opposite extreme stands a case such as that of Greece. There, the fracturing of power into a series of *émigré*, collaborationist and resistance authorities, each of which was highly dependent on external sponsorship, meant that no authority could claim more than a very partial legitimacy. The subsequent civil war resolved eventually the question of who occupied power. But, as the disjointed evolution of the post-war Greek state indicated, possession of power did not bring with it a solution to the more durable issue of where political legitimacy lay.[55]

Given these diverse experiences, the impact of the war on the pre-existing cultures of legitimacy was similarly diverse. In some cases, the traumas of the conflict reinforced hierarchical conceptions of government. The conservative reflex provoked by the material dangers of war gave a new force to 'protective' justifications of government, in which European citizens looked to their rulers to shelter them from the threats of bombs, deportation or expropriation. Pétain's self-presentation as the 'bouclier de la France' had an obvious resonance among the French population in 1940 and had many imitators throughout Europe at the national and, more especially, local level, where mayors, local notables and bishops derived their legitimacy largely from their ability to protect their communities from the depredations of war.[56] In this 'emergency' situation, Europeans were concerned less about their democratic control of government than about how effective these governments were in meeting their needs. When rulers, be they the King of Denmark, the mayor of a town in the Netherlands or a bishop in German-occupied northern Italy, succeeded in that role, they emerged from the war with their legitimacy enhanced. But, when they failed to do so, or preferred to place their personal or political interests ahead of those of the community, they lost whatever legitimacy they had formerly possessed. Such was the fate of a large number of the New Order authorities who came to power in the aftermath of the German defeats of the early war years but who subsequently dissipated their initial legitimacy through their evident dependence on German favour and their crude attempts to carry through an unwanted revolution.[57]

At the same time, however, the war experience also gave new impetus to notions of popular sovereignty. The weakening of the bonds of 'top-down' government during and after foreign occupation restored a primitive autonomy to many European villages, towns and urban neighbourhoods. The villagers of Paulhac in the Auvergne who, as related by Rod Kedward, erected a sign reading 'Ici commence la France libre' at the borders of their commune in June 1944 were doing more than defying the dictates of the German and Vichy authorities.[58] They were also opting out of all government imposed from outside. This was, in myriad ways, the experience of thousands of such communities across Europe from the blasted villages of western Ukraine in the inter-ethnic warfare that gathered pace from 1939 onwards to the neighbourhood and factory committees which flourished in the cities of northern Italy in the spring and summer of 1945.[59] Such liberation, if that is what it can be termed, was generally less sought than imposed, and owed more to the accidents of war than to the belated rediscovery of the traditions of communal anarchism.[60] Its impact was, however, to restore a tangible sense of self-government to communities which felt empowered to negotiate their own relations with external authorities and

Figure 1.1 Philippe Pétain, Head of the Vichy French state. The message to the French population asks 'Are you more French than him?' Courtesy of Archives Nationales, Paris

to regulate their own internal affairs. This was evident in the energy with which citizens banded together to assume collective tasks, such as food provisioning, as well as in the passion they brought to forms of community purging in the aftermath of occupation.[61]

The post-war legacies of these events were less profound than at first sight they appeared. The need for a new political and social order was urgently voiced from all sections of the political spectrum in the immediate aftermath of war, but had given way a few years later to the return of many of the pre-war institutions and mentalities. The much-repeated dictum that 1945 in Germany was not a 'Year Zero' is as true as it is unsurprising. Throughout Europe, the process by which the entirely fractured landscape of the mid-1940s gave way sooner or later to the restoration of state power owed something to the accidents of war and much more to the determination of bureaucratic and military authorities. Except in the mountains of south-eastern Europe, the 'power vacuums' much feared by Allied planners and returning *émigré* governments on the whole failed to materialize.[62] De Gaulle's determination to stamp his authority on liberated Toulouse in September 1944 and the heavy-handed way in which the Allied military authorities neutralized the local liberation committees in northern Italy during the summer of 1945 were indicative of the resolve to re-impose the unchallenged authority of the state.[63] The demons they feared were, however, largely of their own imagination. Once the initial euphoria of the moment of liberation had passed, the crowds largely disappeared from the European political stage. Resistance movements proved unable to project their ambitions beyond the disappearance of a tangible enemy, and only in the local passions aroused by the pursuit of alleged collaborators and the bitter industrial strikes of the post-war years were the legacies of the war years most immediately visible.[64]

It would be misleading, however, to suggest that, even amidst the constitutional continuity of north-western Europe, the war had not given rise to durable changes. As the final chapter will discuss at greater length, the ways in which Europeans perceived and judged their rulers had shifted. From the economic disruptions of the 1930s and the state-led policies of wartime mobilization had arisen an expectation that the state would fulfil a wider range of social responsibilities, not merely protecting citizens against exceptional crises (such as foreign invasion) but also providing a wider security against the more mundane but immediate misfortunes of economic adversity and ill health. The rather partial welfare states of Western Europe and what Jarausch has termed the 'welfare dictatorship' of East Germany (and its East European equivalents) were twin reflections of this change in the 'goods' that Europeans expected their rulers to provide.[65] Alongside that change came, however, also a more circumspect attitude towards the attempts of governments to enrol citizens in their projects. What was termed in Germany the 'sceptical generation' accepted their rulers not on trust but on condition that they delivered tangible benefits. The localism of the war years lived on in a pervasive distrust of the ambitions of ministers, political leaders and civil servants. 'They', be they the rulers of Communist Poland or of Christian Democrat Italy, were assumed by their citizens to be a predominantly self-interested elite, whom their citizens regarded with a wariness born out of the experiences of the preceding decades.[66]

The fourth, and final, theme that we draw from this study must therefore concern the nature of the post-war order. The term is in many ways a misnomer. To suggest that the Soviet-supported Communist regime established from 1947 onwards in Hungary or the Allied-sponsored regime that emerged from the civil war in Greece were victories of 'order' over 'disorder' would be highly misleading. In both cases, as well as most obviously in a defeated and subsequently partitioned Germany, military force rather than the will of the population dictated political power. Franco's consciously triumphal parade through a defeated and subdued Madrid on 19 May

1939 was, in this respect, only the first instance of a ritual that would be imposed many times over on unwilling European citizens during the subsequent decade.[67] Nevertheless, the simple durability of the post-war regimes in almost all of Europe must inevitably raise questions about how far they succeeded, whatever their origins, in rooting their rule in cultures of legitimacy. That, with the notable exceptions of the collapse of the French Fourth Republic in 1958 and the military coup in Greece in 1967, all of the regimes that were in place in 1950 were still there twenty years later marks a moment of 'regime stability' that was unique in Europe during the twentieth century. Many factors did of course account for this political stasis, notably the Cold War and the impact of economic prosperity. But in the homogenous landscape of regimes of parliamentary democracy that emerged north of the Pyrenees and west of the Iron Curtain after the Second World War, there was also a tangible sense that the political and ideological conflicts of the preceding decades had reached a provisional terminus. By combining the rituals of democratic participation with an inclusive politics of social compromises, the post-war West European regimes came to possess a legitimacy more profound than their origins in the defeat of their authoritarian alternatives. The legitimization they sought to derive from looking back to the war years was in this respect perhaps less important for their success than the way in which they were seen to represent a form of government that was both efficient and, however imperfectly, responsible to the people.[68]

There were, of course, clear limits to that success. The demise of the Fourth Republic in France in 1958, as well as the similar crises that threatened to destabilize the Netherlands and Britain in the wake of imperial misadventures in the East Indies and the Middle East, indicated the vulnerability of the imposing post-war state structures to institutional and political crises. There was also the important factor of communism in Western Europe. Most notably in France and Italy but to a lesser degree in other West European states, the Communist parties, excluded from power as a consequence of Cold War alliances, became the vehicles for an alternative form of legitimacy rooted in the memory of resistance and of the ambition of a new social and political democracy that had been defeated, albeit temporarily, by the domestic and international agents of Reaction. Though its political challenge waned rapidly in the 1950s, communism's durability as a 'counter-society' in post-war Western Europe owed much to its possession of an alternative legitimacy.[69] Nevertheless, even notwithstanding these important qualifications, the political history of Western Europe stands in significant contrast to the Iberian peninsula and Soviet-dominated central and eastern Europe. In these regions, the material sinews of authority were of greater importance than the frequently crude attempts of the regimes to legitimize their rule by reference to past history or demonization of the democratic alternative.[70] Yet, even here, the dictatorship of state over society had its limits. By the 1960s the Salazar and Franco dictatorships had begun a tentative process of openness towards new social forces, while in central and eastern Europe post-war Stalinist repression gave way from the mid-1950s onwards to an awareness of the need to encourage forms of limited dialogue with different sections of society and intermediate social institutions. As events in Czechoslovakia during 1968 well demonstrated, the limits of what was and was not possible remained tightly drawn, but the absence of a democratic mandate did not exclude other, albeit limited, forms of legitimacy.[71]

V

The subsequent chapters of this book we hope demonstrate the merit of analysing the phenomenon of legitimacy in mid-twentieth-century Europe. We are by background and training primarily historians but we have also sought to incorporate into our arguments interdisciplinary perspectives derived from political science and cultural studies. The scope of the book is intended to be emphatically European not merely in the now familiar sense of encompassing both east and west but also by including those areas, such as the Iberian peninsula, too often neglected on the basis of their limited role in the military narrative of the era. This broad geographical definition does, however, also dictate the methodological approach that we have adopted. Rather than limiting its scope to a number of case studies, we have preferred to write a series of analytical essays, each of which draws on a variety of 'national' examples to illustrate our 'European' arguments. Given the irreducible diversity of national and indeed local circumstances in different areas of Europe, the subsequent chapters are also to some extent exercises in comparative history. We have, however, been concerned to avoid the constraints inherent to an explicitly comparative approach. To list the manifold similarities and differences between the way in which legitimacy operated within, say, France and Germany during the 1930s and 1940s seems less useful than to seek to capture the broader if also rather elusive shape of the phenomenon of legitimacy over the period. In doing so, there is, however, the concomitant danger that we have been overly neglectful of the nation-state frameworks within which legitimacy was generally defined. This book therefore makes no pretence to completeness. It is constrained by the limits of our collective geographical and linguistic expertise, and we are highly conscious that there are certain regions, notably of south-eastern Europe, which do not feature as prominently as they deserve to do so in our arguments.

Notes

1. See also the case studies presented by the authors of the present volume in the special issue of *Contemporary European History* XIII (2004) No. 4. This chapter draws on some of the arguments initially presented in the Introduction to that collection.

2. To cite particular works might seem invidious. As exempla of the historio-
graphical trends of recent decades, one might, however, consider: V. Mastny
The Czechs under Nazi Rule. The Failure of National Resistance 1939–1942
(New York, 1971); I. Kershaw *Popular Opinion and Political Dissent in the
Third Reich. Bavaria 1933–1945* (Oxford, 1983); P. Burrin *La France à l'heure
allemande, 1940–1944* (Paris, 1995); M. Mazower *Inside Hitler's Greece. The
Experience of Occupation 1941–44* (New Haven and London, 1993); I. Deak,
J. Gross and T. Judt (eds) *The Politics of Retribution in Europe: World War II
and its Aftermath* (Princeton, 2000); R. Bessel and D. Schumann (eds) *Life after
Death. Approaches to a Cultural and Social History of Europe during the 1940s
and 1950s* (Washington DC and Cambridge, 2003).

3. J. Jackson *France. The Dark Years 1940–1944* (Oxford, 2001), pp. 102–11;
M. Conway 'The Greek Civil War: Greek Exceptionalism or Mirror of a European Civil War?' in P. Carabott and T. Sfikas (eds) *The Greek Civil War. Essays
on a Conflict of Exceptionalism and Silences* (Aldershot, 2004), p. 21.

4. H. Graham 'Spain 1936. Resistance and revolution: the flaws in the Front' in
T. Kirk and A. McElligott (eds) *Opposing Fascism. Community, Authority and
Resistance in Europe* (Cambridge, 1999), pp. 63–79; J. Gross *Polish Society
under German Occupation. The General Government 1939–44* (Princeton,
1979).

5. See notably D. Peukert *Inside Nazi Germany. Conformity, Opposition and
Racism in Everyday Life* (London, 1987); P. Willson 'Women in Fascist Italy'
in R. Bessel (ed.) *Fascist Italy and Nazi Germany. Comparisons and contrasts*
(Cambridge, 1996), p. 93; H. Graham 'Popular Culture in the 'Years of Hunger''
in H. Graham and J. Labanyi (eds) *Spanish Cultural Studies. An Introduction*
(Oxford, 1995), pp. 237–44.

6. See pp. 8–11.

7. J. Gross *Polish Society under German Occupation*, pp. 202–3; T. Snyder 'The
Causes of Ukrainian-Polish Ethnic Cleansing 1943', *Past and Present* No.
179 (May 2003), 197–234; K. Berkhoff *Harvest of Despair. Life and Death in
Ukraine under Nazi Rule* (Cambridge MA, 2004).

8. D. Ellwood 'Italy, Europe and the Cold War: The Politics and Economics of
Limited Sovereignty' in C. Duggan and C. Wagstaff (eds) *Italy in the Cold War:
Politics, Culture and Society, 1948–58* (Oxford and Washington DC, 1995), pp.
25–46; T. Barnes 'The Secret Cold War: The CIA and American Foreign Policy
in Europe 1946–1956', *The Historical Journal* XXIV (1981), 399–415 and
XXV (1982), 649–70.

9. For an example of such processes of local adaptation, see G. Bresadola 'The
Legitimising Strategies of the Nazi Administration in Northern Italy: Propaganda
in the *Adriatisches Küstenland*', *Contemporary European History* XIII (2004),
425–51.

10. See the illuminating discussion in J. Watts *Henry VI and the Politics of
Kingship* (Cambridge, 1996), especially pp. 13–80 and M.J. Braddick and

J. Walter 'Introduction. Grids of Power: order, hierarchy and submission in early modern society' in M.J. Braddick and J. Walter (eds) *Negotiating Power in Early Modern Society. Order, Hierarchy and Submission in Britain and Ireland* (Cambridge, 2001), pp. 8–9. See also T. Metzger, *Escape from Predicament. Neo-Confucianism and China's Evolving Political Culture* (New York, 1977).

11. This is, broadly speaking, the interpretation persuasively presented by Michael Mann in M. Mann *The Sources of Social Power* Vol. II (Cambridge, 1993), especially pp. 723–39. For a stimulating if rather diffuse critique of the materialistic account of political power in the modern age, see D. Kertzer *Ritual, Politics and Power* (New Haven and London, 1988).

12. E. Hobsbawm *Age of Extremes. The Short Twentieth Century 1914–1991* (London, 1995), pp. 136–41.

13. I. Kershaw 'War and Political Violence in Twentieth-Century Europe', *Contemporary European History* XIV (2005), 108. See also M. Mazower *Dark Continent: Europe's Twentieth Century* (London, 1998), pp. 161–84; M. Mazower 'Violence and the State in the Twentieth Century', *American Historical Review* CVII (2002), 1158–78; A. De Grand 'Mussolini's Follies: Fascism in its Imperial and Racist Phase, 1935–1940', *Contemporary European History* XIII (2004), 127–47.

14. M.J. Braddick and J. Walter 'Introduction' in M.J. Braddick and J. Walter (eds) *op. cit.*, p. 10.

15. I. Kershaw *Popular Opinion and Political Dissent*, esp. pp. 373–7; P. Laborie *L'opinion française sous Vichy* (Paris, 1990); M. Fulbrook *Anatomy of a Dictatorship. Inside the GDR 1949–1989* (Oxford, 1995), esp. pp. 129–50 and 271–86; R. Gellately *Backing Hitler: Consent and Coercion in Nazi Germany* (Oxford, 2001).

16. P. Laborie 'Vichy et ses représentations dans l'imaginaire social' in J.-P. Azéma and F. Bédarida (eds) *Vichy et les Français* (Paris, 1992), pp. 493–505.

17. I. Kershaw *The Hitler Myth. Image and Reality in the Third Reich* (Oxford, 1987); J.-M. Flonneau 'L'évolution de l'opinion publique de 1940 à 1944' in J.-P. Azéma and F. Bédarida (eds) *op. cit.*, pp. 506–22; P. Laborie '1940–1944: Double-Think in France' in S. Fishman *et. al.* (eds) *France at War: Vichy and the Historians* (Oxford and New York, 2000), pp. 181–90.

18. David Welch, for example, has written about Nazi propaganda that 'Propaganda, if it is to be effective, must in a sense preach to those who are already partially converted': D. Welch *The Third Reich. Politics and Propaganda* (London and New York, 1993), p. 9. See also C. Lévy and D. Veillon 'Propagande et modelage des esprits' in J.-P. Azéma and F. Bédarida (eds) *op. cit.*, pp. 184–202.

19. V. de Grazia *The Culture of Consent. Mass organization of leisure in Fascist Italy* (Cambridge, 1981), pp. 1–23.

20. P. Willson *Peasant Women and Politics in Fascist Italy. The* Massaie Rurali (London and New York, 2002); A. McDougall *Youth Politics in East Germany. The Free German Youth Movement 1946–1968* (Oxford, 2004), p. 3.

21. A. McDougall *Youth Politics*, p. 8. See also the perceptive comments of Corey Ross in C. Ross *Constructing Socialism at the Grass-Roots. The Transformation of East Germany, 1945–65* (Basingstoke, 2000), pp. 203–10. Re. *Eigensinn*, see notably T. Lindenberger (ed.) *Herrschaft und Eigensinn in der Diktatur* (Cologne, 1999).

22. D. Peukert *Inside Nazi Germany*, p. 244.

23. L. Passerini *Fascism in Popular Memory. The Cultural Experience of the Turin Working Class* (Cambridge, 1987), pp. 129–49. See also the comments made regarding East Germany in M. Sabrow 'Dictatorship as Discourse. Cultural Perspectives on SED Legitimacy' in K. Jarausch (ed.) *Dictatorship as Experience. Towards a Socio-cultural History of the GDR* (New York and Oxford, 1999), pp. 196–7 and 208.

24. D. Peschanski 'Legitimacy/Legitimation/Delegitimation: France in the Dark Years, a textbook case', *Contemporary European History* XIII (2004), 409–23; Y. Durand 'Les notables' in J.-P. Azéma and F. Bédarida (eds) *op. cit.*, pp. 379–80.

25. J. Linz 'The Breakdown of Democratic Regimes. Crisis, Breakdown and Reequilibriation' in J. Linz and A. Stepan (eds) *The Breakdown of Democratic Regimes* (Baltimore and London, 1978), esp. pp. 16–18; R. Barker *Legitimating Identities: The Self-Representation of Rulers and Subjects* (Cambridge, 2001); T.H. Rigby 'Political Legitimacy, Weber and Communist Mono-Organisational Systems' in T.H. Rigby and F. Feher (eds) *Political Legitimation in Communist States* (London and Basingstoke, 1982), pp. 1–26.

26. M. Weber, *Economy and Society*, edited by G. Roth and C. Wittich (New York, 1968), pp. 212–99. See also W. Mommsen 'Max Weber's Theory of Legitimacy Today', in W. Mommsen *The Political and Social Theory of Max Weber* (Oxford, 1989), pp. 44–9.

27. M.C. Hudson *Arab Politics: The Search for Legitimacy* (New Haven and London, 1977).

28. R. Barker *Legitimating Identities*; F. Bourricaud 'Legitimacy and Legitimation', *Current Sociology* XXXV (1987), 57–67.

29. R. Barker *Legitimating Identities*, pp. 19–26, 106 and 140.

30. R. Gildea *The Past in French History* (London and New Haven, 1994); H. Rousso *Le syndrome de Vichy* (Paris, 1987); S. Falasca-Zamponi *Fascist Spectacle. The Aesthetics of Power in Mussolini's Italy* (Berkeley etc, 1997).

31. D. Beetham *The Legitimation of Power* (Basingstoke and London, 1991), pp. 7–25.

32. *Ibid.*, pp. 12–20.

33. S. Mikolajczyk *The Rape of Poland. Pattern of Soviet Aggression* (New York and Toronto, 1948), p. 79. Other accounts allege that Stalin made the comment about Poland rather than Germany.

34. See the special issue on 'Democracy in Twentieth-Century Europe' in *European History Quarterly* XXXII (2002).

35. Q. Skinner *The Foundations of Modern Political Thought* Vol. I (Cambridge, 1978), p. x. For similar comments see J. Watts *Henry VI*, pp. 11 and 15.

36. Characteristic examples are R. Gildea *Marianne in Chains. In Search of the German Occupation, 1940–1945* (London, 2002); J. Gross *Neighbors: The Destruction of the Jewish Community in Jedwabne* (Princeton, 2001); S. Aschenbrenner, 'The Civil War from the Perspective of a Messenian Village', in L. Bærentzen, J. Iatrides and O. Smith (eds) *Studies in the History of the Greek Civil War 1945–1949* (Copenhagen, 1987), pp. 105–25.

37. G. Konrád *Geluk* (Amsterdam, 2002), p. 11.

38. See, for example, the diary of two teenage sisters in wartime France or Heinrich Böll's fictional representation of the journey of a German solider returning to the Eastern Front: B. and F. Groult *Journal à quatre mains* (Paris, 1994); H. Böll *The Train was on Time* (republished Evanston IL, 1994).

39. R. Sarti *Long Live the Strong. A History of Rural Society in the Apennine Mountains* (Amherst MA, 1985), p. 227.

40. C.B. Christensen, J. Lund, N.W. Olesen and J. Soerensen *Danmark besat. Krig og hverdag 1940–45* (Copenhagen, 2005), pp. 181ff; D. Barnouw 'Dutch exiles in London' in M. Conway and J. Gotovitch (eds) *Europe in Exile. European Exile Communities in Britain 1940–45* (New York and Oxford, 2001), pp. 235–8; J. Fusi *Franco. A Biography* (London, 1987), pp. 39–44.

41. J. Jackson *France. The Dark Years*, pp. 288–90; M-P d'Udekem d'Acoz *Pour le Roi et la Patrie. La noblesse belge dans la Résistance* (Brussels, 2002); J.-D. Durand 'L'épiscopat italien devant l'occupation allemande, 1943–1945' in J. Sainclivier and C. Bougeard (eds) *La Résistance et les Français* (Rennes, 1995), pp. 95–108; J. Teissier du Cros *Divided Loyalties: A Scotswoman in occupied France* (republished Edinburgh, 1992).

42. M. Anderson *Practicing Democracy. Elections and Political Culture in Imperial Germany* (Princeton, 2000); G. Eley *Forging Democracy. The History of the Left in Europe, 1850–2000* (Oxford and New York, 2002).

43. See for example the studies of local politics in the Weimar Republic in R. Moeller *German Peasants and Agrarian Politics, 1914–1924. The Rhineland and Westphalia* (Chapel Hill and London, 1986); J. Osmond *Rural Protest in the Weimar Republic. The Free Peasantry in the Rhineland and Bavaria* (Basingstoke and London, 1993).

44. M. Mann *Fascists* (Cambridge, 2004), pp. 6–9.

45. R. Paxton *The Anatomy of Fascism* (London, 2004), pp. 40–2.

46. M. Mann *Fascists*, pp. 141–7.

47. M. Conway *Catholic Politics in Europe 1918–45* (London and New York, 1997), pp. 47–95; R. Steigmann-Gall *The Holy Reich. Nazi Conceptions of Christianity 1919–1945* (Cambridge, 2003); R.J. Wolff and J.K. Hoensch (eds) *Catholics, the State and the European Radical Right 1919–1945* (Boulder, 1987); M. Mitchell 'Materialism and Secularism: CDU Politicians and National Socialism, 1945–1949', *Journal of Modern History* LXVII (1995), 278–308.

48. See, for example, A. Schwarzenbach 'Royal Photographs: Emotions for the People', *Contemporary European History* XIII (2004), 255–80.

49. L. Wylie *Village in the Vaucluse* (3rd edition: Cambridge MA and London, 1974), pp. 206–13. See also A. Karakasidou *Fields of Wheat, Hills of Blood. Passages to Nationhood in Greek Macedonia 1870–1990* (Chicago and London, 1997).

50. See pp. 111–15.

51. For examples of this process, see A. De Jonghe 'La lutte Himmler-Reeder pour la nomination d'un HSSPF à Bruxelles', *Cahiers d'histoire de la seconde guerre mondiale* III (1974), IV (1976), V (1978), VII (1982) and VIII (1984); V. Mastny *The Czechs under Nazi Rule*, pp. 45–64, 86–102 and 183–206; H. Umbreit *Der Militärbefehlshaber in Frankreich 1940–1944* (Boppard am Rhein, 1968), pp. 118–50.

52. N. Wouters 'New Order and good government: municipal administration in Belgium (1938–46)', *Contemporary European History* XIII (2004) 389–407; H.F. Dahl *Quisling. A Study in Treachery* (Cambridge, 1999), pp. 253–62 and 311–19.

53. See, for example, J. Guillon 'La résistance au village' in J. Sainclivier and C. Bougeard (eds) *op. cit.*, pp. 233–43; R. Gildea 'Resistance, Reprisals and Community in Occupied France', *Transactions of the Royal Historical Society* Sixth Series XIII (2003), 163–85; F. Maerten 'Résistance et société en Hainaut belge. Histoire d'une brève rencontre' in R. Vandenbussche (ed.) *L'engagement dans la Résistance (France du Nord – Belgique)* (Lille, 2003), pp. 85–96.

54. H. Poulsen 'Denmark at War? The Occupation as History' in S. Ekman and N. Edling (eds) *War Experience, Self Image and National Identity: The Second World War as Myth and History* (Södertälje, 1997), pp. 98–105.

55. J. Iatrides (ed.) *Greece in the 1940s. A Nation in Crisis* (Hanover, 1981); D. Close (ed.) *The Greek Civil War 1943–1950. Studies of Polarization* (London, 1993); R. Clogg *Parties and Elections in Greece. The Search for Legitimacy* (London, 1987), pp. 17–53.

56. *Le procès du Maréchal Pétain* (Paris, 1945), p. 32; Y. Le Maner 'Town Councils of the Nord and Pas-de-Calais region: local power, French power, German power', in T. Kirk and A. McElligott (eds) *op. cit.*, pp. 97–119; J.-L. Clément *Monseigneur Saliège, archevêque de Toulouse, 1929–1956* (Paris, 1994).

57. N. Wouters *Oorlogsburgemeesters 40/44. Lokaal bestuur en collaboratie in België* (Tielt, 2004); P. Romijn 'Did soldiers become governors? Liberators,

resistance, and the reconstruction of local government in the liberated Netherlands, 1944–1945' in C. Brower (ed.) *World War II in Europe. The Final Year* (New York, 1998), pp. 266–87.

58. H.R. Kedward 'Introduction: Ici commence la France libre' in H.R. Kedward and N. Wood (eds) *The Liberation of France. Image and Event* (Oxford, 1995), pp. 1–2.

59. T. Snyder 'The Causes...', *Past and Present* No. 179 (May 2003), 197–234; T. Behan *The Long-Awaited Moment. The Working Class and the Italian Communist Party in Milan, 1943–1948* (New York etc, 1997), pp. 139–74.

60. M. Koreman *The Expectation of Justice. France 1944–46* (Durham N.C. and London, 1999), pp. 8–47. However in areas of Republican Spain, such as Aragon, which were left without any effective government in the early stages of the civil war, local structures of self-government were strongly influenced by Anarchist ideas: G. Leval *Collectives in the Spanish Revolution* (London, 1975), pp. 70–82; J. Casanova *Anarquismo y revolución en la sociedad rural aragonesa 1936–1938* (Madrid, 1985), pp. 60–72 and 106–29.

61. The community dynamics of purging and violence have stimulated a substantial historiography. See, for example, F. Virgili *Shorn Women. Gender and Punishment in Liberation France* (Oxford, 2002); M. Conway 'Justice in post-war Belgium: Popular Pressures and Political Realities' in I. Deak, J. Gross and T. Judt (eds) *The Politics of Retribution in Europe*, pp. 133–56; M. Vincent 'The Keys of the Kingdom: Religious Violence in the Spanish Civil War, July-August 1936' in C. Ealham and M. Richards (eds) *The Splintering of Spain: New Historical Perspectives on the Spanish Civil War* (Cambridge, 2004), pp. 68–89. See also P. Matesis *The Daughter* (London, 2002).

62. M. Mazower *Inside Hitler's Greece*, pp. 265–96; N. Malcolm *Bosnia. A Short History* (London, 1994), pp. 174–92.

63. M. Goubet 'La Haute Garonne' in P. Buton and J.-M. Guillon (eds) *Les pouvoirs en France à la Libération* (Paris, 1994), pp. 482–93; D. Ellwood *Italy 1943–1945* (Leicester, 1985), pp. 184–90; M. Conway 'Legacies of Exile: The Exile Governments in London during the Second World War and the Politics of Post-War Europe' in M. Conway and J. Gotovitch (eds) *Europe in Exile*, p. 263.

64. G. Warner 'Allies, Government and Resistance: The Belgian Political Crisis of November 1944', *Transactions of the Royal Historical Society* Fifth Series XXVIII (1978), 45–60; B. Frommer *National Cleansing. Retribution against Nazi Collaborators in Postwar Czechoslovakia* (Cambridge, 2005), pp. 33–62; R. Mencherini *Guerre froide, grèves rouges* (Paris, 1998).

65. G. Eley *Forging Democracy*, pp. 311–13; K. Jarausch 'Care and coercion: the GDR as welfare dictatorship' in K. Jarausch (ed.) *op. cit.*, pp. 59–60.

66. H. Schelsky *Die skeptische Generation: Eine Soziologie der deutschen Jugend* (Düsseldorf, 1957); T. Toranska *Oni. Stalin's Polish Puppets* (London, 1987);

P.A. Allum *Politics and Society in Post-war Naples* (Cambridge, 1973), pp. 93–100. See also pp. 198–200.

67. P. Preston *Franco* (London, 1993), pp. 329–30.
68. M. Conway 'The Rise and Fall of Western Europe's Democratic Age 1945–73', *Contemporary European History* XIII (2004), 78–87.
69. T. Judt 'Introduction' in T. Judt (ed.) *Resistance and Revolution in Mediterranean Europe 1939–1948* (London and New York, 1989), pp. 4–6; I. Wall *French Communism in the Era of Stalin. The Quest for Unity and Integration, 1945–1962* (Westport and London, 1983), pp. 115–31; S. Gundle *Between Hollywood and Moscow. The Italian Communists and the Challenge of Mass Culture 1943–1991* (Durham NC and London, 2000), pp. 11–41.
70. M. Richards *A Time of Silence: Civil War and the Culture of Repression in Franco's Spain, 1936–1945* (Cambridge, 1998); J. Grugel and T. Rees *Franco's Spain* (London, 1997), pp. 128–42; V. Tismaneanu *Stalinism for All Seasons. A Political History of Romanian Communism* (Berkeley, 2003), pp. 189–91; T. H. Rigby and F. Feher (eds) *op. cit.*
71. M. Pittaway *Eastern Europe 1939–2000* (London, 2004), pp. 133–5; C. Ross *The East German Dictatorship. Problems and Perspectives in the Interpretation of the GDR* (London, 2002), pp. 19–68.

–2–

Legitimacy in Inter-War Europe*

A 'Provisional Regime', 1918–39

The end of the First World War challenged all Europeans to consider and redefine their relationship to their political communities, to the state and above all the nation. From 1914 onwards, the citizens and subjects of the belligerent states had entered the 'Great War' that ultimately destroyed millions of lives, as well as regimes and empires. Those who willingly entered military service in 1914, as François Furet has argued, did not necessarily like the war but saw it as an unavoidable consequence of the existence of nations and therefore, as the ultimate test of citizenship.[1] Socialists famously put aside their disputes with the ruling classes to rally for their nations in 1914. Such solidarity did not survive the gruelling experience of total war, mass casualties, and, for the Central Powers, ignominious defeat. In 1918, at the end of the war, rulers and the ruled all over Europe saw themselves urged to renegotiate the radius of citizenship, including the issue of undivided loyalty to political entities both old and new.

In contrast to the relatively peaceful and stable 'long nineteenth century', the 1920s and 1930s witnessed nearly constant upheaval across the European continent. In the political life of the 1920s and 1930s, Europe's regimes faced regular, repeated and relentless challenges to the legitimacy of their rule. Oppositions not only sought to change individual governments; they aimed to transform or even overturn the existing constitutional system. From the battles, both verbal and violent, surrounding the creation of new states in 1918–21, through the succession of economic crises that impoverished entire countries, to the ultimate collapse into violence from both Right and Left, the continent's rulers faced a series of challenges for which they increasingly seemed to have no answer. Vast numbers of Europeans simply refused to accept the status quo either internationally or domestically.

Internationally, Hungarians and Germans bristled under the Versailles and Trianon Treaties respectively, and dreamed of, or planned for, reversing their countries' wartime and post-war defeats. Internally, Hungarian and German minorities in Czechoslovakia first rejected then grudgingly accepted and then, as a new war was looming ahead, happily buried the state. Rather than arguing within the rules, or even over them, many chose simply to ignore them. Whether we speak of communists and

---

*This chapter was written by Peter Romijn, with Ben Frommer as co-author.

fascists in Italy, Germany or Spain, national minorities in Eastern Europe, or even religiously minded conservatives in France, the opposition aimed not just to replace those in power but to replace the system altogether. And they intended to make that replacement irreversible.

The 1920s and 1930s has come to be known retrospectively as the 'inter-war period,' a teleological moniker that turns these two decades into little more than a tenuous pause between the World Wars. Nonetheless, this term, and the frequency with which it is used, points to the provisional nature of the period. While the Versailles system did not necessarily have to disintegrate, the post-1918 settlement never acquired the sense of permanence that the post-1945 one did (inaccurately, after all, as the events of 1989–91 demonstrated). In many ways, inter-war Europe was a 'provisional regime' writ large, founded on treaties which failed to gain universal approval, on borders that remained open to challenge (despite Locarno), and on a system of government, liberal democracy, that was new, untested, and ultimately unsatisfactory to many, if not most Europeans.[2]

The period began and ended violently; especially in the east, centre and south-west, the years 1918 and 1939 do not mark a clear division between peace and war. In the first few years militias battled across Germany, Hungary was consumed by communist revolution, foreign invasion and a vicious counter-revolution, and Poland fought the Bolsheviks (and Ukrainians) for control of north-eastern Europe's plains. Towards the end of the 1930s the Civil War devoured Spain. In Ukraine, war, collectivization, the Famine and the Great Purge meant that its inhabitants barely experienced a year of secure existence. Moreover, between 1919 and 1922, on the extreme western periphery of Western Europe, Irish nationalists fought a fierce war of independence against British forces. Even during more peaceful times in more peaceful places, violence was never far from the surface. If war is politics by other means then inter-war politics were simply a substitute for unfinished and nascent conflicts, the former mainly national the latter ideological. Politics was a means to manoeuvre and gain position during a lull. At times, this violence did break through, most notably, in the political assassinations that punctuated the history of central and southern Europe.

That many were reluctant to accept the shape of inter-war Europe, especially its eastern half, should hardly come as a surprise. It was new, remarkably so. Before the First World War, the continent was home to only three republics; by the time the dust had settled (temporarily) there were thirteen.[3] Three great empires that had once controlled almost all of Eastern Europe disappeared suddenly leaving new states in their wakes. Some were merely expanded versions of 'old' states such as Romania, Greece or Italy, themselves less than a century in existence. Poland was resurrected after a two-century hiatus. Czechoslovakia and Yugoslavia appeared for the first time on European maps (despite ancient claims to kinship of western and southern Slavs). Austria and Hungary were truncated (and recalcitrant) remnants that, in the former case, had little besides a capital city in common with its pre-war namesake.

Not only new states appeared; their forms of government were also radically altered. Democracy, minority rights and the enfranchisement of women were just some of those changes. In the place of monarchs from ancient families, bourgeois presidents, prime ministers and cabinets governed, or at least attempted to do so. By the end of Emperor Franz Josef's 68-year reign in 1916 only a small fraction of his subjects could remember a time when someone else had ruled them. In contrast, the vast majority of inter-war Eastern Europeans had lived as adults under other regimes in other countries. When Stalin and Hitler convivially agreed in August 1939 to partition Poland out of existence, they essentially returned the map of that area of Europe to that which they had known in their youth.

By the end of the 1930s, few of the newly established regimes could still confidently count on the undivided support of their citizenry. If the ultimate measure of a regime's (and a state's) legitimacy is the willingness of its subjects and citizens to fight for it then the minorities of Eastern Europe, in particular, had qualms about laying down their lives for states that relegated them to second-class citizenship. In September 1938, 50 per cent of Sudeten German reserves did not respond to the mobilization of the Czechoslovak army.[4] In March 1941 large numbers of Croats refused the call to fight for Yugoslavia.[5] At the same time, regimes of the radical Left and Right commandeered ideological support across borders. In 1940, Dutch Nazi leader Anton Mussert told an American journalist that in the event of a German invasion of the Netherlands, he would not support national defence. On the contrary, conservative elites welcomed 'imported' fascist and National-Socialist rule as a lesser evil compared to Leftist governance. By 1939 the so-called Versailles system that shaped Europe in the inter-war period had been buried by opponents and proponents alike. In an attempt to explain the Nazi occupation of Bohemia, on 16 March 1939 Czech president Emil Hácha told his people:

> When twenty years ago all Czech hearts were filled with joy [at the proclamation of national independence], I stood apart from those historic events. My joy about our unbelievable success was overshadowed by anxiety about the external and internal guarantees which would assure the permanence of our success. Now, after twenty years, I can see with grief that my anxieties were not without foundation. What we held for a solution to last for ages proved to be merely a short episode in our national history.[6]

For Hácha and many others of his generation, German rule appeared as a restoration, albeit unwelcome, of Central Europe's natural order.

In the two decades following the First World War, Europeans lived through a prolonged period of political upheaval in which their relationship with their different regimes was subject to often intense strains. In this chapter, the political history of Europe will be observed through the prism of legitimacy, for the purpose of acquiring a better understanding of the primary topic of this volume, the political behaviour of individuals and collectives living under Fascist and National Socialist occupation

Figure 2.1 German forces hold a triumphant parade through the Czech capital Prague on 17 March 1939. Courtesy of Netherlands Institute for War Documentation, Amsterdam

between 1938 and 1945. These many-sided processes of construction, development and destruction of the political order in inter-war Europe will be analysed from the perspective of an enduring crisis in legitimacy, as expressed by fundamental shifts in political domination and political loyalty.

This chapter will argue that the political order of inter-war Europe, seen from the point of view of legitimacy, actually showed many characteristics of a 'provisional regime'. On a continental scale, it suffered instability and, despite temporary consolidation, eventually collapsed in the furnace of the Second World War. At the beginning of that war, the attitude of ruled towards rulers old and new was strongly related to the extent of the crisis in legitimacy and the degree of loyalty towards the 'provisional regime' of the preceding period in specific states. With hindsight, however, there is much evidence that, at least for post-war Western Europe, the collective experience of this very collapse laid the foundation for an unprecedented period of legitimate rule after 1945. In fact, it may be argued that the thorough delegitimation of inter-war Europe was a necessary prerequisite to the creation of a legitimate Western European post-Nazi order. In Eastern Europe the experience of fascist and National-Socialist rule was similarly used by the Communist successor regimes to underline their own legitimacy, ultimately with far less success.

Inter-war Europe faced three distinct but interrelated crises of legitimacy, each of which left a critical heritage for the wartime and post-war years. First, individual regimes confronted challenges to their very claims to rule, related to their constitutional positions as well as to their effectiveness. Second, there was a general challenge to the entire inter-war European order, the so-called Versailles system (encompassing not only the Versailles Treaty, but the concomitant treaties of Neuilly-sur-Seine, Sèvres, St Germain, and Trianon). States (and their borders) faced a crisis of legitimacy along with the regimes that ruled (and ruled over) them. Such phenomena were country specific, but they shared much and were often not self-contained (as shown by Nazi Germany's encouragement of Sudeten demands in Czechoslovakia). Third, the position of Europe as a whole, its imperial powers specifically, but its superior self-imagined culture more generally, within the world was undermined. The continent's dominance over others was coming to an end, even if Europe hardly confronted this particular challenge, nor was often even aware of it.

'Conditional Legitimacy'

At first sight, in 1917–18 the old political order in Europe largely fell apart. Dramatic changes were followed by uneasy settlements. Windows of opportunity were used to force decisions about statehood and territorial issues as *faits accomplis* upon both the vanquished and the bystanders. The conclusion of the peace treaties took quite some time. Most were signed in 1919 and 1920, although several boundary settlements, like the Italian-Yugoslav border in Fiume, took until 1924. The 1925 Treaty of Locarno more-or-less solidified the international post-war settlements for Western Europe, but the mutual system of guarantees failed to endorse the borders of eastern Europe. In central and eastern Europe especially, disputes about borders and state-building continued.

The internal crises of legitimacy in the inter-war European states largely differed in manifestation and intensity. What they had in common was a fundamental controversy about relations between rulers and the ruled. Crucial and heavily contested issues were the definition of the boundaries of political communities, inclusion and exclusion in citizenship, political participation and representation, and, last but not least, the overall performance of governments. Liberal representative democracy, in particular, a relatively new political concept, went through a severe crisis of confidence.[7] Still present, below the surface of day-to-day politics in the inter-war period, and often hidden by the new and inherited problems, was the influence of inherited tradition at work in the political process. Europeans necessarily reflected upon the relations with their rulers and, thus, existing notions of legitimacy set constraints and limits to the shape of what was new.

In the inter-war period, the relationship between the rulers and the ruled developed. The space in which the political process took place, where policies were formulated and consent was expressed or withdrawn, expanded significantly. Across Europe, three long-term developments reached new heights and became more intertwined than before: the emergence of modern mass politics; the evolution of the role of the state in society and the progressive politicization of social life. Conventionally, political space is identified with the institutional order that structures the process. Between 1914 and 1918, the need for organization of societies and their productive capacity towards a maximal war effort had called for unprecedented growth of state regulation and bureaucracies. While institutions and political leadership had been invigorated, the potential for influencing the course of politics had been narrowed.

When the war was over, the search for a new equilibrium between the institutional order and political representation, participation and mobilization began. The state, and consequently politics, penetrated the private sphere. An important corollary of this process was how relations developed between the state and civil society, as the intermediate sphere between families and state bodies. In an open society the credibility of rulers is tied to their ability to convince the citizens that the state is supportive of their free associations to promote their social, cultural and religious goals. In contrast, the authoritarian regimes, which developed in the inter-war years, applied different degrees of *Gleichschaltung* and mobilization of society to their political expressions and ambitions, in the process destroying the autonomy of civil society to large degrees. These regimes were of a fundamentally new and innovative character and generated an appeal that went far beyond the states that had produced it.

For evident reasons, contemporaries and historians alike have focussed more on abrupt changes than on continuities. Regimes deliberately chose to call for a new beginning and thus contributed to this perspective.[8] They did so by playing upon the general urge among Europeans to look forward to a brighter future and to avert collective memory from the recent catastrophe. Nonetheless, in the aftermath of the Great War, an urgent need for stability was felt everywhere, producing a mixed ambition to build upon heritages in political legitimacy on the one hand, and to create the preconditions for making a new start on the other, in order to overcome the war's destructive effects on personal and social life. Such a forward-looking mood certainly contributed to acceptance of regimes, for the time being, to wait and see, to tolerate the rulers and judge their performance. Thus, legitimacy became related to the power of regimes to promote stability in political and social life and 'good government' in general. Under the 'provisional regime' of the 1920s and 1930s, these issues produced a sense of what might be called 'conditional legitimacy'.

The political order in inter-war Europe developed into three distinctive forms: 'old regimes' that survived and continued without fundamental change in their political orders; 'new regimes' that took over existing states and went through a transition towards a new political order; and 'new states' that had to establish themselves and their political order from the rubble left over by the collapse of their predecessors. All three categories of political communities included strong notions about how the state should work and what had been wrong in their functioning under the pre-existing order. Such notions could be normative and material. The normative ones could be closely connected to the inherited values of the pre-existing political systems. Legality of the regime was at the centre of such notions, being connected to the way in which the system operates: procedures for political succession, opportunities for participation and representation through the exercise of basic civil rights such as suffrage and freedom of speech and association; the degree to which the rule of law is applied; the impartiality and professionalism of the civil service; the monopoly of the state to apply violence and civil control of the military and police. These issues were not limited to regimes that aspired to be democratic in the traditional liberal sense alone. Legality is not an equivalent of democracy. Authoritarian regimes may uphold certain standards of legality, apart from civil rights, in order to provide for predictability, by means of due bureaucratic procedures, the maintenance of property rights and the like.[9]

Inherited political traditions cannot be seen solely as impediments for the immediate rethinking of the political order. Potentially, such traditions could also be turned into assets for new regimes. A key element of this inherited legitimacy was respect for legality, the way in which government was conducted internally. But also central was the way in which they responded to the urgent issues of the day. In many respects, in the aftermath of the First World War, the regimes' performance was put to the test. This specifically related to the ability to deal with border disputes, streams of refugees, food shortages and other social emergencies, political upheaval, and economic crises. In the inter-war years of 'conditional legitimacy' such collective experience of hardship and turmoil sharpened thinking about what it exactly was that constituted legitimate rule.

Notions of political legitimacy were therefore partly inherited, but were also newly formulated. These inheritances from the 'old regime' aggregated over the course of time and continued to affect fundamentally political life in the context of fascist or National-Socialist occupation and rule. After all, political legality as such has a persuasive power of its own. Continuity of a state, its symbols and constitutional order are important assets for political stability, even if the ruled are not particularly enthusiastic about the incumbent regime. On the other hand, the destructive effect of a lost war on the legitimacy of a regime should not be underestimated. Hannah Arendt pointed to the 'perverted relationship' between the military and political classes, that since the Franco-Prussian war of 1870 made the positions of civil rulers untenable in the wake of military defeat.[10]

Defeat in the First World War strongly contributed to a series of dramatic regime changes immediately after the war ended and to the loss of legitimacy of the 'provisional regime' over the long run. In Hungary, for instance, the Horthy regime instituted the annual 'Day of the Heroic Dead', which it used to underline its message that brave soldiers had been betrayed by 'internal enemies' at home. The problem is not only that people who have sacrificed their blood and belongings will blame their rulers for failed management of the war. Just as important is the factor expressed by Fred C. Iklé: 'Nothing is more divisive for a government than having to make peace at the price of major concessions.'[11] In such situations, owing to internal dissension, rulers may quickly lose control over political developments, as well as their perspective about what can be done, and decide that devolution of power is a way to end a dead-end situation.

In the victorious states, and even in the neutral ones, the war had caused much grief and hardship, factors that remained close at hand in the memories of those who had lived through the ordeal. They were subject to the same continuity of social tensions that had risen throughout Europe in the first decade of the twentieth century. Just as in defeated Germany, class-based challenges in Britain or Italy provoked varying degrees of violent response. As long as victorious governments kept the military intact, exerted political control over it and employed it to suppress political dissent, they managed to remain in control of the state. Thus, in 1919 and 1920, both France and Italy faced massive social and political unrest. The French government managed to contain the threat when it called upon voluntary units of civil guards, under control of the *préfets*, and let them take over vital social services and constitute a counter-force. By contrast, the Italian governments of the day, weakened by disputes about the conditions for peace, left the issue to independent squads of former soldiers. The upper classes employed these *squadristi* to crush the socialist and syndicalist strongholds by means of violent terror and thus paved the way for Fascism to take over.[12]

Neutral Holland followed the French example. When in November 1918, P.J. Troelstra, the leader of the Social Democrats, announced in Parliament that 'the revolution would not stop at the German-Dutch border', a conservative and royalist counterrevolution was organized by calling up a civil guard. Thousands of young men poured into the seat of government at The Hague to get arms and counter the threat of a socialist takeover. Many of them were subsequently incorporated into more permanent civil guards. These units were employed as a police reserve when the establishment saw its position undermined in the 1920s and 1930s. The November 1918 scare was to be an important determinant in Dutch politics until the end of the Second World War.[13]

By remaining in control, rulers could also shape collective memory and give meaning to recent experiences. Antoine Prost has pointed to the contradictions in the representations of the Great War in France during the inter-war period. Pre-war values of heroic and offensive spirit were discredited and the ability to suffer in the trenches and ultimately to give one's life for the good of the nation became civic virtues.[14] Rulers in defeated states offered an alternative version of the recent past: Ludendorff's 'stab-in-the-back' theory was a fatal contribution to the discourse of defeat.

Heritages in legitimacy are thus a multi-facetted phenomenon. In a broad sense, such heritages relate to state- and nationhood, political systems and political culture, or national and ethnic identities. These matters are all part of the self-understanding and self-definition of political communities, providing both rules and historical justification for a given political order. The sphere of legality is the most tangible aspect of heritages in legitimacy. This concerns what keeps the political system going, by providing rules for decision-making, participation and representation, and political succession. More broadly, in any political community the sense of legality is about proper and fair procedure in order to reach binding decisions. In this perspective it constitutes the starting point for seeing how the continuous efforts of regimes worked to justify their position and in which ways the political space for allegiance and discontent was exploited.

Aside from persuasive power, the continuity of institutions carried a certain amount of regenerative power. The United Kingdom, the Netherlands, and the Scandinavian states, which all enjoyed long-lasting and stable political development, were generally better able to absorb political shocks than those countries whose point of departure was more recent and troubled. Thus, profound uncertainty about the economic viability of the national economy in the first Austrian Republic, the state's much discussed and bemoaned *Unfähigkeit*, fundamentally undermined the authority of rulers and institutions across the political spectrum.[15] After the First World War, new states and new regimes took care to absorb institutions and administrative traditions from their predecessors. Thus, inter-war Poland was obliged to cope with different legal and bureaucratic systems, inherited from the former Russian, Habsburg and German rulers. The enormous task that faced Poland is well illustrated by the fact that at one point the country had six currencies in circulation.[16]

This issue even can be perceived in Soviet Russia and Germany, where military collapse and political revolution had produced radically different regimes in the short term, and quite comparable and destructive dictatorships over the long run. They represented moments in time when progressive erosion of the rulers' legitimacy became irreversible. In the Soviet Union, the Bolshevik government, under the name of the Council of People's Commissars, set out to govern by means of decrees. It established a new concept of political legality, which step-by-step assumed the shape of a dictatorial and highly centralized government structure. Its claim to legitimacy was built on serving as the sole representative of the working class in its revolutionary creation of a non-exploitative, just society.

In defeated Germany the Imperial Government was replaced by civilian politicians from bourgeois and labour backgrounds. They decided to accept the responsibility for surrender and for coping with the conditions and consequences of it, both of which proved to be extremely burdensome. In Weimar a new constitution was formulated and a new republic founded, which despite its democratic framework was also, in many respects, a continuation of the empire's political and administrative system. Of course, short-term acceptance of new institutions and their personnel after revolutionary upheaval was enforced by violence or sheer necessities. Over the long term, however, established states felt the need to organize the internalization of national and civic values – a drive that already had occurred in many European nations by the turn of the century.[17]

Thus, in the inter-war decades, the political space in which authority generally is produced, reproduced and challenged, proved to be unstable and malleable. A symptom, and a reason at the same time, was the dramatic expansion of propaganda as a means of organizing political opinion and support, by means of mass communication (radio, the printed press), architecture, sports and the arts. Another field of expansion and innovation of political space was represented by the different forms in which political dissent, or subversion, were organised: the occupation of factories in France and Spain, the employment of 'storm troopers' by both the extreme Right and Left, first in Italy, Germany, and Russia, and later in many other nations.

At the end of the First World War, the political order in Europe in general and in many of its states, was fundamentally challenged. Territories were disputed, political space was fluid, and legitimacy heavily contested. Whereas American President Woodrow Wilson had declared the purposes of the victorious Entente powers to 'make the world safe for democracy', the collapse of the Russian and German empires was a starting point for producing the most fundamental alternatives for, and challenges to, this concept of post-war order in Europe. The contested legitimacy of the era was to be manifold and elusive at once. In this way, it was a precondition of the political confusion to which societies were subjected when they came under fascist and National-Socialist rule.

1918–22: Uneasy Settlements and Political Legality

In terms of the establishment of a post-war political order, the challenge for regimes was to produce a sufficient degree of political legality to enable new states to begin functioning and to let the existing ones maintain the *ancien régime*. The viable operation of a system implies that the rules of political participation and representation are considered satisfactory by a large majority of the political community. Principles of legality bind both rulers and ruled to proper procedures of political decision-making. It is useful to distinguish between legitimacy and legality to understand how in times of crisis political or social groups temporarily subordinated their sense of what was appropriate in the existing legal order in order to defend their essential interests considered as legitimate.

Periods of transition to the post-war order often started before the end of the fighting and continued a great deal longer. In Russia, or Italy, stabilization of the political order remained a distant prospect. In the immediate aftermath of the Great War, the Hungarian counter-revolutionary elite abandoned legality in acting against the workers movement, secessionist tendencies in Burgenland and ultimately the King. Only after the constitution of a state they regarded as politically legitimate, did this elite return to a brand of legality under the István Bethlen government in the 1920s.[18] In many states a certain degree of stabilization was reached during the first post-war decade, in which rulers operated in more or less well-defined political orders under generally accepted rules of the game. Yet, even in Europe's more stable corners, such stability was eroded as a result of structural political discontent. Political actors broke constitutional rules and sought more authoritarian solutions. Thus, the 1930s comprised a second, increasingly more radical decade of post-war reconstruction of political systems in Europe. Constitutional law as the foundation for political representation and participation was destabilised. Legitimacy was sought in strengthening the executive powers, the direct identification of masses with leaders and the performance of the regime.

The end of the war did not lead to immediate peace everywhere in Europe. A number of civil wars followed the Great War: the bloodiest in Russia, where the Bolsheviks took over, and lesser conflicts in Finland, Hungary and parts of Germany, where revolution was defeated. Opportunistic wars of intervention were engaged in by the Entente against Soviet Russia, by Soviet Russia and new-born Poland against one another and by Greece against Turkey. Romania invaded Hungary (with French support) and Italian ultranationalist mutineers tried to incorporate Fiume/Rijeka by force into their nation. At the western edge of Europe, the British government and separatist Irish nationalists struggled to a standstill before they grudgingly accepted an incomplete solution for Irish national independence. These conflicts made clear that normalization of societies, political stability and constitutional order were not within reach before military decisions had been reached. Even the regime of the Soviet Union, which represented the most radical break with pre-war political order as people knew it, took steps to build, after the conclusion of 'War Communism', a governing structure that at least tried to relate to the issue of the legitimacy of their rule. Soon, Stalin turned away from the Bolsheviks' dreams of world revolution and adopted a policy of building 'socialism in one country' first.

The first category of transitions was negotiated diplomatic arrangements. To conclude the state of war and to establish the price of peace to be paid by the vanquished, a series of treaties was signed in Versailles and at four other locations around Paris (Neuilly-sur-Seine, St. Germain, Sèvres and Trianon). The victorious Entente intended that the so-called Versailles system should establish a framework for the post-war international order in Europe. These treaties had fundamental weaknesses, in so far as that many conditions were determined by the victors' most radical political war aims. President Wilson's 'Fourteen Points' programme espoused the principle of self-determination of nationalities and the establishment of liberal democratic states without taking account of the difficulties inherent in the redrawing of political borders. The British and especially the French wanted to finish off Germany as a military and economic power, while the French and Belgians demanded huge and debilitating compensation. Behind all idealistic phrasing, the utterly punishing conditions of the Versailles Treaty undermined the establishment of a viable democratic Germany.

In 1919 John Maynard Keynes bitterly analysed and presciently prophesized that the origins and consequences of this 'Carthaginian Peace' had not been well thought through:

> Reparation was their main excursion into the economic field, and they settled it as a problem of theology, of politics, of electoral chicanery, from every point of view except that of the economic future of the States whose destiny they were handling... The danger confronting us, therefore, is the rapid depression of the standard of life of the European populations... Men will not always die quietly... [In] their distress [they] may overturn the remnants of organization, and submerge civilization itself in their attempts to satisfy desperately the overwhelming needs of the individual.[19]

The other four treaties had the same effects by creating a whole set of conditions that humiliated the vanquished and egged on the hubris of the victors. Romania, for instance, took Transylvania from Hungary and southern Dobruja from Bulgaria. The result was endemic crisis and long-lasting sentiments of *irredenta* in both states. Hungary emerged from the settlements with a sense that it was the biggest loser of all: it surrendered two-thirds of its prewar territory and three-fifths of its pre-war population. The rump state that remained was smaller than the Transylvanian region it had forfeited. One-third of all Magyars found themselves outside of the borders of Hungary. Various constituencies used irrendentism to advance essentialist visions of Hungarian society. The Hungarian slogan *Nem, nem, soha* ('No, no, never' to acceptance of the Trianon Treaty) captured the sentiments of revisionists across Europe.

The Hungarians' fervent desire to expand the state's borders to encompass the entire nation epitomizes the foreign policies of Central and Eastern Europe. Ernest Gellner's succinct definition of nationalism is applicable here: 'Nationalism is primarily a political principle, which holds that the political and the national unit should be congruent.'[20] The dominant perception in the immediate aftermath of the First World War was that the political community was tied to a specific territory. Even Nazi Germany, in the course of the next World War, would define its ambition as to extend its territory in order to create a Third Reich for all 'Germanic' peoples. Only the new Soviet Union, while tied to the territory of the core of the former Russian Empire, embodied its purpose to be the Fatherland of all Proletarians. Nevertheless, when pushed to the wall in the summer of 1941, even Stalin fell back on Great Russian nationalism and its eternal struggle against the Teutons from the West. In many ways, the inter-war period was the heyday of nationalism in Europe.

Italy was a special case. As part of the winning alliance it gained territory in the postwar settlement and might have been expected to be satisfied with the war's outcome. However, the catastrophic defeat of the Italian Army in the battle of Caporetto/Kobarid in 1917 initiated a crisis in the legitimacy of the Italian political establishment that fatally hampered its stabilization. At the end of the war, many Italian soldiers felt betrayed by their own government, which was not able to counter effectively economic hardship and social divisions. Despite Italy's considerable territorial gains, radical nationalists there remained highly dissatisfied and acted accordingly. By means of the seizure of Fiume, Gabriele d'Annunzio and his troops announced that they denied the Italian government the moral authority to enter into an international agreement over the definition of the nation's territory.

Not all treaties decided matters all at once. A second category of settlements consisted of plebiscites held in various territories across Europe in which populations were asked to choose a country. The vote was often manipulated in such a way as to make clear that the rules were once again set by the victorious powers. This caused much resentment and undermined the legitimacy of the new arrangements. At a later stage, this instrument was turned against the old order by whom it had been invented. The Saarland referendum of 1935 was the last plebiscite to settle the status of a specific territory as a result of the Versailles order. The decision of the Saarlanders to return to Germany spurred Hitler to call for plebiscites to bring Danzig and Memel back into his German empire. The Nazi invasion pre-empted Schuschnigg's 1938 attempt to ask the Austrian people to support their country's independence. The Nazi plebiscite that followed ushered in a new age of post-hoc affirmations.

The domestic counterparts to international plebiscites were the holding of elections and the formation of governments. The first post-war general elections in former belligerent states occurred within such a framework in December 1918 in the United Kingdom. In 1919 followed France, Belgium, Romania, Bulgaria and Greece. Poland also held hasty elections to a multiparty constitutional assembly in February 1919. Czechoslovakia and Yugoslavia followed in 1920. Neutral states, which had usually maintained an internal political truce in the face of external threat, continued as they were. But in these states war also hastened the pressure for more democratic processes. In this respect, different aspects of modernity merged: the advance of mass politics, the mobilization of all citizens for the war effort, both in uniform and in the war economy, and the idea of general representation and participation embodied by the principle of one-man-one-vote (in fact, in many countries one-person-one-vote for the first time). In 1917, in the neutral Netherlands, a compromise was reached in Parliament that established general suffrage and proportional representation. Likewise, in the UK the 1918 Great Reform Bill was introduced. The dominant concept of political participation by – and representation of – the whole political community, including women, determined the first stage of post-First World War politics.

In the first decade of stabilization after the War, the parliamentary concept prevailed in the 'old' states, as well as in the successor states and the newly established states, the Soviet Union being a notable exception. Governments across the continent depended on coalitions for political support and were required to step down when they had lost the confidence of parliamentary majorities. The Weimar Republic and the new states in Eastern and Central Europe opted for constitutional government, dominated by parliament. The legitimation of the latter derived additionally from the ambition to constitute political communities out of national communities. In the struggle for nationhood, any individual counted and was counted, so general suffrage and the parliamentary system were the most obvious way to organize participation and representation. The most visible consequence of this parliamentary political culture was however the inherent weakness of governments, not exactly an asset in a period of reconstruction.

In contemporary criticism of politics all over Europe, the sheer number of registered political parties was generally presented as an argument in itself that the system did not work. The same argument was used for the number of government changes, which were most spectacular in the Baltic states: twenty-one in Estonia between 1919 and 1934; eighteen in Latvia in the same years; eleven in Lithuania between 1918 and 1926. But even the remarkably stable British parliamentary system was subject more than previously to changing coalitions, climaxed by the appearance of National Governments in the 1930s. Such parliamentary systems could be stable enough, if the political parties that really mattered were limited in number, if the successive coalitions gravitated to the political centre, and if political leaders accepted the constitutional framework. In theory, parliamentary governments in the 1920s tended towards political moderation and the implementation of practical tasks like mending war wounds, nation building and taking care of economic recovery and providing elementary forms of social security. In practice, contrary phenomena occurred as well, when, for instance in the United Kingdom or Holland, Right-wing majorities rejected rapprochement with moderate social democrats.

A first stage of parliamentary political reconstruction ended in many states with a turn towards authoritarian rule. Fragmentation and a quick succession of governments wore down political systems. In such cases, the persuasive power of inherited legality was eroded and turned from a political asset into political dead weight. New and radical solutions consisted of strengthening the executive at the cost of the legislative power, and very often, of political liberties in general. 'Strong men' emerged to 'save the nation' (from disintegration and from enemies without and within) and assumed full responsibility for the establishment, temporarily or permanently, of a new political order. In the course of the 1920s, a succession of such leaders stepped forward. The first and most prominent of these, and an example for many others, was Benito Mussolini, who in 1922 assumed power in Italy by means of a 'legal takeover'. In order to assume control of the political process, he set out to bend constitutional law to fit his purpose of authoritarian rule.

In essence, the 'strong men', be they civilian or military, belonged to two different types: the arbiter and the ruler.[21] The 'arbiter type' of leader justified his authoritarian rule as a means to end political stalemate in cases where all other options seemed to be unviable. Such strong men nominally still believed in the rules but blamed the politicians in the first place for stretching those rules for their own benefit and group interest. Their purpose was allegedly limited: to produce a shock effect upon the political elite, or to reduce them to inactivity for a while in order to reinvigorate the political system. Those of the 'ruler' type knew better than to hand over power once the cleanup had been accomplished. Their purpose was power in itself, to carry through a revolution from above and reshape the political system.

In 1926, Polish President Pilsudski displaced a legally elected government by means of a *coup d'état* in order to establish a technocratic regime – the start of a period significantly named *sanacja* (the cleansing). A second attempt at *sanacja*, in 1930, completed the transition of the elderly Marshal into a ruler-type figure. He installed a military regime and strongly expanded the powers of the executive against Parliament. In 1935, at the end of Pilsudski's life, he introduced a new constitution that established a strong presidential system, in which the President of the Polish Republic was solely responsible 'to God and History'.[22] The 'arbiter' had definitely turned into a 'ruler'.

Thus, when the old rules were set aside, the legitimacy of regimes came to depend on the executive power's ability to appeal to a common purpose and set of values. In the longer run, such justification could only be effective if the regime was able to perform. The inter-war period produced a cohort of 'ruler-type' political leaders, not just strong men within the given political field of influence, but men who also developed new forms of political leadership. Mussolini and Hitler were the most prominent examples who served to inspire, guide, and ultimately dominate their peers in Eastern Europe. At the same time, they were not alone. Extra-legal and/or pseudo-legal transfer of power towards authoritarian rulers occurred in Russia (1917), Hungary (1918/1919 three times, and 1922), Germany (1933), Romania (1920 and 1937), Italy (1922), Turkey (1923 and 1939), Bulgaria (1923, 1934, and 1935), Poland (1926, 1930 and 1932), Lithuania (1926), Portugal (1926), Albania (1928), Yugoslavia (1929 and 1934), Estonia (1934), Latvia (1934), Austria (1933 and 1934), Greece (1936), Spain (1936–9), and Czechoslovakia (1938). One of the fascinating aspects of these changes from a longer-term perspective is how under such oppressive circumstances, and under the hegemony of state-supported political parties, remnants of political pluralism could nevertheless survive and still contribute to notions of legitimacy in politics.

Underlying Political Problems of the Era

The heritage of legitimacy, in itself a rather abstract category, became manifest in the way politics worked in the inter-war years. The rulers and the ruled in Europe had to cope with a large number of underlying problems. Some were inherited from the previous era, others resulted from the political transitions that had occurred since 1917–18. Three categories are examined here: the issue of territory and nation; economic development and class antagonism; and brutalization of politics. The way in which these problems were handled, or not, contributed to the longer-term struggle for legitimacy which continued into the 1940s.

Issues of nationhood, *irredenta* and *Lebensraum* constitute the first set of inherited problems that ensued from the redrawing of the political map after the collapse of the Hohenzollern, Habsburg, Romanov and Ottoman empires. New states emerged in central and eastern Europe as an expression of the right to self-determination of nations. Finland, the Baltic states, Poland, and Czechoslovakia were the fulfilment of national ambitions and they optimistically embarked on processes of nation-building. Nevertheless, an inherent problem was the position of the larger national and ethnic minorities within those nation states: in Finland the Swedes, Germans in Yugoslavia, Hungarians in Romania. More than a third of Czechoslovakia was composed of national minorities (mainly German, Hungarian, Polish, and Ukrainian). Not counting the Slovaks, barely half of the country was Czech. Poland, the national state of the Poles, was only 69 per cent Polish; the remainder of the population comprised mainly Ukrainians, Germans, and Jews.

Moreover, parts of states that were on the losing side went over to the winners of the First World War: Alto Adige and Fiume from Austria to Italy; western Prussia and eastern Silesia from Germany to Poland; Transylvania from Hungary to Romania, to mention some of the largest. Sometimes so-called victors bickered over the spoils, for example, Czechoslovakia and Poland in the case of Teschen. Hungary, considered a defeated state, even lost half of the Burgenland to Austria, another defeated state. Each of these changes created new national minorities that contributed – together with frustrations about manipulations in some of the plebiscites – to a further erosion of the legitimacy of the post-war peace settlements. Even so-called titular nations found themselves at odds with their supposed nation-states. Although the Czechoslovak constitution proclaimed the existence of a 'Czechoslovak nation,' in time most Slovaks came to disagree with the unitary concept espoused by Edvard Beneš. The Croats likewise had difficulty in reconciling themselves to a Yugoslav state that was increasingly little more than greater Serbia, with a Serbian King, officer corps and capital city.

Finally, some of the 'losers' had to reinvent the foundation of state- and nation-hood. Whereas the Soviet Union defined itself as the Fatherland of all proletarians, and Atatürk started to build a modern secular state for the Turks, Germany was left maimed and frustrated, prone to revanchism and ultimately underpinned by a revolutionary concept of *Lebensraum*. The meagre remnants of Habsburg Austria were cobbled together into a new Republic, which many of its inhabitants considered to be illegitimate and unviable. In particular, a profound uncertainty about the national economy's potential and international trusteeship over the state finances in the longer run fundamentally undermined the authority of the country's political class and institutions.[23]

Of all the states in inter-war Europe, Austria typifies (in the extreme) the disloca-tion following loss of empire and overthrow of the old regime. Many regimes faced challenges to their right to govern; many states (especially in the east) faced challenges from national minorities to the right to certain territory; Austria's very existence was doubted, or contested, by most of its people (at one point or another). Unlike Czechoslovakia, the titular people of Austria, not its national minorities, ultimately rejected the state. Moreover, that majority, it could be argued, also rejected the nation. Many Austrians were not sure that they were even Austrian, a term used hitherto to describe a nationally indeterminate citizen of the western half of the Habsburg Monarchy (Bohemia and Galicia included). Many residents of post-imperial Austria saw themselves simply as Germans, or German-Austrians, while many others identified simply with their region as Tirolians, Styrians and so on. The people of Voralberg even attempted to become Swiss at the end of the First World War. For the 200,000 Czechs who relocated to Czechoslovakia, the decision may have been clearer, but the German-speakers of Italian-annexed south Tirol could not be sure whether they belonged in Austria, Italy, or Germany.

The second set of inherited problems concerns those of a social and economic nature. Charles Maier has pointed to the phenomenon that in the aftermath of many European wars an initial period of economic hardship and political turmoil was followed by a swing towards political moderation and consolidation. The ability of 'Bourgeois Europe' to overcome radicalism from the Left and from the Right was in his view essential to achieving political stability and economic growth.[24] Nevertheless, in the 1920s social and political turmoil was widespread in many European states. The impact of the economic crises on the middle class moved that class out of the political centre towards the radical Right. The most prominent example was Germany, where economic hardship for many occurred against a background of political and social upheaval, in particular during the Ruhr crisis of 1923 and several armed risings. Hyperinflation became a political weapon that destroyed the texture of society. Consequently, the state was blamed for its failure to protect the value of money, and thus, the self-esteem of its citizens. When the *Reichsmark* collapsed, Germans felt degraded and devalued as human beings.[25] Henceforth 'Weimar' would be tainted by the spectre of inflation and lasting dissatisfaction over its performance.

As a part of the modernization process in Europe, the state and its subsidiaries had assumed more and more responsibilities in the socio-economic sphere. War and recovery required very strong organization and regulation of the economy. Faced by mass unemployment and economic crisis all over Europe, the idea of a planned economy appealed to many who rejected being subject to the seemingly arbitrary and manifestly unjust invisible laws of supply and demand. The Soviet Union's Five Year Plan was just the most ambitious (and destructive) of state plans to control and expand the economy. The Nazis, who according to Tim Mason were not very competent in matters of economic planing, tried to establish the primacy of politics over economy by creating a special authority for the Five Year Plan under Goering.[26] Thus, their method of structuring economic life closely corresponded to the way in which politics was organized within the Third Reich and which was dubbed 'organized chaos'.[27] Horthyite Hungary approved its own Five Year Plan in 1938.

In the world economic crisis of the 1930s, regimes of all ideological persuasions attempted to assert the primacy of politics over economy in order to produce results that could legitimize their rule.

A third set of inherited problems were related to the demobilization of armies. In the victorious states, demobilization and return to civilian life was less complicated than in those that had lost the war and were the scenes of unsettled transitions, large-scale unrest and civil war. Still, in Great Britain and France, unrest and public violence occurred on a much larger scale than before the war.[28] In Germany and Austria, large numbers of demobilized troops remained more or less together in the post-war revolutionary period and accounted for the process of 'brutalization' of politics that followed. This also occurred in Italy, where veterans strongly contributed to Mussolini's Fascist fighting squads, which violently intimidated and killed their enemies in the streets while the Duce operated in the political arena. In formerly imperial Vienna, demobilized bureaucrats, used to tending to far-flung provinces, provided another tinderbox for extremist politics. They, like their counterparts in Germany and frustrated members of the so-called free professions throughout Europe, proved amenable to using racial persecution (purges of Jews) as a means to professional advancement.

The German and Austrian Right-wing labelled themselves as *Freikorps* to indicate that they were operating independently of any state authority. They fundamentally rejected the Weberian monopoly of violence that the state traditionally claimed and refused to recognize its authority. On the far Left appeared the forces who took their example from the Russian Bolsheviks. They initiated short-lived communist republics in Bavaria and Hungary, risings in other parts of Germany and a civil war in Finland. After a number of failed *coups d'état* from the extreme Right, this *Freikorps* tendency was more-or-less domesticated, at least for the time being. Political upheaval was, however, not averted for long, and from the end of the 1920s, many of the supporters found their way into National Socialist and fascist movements and fighting squads. Their fundamental rejection of the post-war political order of Weimar (and Vienna) was a phenomenon that the new republics never overcame.

Though governments tamed paramilitary forces by the early 1920s, political violence was never far from the surface. Occasionally it broke through in the assassinations that punctuated political life in Central and Eastern Europe. Building on the traditions of nineteenth-century terrorism (for example, the murders of Tsar Alexander II, Austrian Empress Elisabeth, Italian King Umberto, and, ultimately, Archduke Franz Ferdinand) the new wave of assassins focused as much on ethnic as ideological enemies. The murderers of Walther Rathenau were as likely to have been incensed by the Weimar Foreign Minister's Jewish background as by his adherence to the terms of the Versailles Treaty. The killing of Poland's first president, Gabriel Narutowicz, five days after his 11 December 1922 inauguration similarly revealed the xenophobic base of that country's emerging political culture. Polish nationalists, including the assassin, rejected the esteemed scientist's election because his parliamentary majority rested on the votes of national minorities.

Political assassinations became an instrument of choice of the political extremes in other parts of Europe as well. In Spain, killings such as those of the Cardinal-Archbishop of Zaragosa (1927), Right-wing politician José Calvo Sotelo (1936) and poet and playwright Frederico Garcia Lorca (1936) by Falangists – only to mention a few of the more 'spectacular' cases – belonged to the process of brutalization of politics that anticipated, if not provoked, the civil war. The infamous killing of Italian Socialist deputy Giacomo Matteotti by radical Fascists was a low point in the violent intimidation of political opponents and at the same time forced Mussolini to distance himself from the radicals in his movement. Sebastian Haffner has, while writing his memoirs of the murderous campaign of the Nazi *Sturmabteilungen* in early 1933, linked the revolutionary and the instrumental shapes of terror: 'Die eine ist der zügellose Blutrausch einer losgelassenen, siegestrunkenen revolutionären Masse; die andere ist die kalte, überlegte Grausamkeit eines siegreichen, auf Abschreckung und Machtsdemonstration bedachten Staatsapparats.'[29]

Political assassinations justified the passage of measures restricting civic rights. After a young anarchist murdered Czechoslovak finance minister Alois Rašín, the country's parliament passed the 1923 Law for the Protection of the Republic, which toughened penalties for acts against the constitution, the democratic system, the state's integrity, and public officials. The law, modelled on a similar post-Rathenau measure in Germany, was designed to prevent extremism on both the Left and the Right and to secure the state against national minorities' attempts to undermine it.

Vectors of Legality

In the European power struggles of the inter-war years, heads of state could play an important role as vectors of legality. Europe after the First World War was partly monarchical, partly republican. Some states were formally a kingdom but *de facto* a republic (Spain and Hungary). Generally, the position of republican leaders in bourgeois states allowed less appropriation of power from traditional forms of legitimacy. Their own political succession operated according to strict rules and remained limited in time; it was empty in the sphere of magic and charisma was only a personal and not a functional capacity. Since the nineteenth century, emperors and kings were represented in ceremonial military uniforms. Presidents and prime ministers had their ceremonial uniforms too but not specially of a military character. Their public dress was bourgeois: tail-coat and top-hat, epitomized ironically by a former officer, Mustafa Kemal. The Weimar political leadership wore a mixture of top-hats and wide-brimmed hats and V.I. Lenin and the German Spartakists kept their class distance by wearing a working-man's cap. In the 1930s especially, years that saw a huge increase in the use of military uniforms by political leaders, the military cap was to characterize a whole new wave of authoritarian leadership.

From the perspective of political continuities embodied by the rulers themselves, there seems to be good reason to assume that dynastic rule was a strong asset for political stability. Even in autocratic systems, princes exploited the myth of the 'good emperor' or the 'good king', who in times of trouble could claim that they had been disappointed or betrayed by their ministers. In theory, at least, the latter were exchangeable at the whims of the monarch, or as a result of a more regulated political process of denying them further trust and mandate. Under these terms, the prince was able to remain in place, to embody the sovereignty of the state. Succession was meant to be unproblematic, as a consequence of the hereditary principle, and therefore to happen outside the political process.[30] Complications, however, could arise in cases when there was a lack of suitable offspring or when pretenders were put forward by warring political factions. In theory, monarchs embodied continuity of their political entity, almost apart from the questions of time which applied to ordinary mortals. Only their physical demise was to change matters. This implied a fundamental risk, as it accounted for the efforts of Russian revolutionaries in the nineteenth century to assassinate the Tsars in order to finish off autocratic rule. The same phenomenon occurred in Italy (1900) and Portugal (1908). As we have also seen, since the beginning of the twentieth century, political murder was 'democratized': would-be killers did not want to wait for civilian politicians to reach the end of their term in office.

Crowned heads of state who, in the aftermath of the First World War formally abdicated, underlined by this gesture that the old order had stopped functioning and was no longer acceptable. Significantly, attempts in Russia, Germany or Austria to put forward other members of the royal families proved hopeless. The same was true when former Habsburg Emperor Karl of Austria tried in 1922 to bring about his restoration to the Hungarian throne. Though he failed, inter-war Hungary formally remained a kingdom, with strong man Admiral Horthy as the 'Regent'. Karl's attempts divided the governing elite in Hungary, and Horthy had to resort to paramilitaries of the radical Right for military support against royalist troops. As Italian Foreign Minister Ciano mocked in his memoirs, Hungary was a kingdom without a king ruled by an admiral without a navy.[31] A failed restoration could be a breakthrough that enabled a nation to deal with new realities and adapt its political system accordingly. In most regime transitions, however, a tendency prevailed to connect the legality of new states with the one of the old order, by means of governmental proclamations, parliamentary pronunciations and plebiscites.

Dynasties could serve as stabilizing factors in a given political order, as a seemingly timeless vector of legitimacy. Although in many cases a nineteenth-century invention, or re-invention, monarchy as such was surrounded with a golden glow of, in Max Weber's words, the 'sanctity of immemorial traditions'.[32] The Habsburgs and the Romanovs had ruled for centuries and in the eyes of their subjects they had dominated the image of what constituted the state and political life. In the republics that followed, the populace looked upon founders as *ersatz* kings embodying traditional legitimacy. Following the death of Franz Josef and the demise of the Habsburg Monarchy, Tomáš G. Masaryk became the surrogate 'little father' of his people in the new Czechoslovakia. Similarly, Pilsudski's ability to shape and reshape Poland's polity stemmed from his position as the father of modern Poland. Ultimately, Stalin too stepped intentionally and manipulatively into the role of Soviet father, albeit an exceptionally cruel one, whose errors could be attributed to evil advisors.

Moreover, modern politics created a class of professional politicians and bureaucrats, who developed a potential for independent action. When politics as such became within reach of the masses, and when nationalism and imperialism grew to be driving forces in society, monarchs needed to adapt and fill the new political space. They transformed themselves from dynastic operators into national symbols par excellence. Benedict Anderson has pointed both to the necessity to do so in times of rapid modernisation of society, when their authority 'could less and less safely rest on putative sacrality and sheer antiquity', and to the inherent dangers that were involved in such a process.[33]

As a matter of fact, the position of the monarch would be as strong as the political order itself, and just as much affected by events in the political arena. In times of stability, they reinforced the legitimacy of the order as agents of identification. During upheaval, however, to challenge their position represented the very will to break with a given political order. Regime change would at least imply their reduction to the status of ordinary citizens by means of abdication and banishment (William II, Karl I, the Ottoman Sultan) and potentially the killing of the former sovereign. The execution of Nicholas II of Russia and his entire family symbolised the most radical break with the imperial past. According to Richard Pipes, this was brought about by the desire of the Bolshevik leadership to impose upon their followers a bond of collective guilt.[34] This was a radical way of severing the remaining ties with the old political order, much like the revolutionary killings of British and French kings in earlier centuries.

In the inter-war period, monarchs were no longer sovereign in the established sense of the term. Their function was a part of constitutional systems (democratic or not) in which their influence was defined and confined by written and unwritten rules. Their authority was generally limited and often more than a little irrelevant. Nevertheless, under stress of internal crisis or the threat of war, some crowned heads moved, or were moved, forward to offer themselves as saviours of the nation. By doing so, they claimed extra-legal authority once more, engaging themselves over the head of the political class with 'the people' and 'the nation'. Under such circumstances, a special relationship with the armed forces or the formal ties of an oath of allegiance might be quite instrumental. Thus, in 1922 King Victor Emmanuel of Italy played a role as an arbiter, although not an impartial one, in Mussolini's rise to power. The King's constitutional function in the process of political succession was fully exploited by Mussolini in order to establish himself as the only viable alternative to the political stalemate of the time. In several times of tension, the not-very-powerful British King George V took steps to cover by means of the prestige of his function political courses that he considered desirable, such as the 1921 appeal for forbearance and conciliation with the Irish Free State, and his support in 1931 for the formation of a National Government.

In 1929 King Alexander overthrew the rules in Yugoslavia: he suspended the constitution, banned religious and ethnically based parties and declared himself to be the sole source of legal authority in the country. In 1935 King George of Greece was restored to his constitutional position after a failed *coup d'état*. His intervention worked to end a stalemate in national politics by giving his prime minister, Metaxas, the authority to set parliament aside. Kings also intervened in foreign policy by pointing to their supposed special responsibility for the defence of their nation. In the stressful circumstances when the Germans renounced the Treaty of Locarno and re-militarized the Rhineland, King Leopold III of the Belgians made himself the spokesman of a strong neutralist policy. Consequently, the Belgian orientation towards France was abandoned in order to stress defence of its own territory and to foster the unity of the French- and Dutch-speaking communities. The 1939 appeal for peace by the monarchs of Holland and Belgium, supported by the Scandinavian kings, remained without any tangible effect and indicated, in a rather pathetic way, that in modern international politics their prestige was to remain without impact. On national levels, however, such interventions were perceived quite favourably. These monarchs were seen as protectors of international peace and national independence. In those smaller nations, such actions fostered national unity, while facing the threats of the outside world.

Nevertheless, when war brought about National Socialist and fascist rule and produced crises in legitimacy of the old political order, the crowned heads of Europe had great difficulty in maintaining their positions as vectors of legitimacy. Some escaped into exile, others accommodated themselves to the establishment of the New Order in Europe. Their standing was harmed in different ways. When Queen Wilhelmina of the Netherlands and her government fled to London, this move was widely criticized by many of those who remained in the occupied Netherlands. Many Dutch praised King Christian of Denmark and King Leopold III of the Belgians, by contrast, for their decision to 'share the fate of their peoples'. The indigenous National Socialists made much of the flight of Wilhelmina and claimed that she had severed ties with the nation. Her choice was portrayed as the symbolic ending of the old order and irreversibly gave way to the new Nazi order. Leopold, on the other hand, was to remain separate from his government in France, then in London, and found himself in an impossible political position that was to produce a crisis of the Belgian monarchy after the war. By that time Wilhelmina had returned with glory and nobody dared to doubt the wisdom of her decision to leave – it was even represented as something that had happened against her personal will.[35]

In Yugoslavia, military officers overthrew Prince Regent Paul when he seemed to be prepared to bring his country into the war on the side of the Axis powers. A military putsch in March 1941 placed the young Crown Prince Peter on the throne, a figurehead perhaps but still the personification of legal continuity. Within a fortnight he was forced to flee and reigned thereafter only in exile. Another figurehead-as-king during the Second World War was the Italian Duke of Spoleto, who never managed to gain access to his territory, let alone any legitimacy, during his nominal reign over the Croatian Ustashe-state under the name of Tomislav II (1941–3).

On the other hand, the presence of crowned heads would be an asset for some governments-in-exile (Wilhelmina of the Netherlands, Haakon of Norway) in their struggle to reconstitute their legitimacy, while others were rendered irrelevant because of the way in which the war and international politics developed. Peter of Yugoslavia offended Serbian national tradition by marrying in times of national crisis and, moreover, did not manage to maintain a government in exile of sufficient political stature.[36] It hardly helped his cause that the British and Americans threw their support behind Tito and his Partisan movement. King George II of Greece had been exiled before, in 1923, owing to a political crisis. After being restored to the throne in 1935, he escaped the German occupation in 1941, only to return in 1946 as one of the leading figures in the Greek civil war.[37] The most and least successful royal intervention took place in Romania, where the young King Michael helped to overthrow the Antonescu regime and switch his country to the victorious Allied side only to be sidelined and exiled by the Communists after the war.

Republican leadership, by its nature, worked in more businesslike and less 'magic' ways than monarchical rule. In general, in the nineteenth century new states set out as monarchies and found themselves a dynasty, especially in one of the German princedoms (Belgium, Romania, Bulgaria, Serbia). In 1905 the Norwegians separated from Sweden and chose a Danish Prince, who assumed the Crown under the name of Haakon VII – thus creating a continuity with medieval times. After the First World War, by contrast, most of the new states opted for the republican model, in accordance with the post-war spirit of self-determination of nations and liberal democracy.[38] Moreover, the development of the modern state and bureaucracies as machines of government, made presidents, heads of government and cabinet ministers look more or less interchangeable.

In fact, constitutional legality dominated the states' operation by providing the rules for the political game and safeguarding the lines of succession. The same holds true for the political classes working in the constitutional monarchies. In both cases, besides legality, the first claim to authority of politicians in the era of developing mass politics was performance, in the sense of representing the ambitions of political constituencies and bringing their programmes to fruition. In the aftermath of the First World War, however, republican national leaders such as Masaryk of

Czechoslovakia, Pilsudski of Poland and Atatürk of Turkey were strongly connected to founding myths that embodied the national ambitions of recently formed states. By contrast, leading politicians in the Weimar Republic, such as Ebert, Scheidemann and Rathenau, remained highly contested personifications of a highly contested new political order.

Weimar's legitimacy was hampered not just by its origin in a lost war but also by the republican and liberal-democratic basis of its constitution. From the beginning, reactionary and revolutionary tendencies rejected the legality of this foundation, including the newly established democratic rules. They were prepared to use these rules as an instrument in order to enhance their power and undermine the democratic system, but sought to rid themselves of the very same rules as soon as possible. In Weimar a pattern of socio-political upheaval developed that has been characterized by Karl Mannheim as a transition in society 'from the stage of unorganized insecurity into that of organized security'.[39] In this way, he alluded to a fundamental restructuring of politics, of society and of human relations. This was reached by imposing upon society the military discipline and technocratic procedures reminiscent of wartime.

As an alternative to republican modernity and as a complement for constitutional monarchy, new mythical representations of nationhood were developed. Thus, the new authoritarian, fascist and National Socialist states produced self-images of historical essentialism. This was intended both to exclude 'others' and to underline new ways of bonding between the leadership and the people as a whole. Mussolini's evocation of the Roman Empire's properties in Fascist Italy or Franco's emphasis on Spain immortal and Catholic served the same purpose as Hitler's assumption of the 'Germanic character' of people and culture. By doing so, they reached back over their immediate predecessors to find a legitimacy connected to the essence of national histories, in sources such as *Volk*, religion, or class.[40] Corneliu Zela Codreanu (born of German and Polish-Ukrainian parents), the father of the Romanian Iron Guard, commented that the nation included 'the souls and tombs of … our ancestors' and explained 'When we speak of the Romanian nation we refer to all Romanians, dead or alive, who have lived on this land of ours from the beginnings of history and will live on it also in the future.'[41]

This phenomenon was not restricted to fascism and National Socialism. Many smaller nations connected the notions of legitimate political order with ideas about national character or identity. Thus, in the inter-war years, a sense of 'Belgianness' was cultivated to indicate a prevalent sense of national community.[42] Yugoslavia's tortured attempts to create an identity to match the new state revealed a rootlessness that plagued the country until its final demise. Though the country switched its name from the Kingdom of Serbs, Croats and Slovenes to the Kingdom of Yugoslavia and attempted to reorganize its territorial divisions on non-national lines, pre-existing and continually evolving forms of ethnic allegiance thwarted half-hearted measures to create a unified identity (attempts that, in any case, never sought to give non-Slavs a place in the official culture). Ultimately, during the Second World War in particular, even the Soviet Union would re-exploit Russian nationalism parallel to class chauvinism as an asset inherited from earlier Tsarist times. Such issues were especially complicated in multi-ethnic states, where local and regional autonomism and separatism could work as disintegrating elements, just as conflicts of language, religion and ethnicity did.

Thus, the call for leadership and guidance provided new interpretations of citizenship and participation. In the 1920s and 1930s, authoritarian leaders who had conquered political power portrayed this not in terms of legal procedure. They preferred instead to stress this as the outcome of struggle between defenders of an outmoded order and 'the people' who knew their best interest. Significantly, both Mussolini and Hitler could have claimed that they had come to power by legally manipulating the constitutional process, but they preferred to establish the myths of the Fascist 'March to Rome' and the National Socialist *Kampfzeit*.

In the inter-war years authoritarian political leaders came to represent new political styles and content. Two types of authoritarian leader were visible, the military *caudillo* and the civilian leader. The first were professional soldiers who used their uniform and troops to assume power, in order to save the nation by enforcing 'unity'. Examples are Horthy in Hungary, Antonescu in Romania, Franco in Spain. Significantly enough, during their rule they appropriated the golden glow of royalty, especially while the throne remained formally in existence in their states. The second type was represented by professional agitators-turned-politicians assuming the role of redeemers, such as Mussolini and Hitler. These types mutually influenced each other and generated epigones at the same time: Salazar in Portugal, Dollfuss in Austria, Metaxas in Greece, and a number of leaders of the different fascist and National Socialist parties throughout Europe.

The ultimate form of this new kind of leadership in a new kind of political community was the *Führer*-principle in Adolf Hitler's Germany. It worked on different levels: the leader was to be a dictator, the one and only decisive authority in the political community, at the same time responsible for both the largest and the smallest of issues. More than that, he was the embodiment of the collective will of the people and their common interest. He was the one who had the capacity to guide all political activity towards radical visions of the future – and all members of the community, state-officials and all others, were challenged, in Ian Kershaw's words, to 'work towards the Führer'.[43] In short: 'Ein Völk, Ein Reich, Ein Führer.'

In Weberian terms, the authoritarian leaders may have represented a development towards charismatic leadership. Charisma in political leadership is connected to giving the impression to the ruled that their ruler is able to work miracles in their name. Such a capacity is supposed to happen outside the everyday routine of the rational and profane political sphere, and thus seen as sharply opposed to traditional authority and bureaucracy.[44] At the same time, charisma is not the only relevant capacity, nor is it limited to authoritarian leaders alone. The fascist and

Figure 2.2 The Spanish leader Franco in military uniform but with his wife and daughter. Courtesy of Netherlands Institute for War Documentation, Amsterdam.

National Socialist regimes in Europe essentially constituted new states, built on different concepts of legality and its sources, but at the same time on elements of the preceding order.

'New Politics' of the Radical Right

The authoritarian – and extreme – Right came to power both as a response and a challenge to the liberal concept of political order and legitimate rule. These tendencies addressed, each in their own mixture, the political problems and public frustrations of the inter-war years. Consequently, they were indeed attractive, in so far as they carried a credible promise to re-negotiate the uneasy settlements of the post-1918 'provisional regime'. The first set of challenges in societies and responses from the extreme Right concerned the ambition to regain and recover, or otherwise to conquer and expand territories. This implied revanchism and outright rejection of the Versailles system, intended to produce an aggressive boost of collective morale. The *Lebensraum* issue was a central issue in Fascist and National Socialist political discourse and consequently, occupies a central position in the historiography of the era.[45] At the same time, the heritage of lost territory and the ambition for empire did not remain limited to Mussolini's Italy or Nazi Germany. Political frustration transformed patriotism into aggressive nationalism in Croatia, Hungary, and Romania as well.

A further expression of the urge for national survival was the search for empire. This remained not just a project to enlarge the economic and political potentials of a state; it could equally be portrayed as a moral project, in order to mobilize the best energies of the nation, to give purpose to national communities and revitalise them. The golden age of European imperialism predated the First World War, but the inter-war years in fact witnessed an expansion of the British and especially French empires as they picked up lands stripped from Wilhelmine Germany and the Ottomans. In the 1930s a new imperial actor appeared very late on the scene: Mussolini's war for empire in Africa has been interpreted as an essentially modernist project.[46] Hitler's conquest in Eastern Europe, on the other hand, was much more an expression of social Darwinism. In any case, matters of race and racism were very strongly present, not just in the inherited nineteenth-century ideas about racial hegemony, but also in the fundamental rethinking of human relations (*Weltanschauung*) in predominantly racial categories as a driving force for political adventures of conquest, colonisation and elimination.[47]

In Nazi Germany, the drive for war production probably contributed more to the sharp rise in employment in the 1930s than economic planning as such. Nevertheless, this was used for propaganda purposes and internationally recognised as a huge success of the regime. In occupied Europe in the early 1940s, conquest by Nazi Germany seemingly offered new opportunities for the unemployed in at least some countries. Politically, this served to calm down opposition, as for instance was the case in the Netherlands, where German and Dutch authorities immediately made a connection between solving unemployment and the maintenance of public order. It would be the forced transfer of workers to Germany – and the harsh treatment of those from central and eastern Europe – that reversed the advantages of what the occupier had to offer to labour in terms of new forms of disciplining and organizing the labour force. Economic planning, however, was only one part of the policies employed by rulers in the 1930s to organize socio-economic life, both under democratic and authoritarian regimes. In particular, the disciplining of labour in the fascist states stands out as an example of how to take control in this sphere, in exchange for the prospect of social security for those accepted as members of the body politic.

Part of the bid for power from the radical Right was to resort systematically to political violence. The widespread brutalization of politics related to a process of the re-division of political space. Political action increasingly took place outside the institutions and beyond the rules of the system. Thus, politics as a process were made visible and concrete when political uniforms and new political symbols were introduced. Such paraphernalia were intended to claim that the political process was relocated 'from the backrooms to the street'. Significantly, the old order tried to defend itself, for example in the Netherlands in the 1930s, by banishing the public wearing of political attire. It was even forbidden to have little flags attached to a bicycle if they represented any ideological tendency. Nevertheless, the new political styles replaced inherited legality by revolutionary legality. This was the clear expression of a *fait accompli* resulting from a newly established political order that brandished the old one as obsolete. In place of the old rules, revolution as such was the source of the new legality, as substantiated by multitudes of ceremonies, invented rituals and, if necessary, new calendars as well.[48]

Thus, liberal parliamentary regimes were fundamentally challenged throughout Europe. Emancipationist socialist or religious movements focused their attention on parliamentary representation as the quickest way to fulfil their political ambitions and their electorate's interests. But, as frustration grew, radicals from the Right and Left of the spectrum used parliaments as a forum for their positions and a stage for agitprop. At the same time, the development of universal suffrage was a reason for concern on the part of ruling elites who wondered how to maintain their predominance in the face of ambitious mass parties demanding at least a share in power and the implementation of policies of vital national interest. This in turn encouraged an ideological critique of mass democracy and encouraged debate about the desirability of some forms of 'guided democracy'.

While general acceptance of democracy remained problematic, disappointment in the performance of the system in the face of the world economic crisis added to what was considered by many to be the crisis of democracy. The radical Right was not the only response to the challenges that were posed by the inherited problems of the 'provisional regime'. Several sets of ideas were promoted in order to adapt the liberal system or change it from within. One was introduction of the (originally Roman-Catholic) principle of subsidiarity in order to connect the political and socio-economic orders. The corporatist experiments in Portugal and Italy were observed with strong interest in other parts of Europe. This was especially the case as a result of the system's claim to have abolished class struggle in economy and politics. Another parallel tendency added more technocratic or 'plannist' approaches (such as that of Hendrik DeMan in Belgium).

A radically different solution was a temporary coalition of the Left: Left-wing liberals and social democrats, together with the radical Left and communists. Despite revolutionary romanticism, the 'Popular Fronts' were very unlikely formations. They resulted from defensive tactics against the threat that was posed by the radical Right and were only made possible when the Comintern decided to draw its conclusions from the defeat and take-over by Nazism of the political movements of the working class in Germany. In Spain, the many-coloured Popular Front Government was confronted by military risings and a civil war, severely hampered by internal divisions, and ultimately destroyed as a result of both. The Popular Front in France governed within the conventional political order, and fell apart too. In fact, the concept did not pose a sufficient defence against the radicalism of the Right. In Northern and Western Europe, and in Czechoslovakia, liberal-democratic legitimacy was safeguarded for the time being by strong coalitions of the political centre. When in the 1930s, the danger of National Socialist conquest became more and more imminent, moderate Social Democrats linked up with the centre.

Fascism came to power as a new method of political rule and state-building, even if in the process it undermined the organization of the state. Earlier authoritarian states have been identified as its predecessors – such as the French Second Empire or Bismarck's Germany. These precursors were, however, primarily étatist experiments in political representation and social engineering. What made fascism and later National Socialism similar but different was especially the elusive character of the state and its relationship to the leading political movement. In 1917, Lenin had stated in his famous theoretical treatise on *State and Revolution* that after the socialist revolution the state would simply vanish and be replaced by the associations of workers' interests. Even if the outcome of the process that he tried to lead was completely different in reality, the worst reproof against the Bolshevik leadership was to say that they had successfully taken over political power in former Russia. On the contrary, fascism and National Socialism had a political ideology of which the driving force was the very struggle for power. This was seen as a necessity to forge and harden the movement and its membership.

'Normal' or 'classical' authoritarian political takeovers were usually legitimized by specific political urgencies, such as the ineffectiveness of the incumbent regime, or the need for action in the face of military defeat. In contrast, the new post-First World War movements legitimized their takeovers by the urgency of their aspiration to rule, their *Wille zur Macht*. Political violence was not just accepted as a necessary means to an end, but was seen as a purpose in itself, as a way continuously to generate and regenerate power. Therefore, there was to be a continuity of intimidation of adversaries, neutrals, and even partisans before, during and after fascist and National Socialist takeovers. This was a product both of the nature of the movements and the political situation during their assumption of power. As Stalin explained in the not dissimilar Soviet context:

The History of the [Communist] Party further teaches us that unless the Party of the working class wages an uncompromising struggle against the opportunists within its own ranks, unless it smashes the capitulators in its own midst, it cannot preserve unity and discipline within its ranks, it cannot perform its role as organizer and leader of the proletarian revolution, nor its role as the builder of the new, Socialist society.[49]

Mussolini and Hitler, for their part, came to power as a result of coalitions with the conservative bourgeoisie. Under those circumstances, they were in need of continuing the struggle for absolute power, at the same time against their temporary partners and against radicals within their own ranks.

More than Hitler, Mussolini followed the path of taking over power within the state's procedures and structures, before he managed to stabilize his personal position as the *Duce*. Hitler assumed full powers in the German *Reichstag* by means of the 1933 *Ermächtigungsgesetz*. Despite this legal varnish, the Nazi party quickly set out not just to take over the state, but to replace it. As A.J. de Grand has argued: 'Ten years of experimentation by Mussolini in the techniques of authoritarian rule gave Hitler important advantages.'[50] Thus, a clear-cut distinction between movement and state could disappear, and was even considered to be undesirable. In this respect, the 'snatching of the body of the state' (to employ the title of a horror picture) by fascism and National Socialism radically transformed political space into a voluntaristic adventure, driven by a cult of leadership. The state, however, did not completely wither away under these movements. On the contrary, it would remain indispensable in specific crucial aspects, like police, armed forces, economy and the like.

After the takeovers in Italy in 1922 and Germany in 1933, the radical wings of the respective movements tried to perpetuate their revolutions and win for their rank and file the influence and positions of which they had dreamt. This development posed a serious dilemma for the leadership who had to find a balance between permanent revolution and consolidation of power. In Italy, the radical Fascist *Squadristi* forced Mussolini to opt for a more radical implementation of the Fascist programme. In the long run, however, revolutionary spirits did not automatically count as a political bonus in the New Order, as radical contenders from their own ranks, such as Farinacci in Italy or Röhm and the Strasser brothers in Germany learned.

The Italian Fascist regime needed two or three more years to consolidate and to transform the state institutions into instruments of repression, both of the old enemies and its own radical wing.[51] In Germany, the Nazi revolution from below was damped down in the course of 1933 to such a degree that discontent spread among the rank and file. The Night of the Long Knives was organized both to domesticate the *Sturmabteilungen* and to spread fear among fellow-travellers from the old regime, who started to feel uneasy. After consolidation of the regimes, the Fascist and Nazi revolutionary zeal were directed towards internal enemies (the political Left, the Jews in Germany) and more and more outward, especially in the struggle for empire and *Lebensraum*.

The authoritarian tendency in the inter-war period was primarily oriented towards taking over the state. The purpose was to strengthen the executive power at the cost of political liberties, including the role of parliament, political representation and freedom of association, freedom of speech and the rule of law. From 1921 onward, Hungarian Prime Minister Bethlen reorganized the political system in such a way that the landed interests could control politics and bureaucrats lead the administration.

Significantly, his 'Unified Party' which merged the Smallholders' and Christian National Parties, became known as 'The Government Party'.[52] Likewise, in 1932 Antonio Salazar adapted the Portuguese constitution. This was the legal foundation intended to consolidate his dictatorship, which expressed the political and economic aspirations of the aristocracy and bourgeoisie. Salazar's corporatist regime as an authoritarian expression of Roman Catholic social doctrine was strongly supported by the Church. Engelbert Dollfuss tried to guide Austria in similar directions.

Such corporatist, authoritarian regimes depended strongly on support from the vested interests in their societies: aristocracy and landowners in general, upper middle classes and professionals, and last but not least, the Church. The shared values to which they appealed were promotion of economic stability, social hierarchy and the Faith. This implied repression of the industrial and agricultural working classes in the first place, and of secularism and liberalism in general. At the same time, these regimes rejected the movements of the more extreme Right. They deplored the destruction of the existing social and economic order and the challenge to the church's moral authority. Thus, Regent Horthy clashed in the 1930s with the Hungarian extreme-Right leader Gömbös, Salazar banned the Fascist Party in Portugal, and Dollfuss was assassinated by Austrian Nazis after he had banned them. On the contrary, Mussolini's and Hitler's dictatorship can be seen as a new kind of mixture of personal dictatorship, management of parallel interests and aspirations, and administrative continuity. Mussolini's state remained halfway between authoritarianism and corporatism on the one hand, and Hitler's model on the other. He tactically consolidated his regime by the 1929 Lateran Treaty with the Vatican, but also initiated a radical project of modernization of society, that left morality with the Church, but action with his movement.

For Hitler, the conquest of state power was not a purpose in itself. Despite the name of the NSDAP, National Socialism was presented as a movement more than as a conventional political party. In 1933, the movement assumed political power, but expanded its position by taking over more and more of the state functions by means of parallel organizations. Even the police and armed forces would be sapped of their power by Himmler's *SS und Polizei* machine, including the *Waffen-SS*.[53] From the theoretical perspective of crude social Darwinism, the chaos was not unintended, nor considered to be too harmful. It was seen as a by-product of struggle, which was, within the regime as well, identified as the constructive force of National Socialism. In the end, the Nazi dictatorship practised an inefficient 'organized chaos'.

Recapitulation: Legitimacy in Inter-war Europe

In many respects, the provisional regime in inter-war Europe had an experimental character. As far as legitimacy in politics is concerned, three main tendencies can be discerned, which occurred in either a serial, or a parallel mode: the liberal-parliamentary experiment, the authoritarian experiment and the fascist experiments. Some states progressed in a linear way through all three of these modes: Germany evolved from Weimar parliamentarism, via the rule by Enabling Act of the last years of the Republic, to Nazi rule. Other states experienced one dominant pattern, with the others as aberrations on the margin. Thus, in the relatively stable parliamentary regimes of Northern and Western Europe, the extreme Right could only (and in part) assume power as a result of foreign invasion.

The parliamentary experiment sought legitimacy through representation. Parliament as a representative body of the electorate was to have the last word in government formation and succession. The political space was – in theory at least – primarily within the parliamentary system. Political justification appealed to playing by the inherited rules, and to the principle of 'unity in diversity' within the nation. The agreement to differ and the loyalty of opposition to the system were presupposed. While dramatic expressions of discontent could occur, these did not transgress constitutional limits.

The authoritarian experiment sought to legitimize its rule through an appeal to tradition, as indicated above by their tendency to appropriate the 'golden glow of royalty'. It stood for a return to pre-existing notions of stability and order (even if those only lived in people's minds). The offer to make things better was based upon the 'lesser-evil' argument. Authoritarians revived a repressive tradition against the new radical Left (communism) or Right (fascism) and warned the political centre that the only alternatives to authoritarianism were much worse. Shared values were sought in stressing national identity and national symbols or a unifying religion. Political action, including the attribution of consent, was state driven and thus the withdrawal of consent would be perceived to be against the interest of the state and the ruling elites, and therefore punishable by law. Their claim to performance was limited and reactive: preventing social upheaval and territorial losses.

The fascist and National Socialist experiments promoted legitimacy through identification, that is by introducing the leader principle. Political space was transformed in a continuous process of reference to the leadership's guidance and intentions, 'working towards the Führer' in the words of Ian Kershaw. Justification was couched in terms of newly constructed totalitarian ideologies that in fact were packages of different elements covering all aspects of social life. In contrast to the authoritarian brand of leadership, fascists engaged strongly in performance legitimacy. They promised to 'make the trains run on time', engineered economic recovery and made territorial conquests. Political action was stronger than under 'authoritarian only' regimes, and directed to continuous collective attribution of consent, and as such it was movement driven. Withdrawal of consent was seen as a threat to the movement, and therefore punishable by elimination.

In hindsight, the post-Second World War order was built not only on the ruins of Nazi Europe. It was also constructed on the ruins of inter-war Europe. In many countries, post-war leaders rejected not only Nazism and its collaborators – they also rejected the idea of restoring what had come before. In politics and civil society, democratic leaders felt responsibility for their failure to counter political extremism in the 1930s. At the same time, however, they adopted much from both periods; historians have found numerous continuities in both policies and personnel that often dwarf the discontinuities. Those areas where the inter-war order had already by 1939 lost legitimacy witnessed the most radical post-1945 transformations. Where, by contrast, the inter-war order had maintained legitimacy, sometimes even despite defeat, regimes and individuals reclaimed power after the war. In a simple typology, legitimacy led to restoration, while delegitimation resulted in revolution (with many intermediate outcomes).

The crisis of European rule in the inter-war period was not limited to Europe itself. At the same time (and not wholly coincidentally) as Europe was consumed by internal conflict, it faced rising challenges from beyond its shores. After a century of imperialist expansion, which culminated in the post-First World War mandates (leaving to one side the short-lived Italian conquest of Ethiopia) in the Middle East and Asia, the 1920s and 1930s witnessed the dynamic expansion of calls for decolonization and the exponential growth of liberation movements. If individual European regimes confronted threats to their rule at home then Europe as a whole faced an unprecedented challenge to its hegemony over much of the world. The traditional assumption in the colonies that skin colour legitimated power, that Europe equalled civilization, was eroded irreversibly. Like so much else, the inter-war period thus laid the groundwork for the *coup de grâce* administered by the Second World War.

In many ways, this is a familiar story and one that runs counter to recent attempts to resurrect the inter-war period as a legitimate historical topic in its own right. If we aim to rescue Wilhelmine – and Weimar – Germany from *Sonderweg* theses, we should also not view Europe as a whole exclusively through the teleological lens of the Second World War. Nevertheless, the focus of this particular book, with its interest in wartime and post-war legitimacy, necessitates the search for heritages in political legitimacy. In the longer run, this heritage does not need to be perceived as, and was not, wholly negative. The inter-war period not only delegitimized various answers to Europe's problems, or experienced crises that the post-war period sought to avoid. The inter-war period not only cleared the decks. To mix a metaphor, it also stacked them. After all, the post-war leaders without exception had either been adults or had grown up in the inter-war period. They had been at the least affected, if not formed by that time.

Despite the contested legitimacy of the Versailles settlement, the map of Europe in 1945 looked remarkably similar to that of 1918. Alsace-Lorraine was back in French hands; Czechoslovakia (that 'bastard of Versailles') had been re-established along with 'artificial' Yugoslavia; Romania retained Transylvania (and its disgruntled Hungarian population); upper Schleswig-Holstein remained Danish; Finland survived as an independent state; the victors reaffirmed their commitment to a separate Austria. Of all of inter-war Europe's new states, only the three Baltic countries disappeared from the map. Despite the undeniable shortcomings (even failures) of Eastern Europe's new states, Joseph Rothschild finds that they had one significant inter-war success: 'they legitimated their sovereign existence in the world's eyes beyond Nazi or Stalinist capacity to obliterate.'[54]

Much the same could be written of the so-called Versailles system as a whole. The states of post-war Western Europe committed themselves to democratic forms of government once again. Although some remained in theory limited monarchies, in practice republics became the norm. In Eastern Europe democracy acquired a new, widely debased meaning but the Communist governments behind the Iron Curtain always paid lip service to the idea of popular sovereignty exercised through the ballot box. In terms of justice, the attempts after 1918 to hold the Kaiser and his supporters accountable for war crimes failed miserably but the concept of retributive justice gained new life in 1945 with the Nuremberg Tribunal and thousands of other retribution trials held throughout Europe. The concepts of collective security and international organization enshrined in the League of Nations re-emerged in the United Nations and ultimately in the European Union. Although few leaders in 1945 looked admiringly to the post-First World War settlement, they were nonetheless limited and guided by it.

Notes

1. F. Furet *Le passé d'une illusion. Essai sur l'idée communiste au XXe siècle* (Paris, 1995), p. 51.
2. M. Mazower *Dark Continent. Europe's Twentieth Century* (London, 1998), xi–xii; J.J. Linz and Y. Shain *Between States. Interim Governments and Democratic Transitions* (Cambridge, 1995), pp. 7–21.
3. M. Mazower *Dark Continent*, pp. 1–2.
4. I. Lukes *Czechoslovakia between Stalin and Hitler: The Diplomacy of Edvard Beneš in the 1930s* (New York, 1996), p. 237.
5. J. Rothschild *East Central Europe between the Two World Wars* (Seattle, 1974), p. 263.
6. V. Mastny *The Czechs under Nazi Rule: The Failure of National Resistance* (New York, 1971), p. 58.
7. As argued by P. Laborie for France: P. Laborie *L'opinion française sous Vichy* (Paris, 1990); and by P. de Rooy for Holland: P. de Rooy 'Een zoekende tijd. De ongemakkelijke democratie, 1913–1949' in R. Aerts et al. (eds) *Land van kleine gebaren. Een politieke geschiedenis van Nederland, 1780–1990* (Nijmegen, 1999), p. 193. It is, however, applicable to most Western European states.

8. M. Mazower *Dark Continent,* pp. 4–8 emphasizes the general urge in 'new states' to make a start by adopting a liberal constitution.

9. J.J. Linz *The Breakdown of Democratic Regimes*: *Crisis, Breakdown and Reequilibration* (Baltimore and London, 1978), p. 15.

10. H. Arendt *Über die Revolution* (Munich, 4th edn, 2000), p. 14.

11. F.C. Iklé *Every War Must End* (second revised edition: New York, 2005), p. 59.

12. A. Wirsching 'Political violence in France and Italy after 1918', *Journal of Modern European History* I (1) (2003), 67–8.

13. E. Kossmann *The Low Countries 1780–1940* (Oxford, 1978), pp. 557–60.

14. A. Prost 'Representations of War in the Cultural History of France' in J. Winter and H. McPhail (eds) *Republican Identities in War and Peace* (Oxford and New York, 2002), pp. 98–9.

15. P. Berger 'The Austrian Economy, 1918–1938' in J. Komlos (ed.) *Economic Development in the Habsburg Monarchy and in the Successor States* (New York, 1990), pp. 270–84.

16. R.J. Crampton *Eastern Europe in the Twentieth Century – and After* (London and New York, 2nd edn, 2004), pp. 40–1.

17. E. Weber *Peasants into Frenchmen: The Modernization of Rural France* (London, 1977); H. te Velde *Gemeenschapszin en Plichtsbesef. Liberalisme en Nationalisme in Nederland, 1870–1918* (The Hague, 1992) as stories of relative success, or F. Sabetti *The Search for Good Government. Understanding the Paradox of Italian Democracy* (Montreal, 2000) for the contrary.

18. See pp. 58–9.

19. J. Maynard Keynes, *Economic Consequences of the Peace* (New York, 1920), p. 227.

20. E. Gellner *Nations and Nationalism* (Ithaca NY, 1983), p. 1.

21. A. Perlmutter *The Military and Politics in Modern Times: On Professionals, Praetorians, and Revolutionary Soldiers* (New Haven, 1977).

22. R.J. Crampton *Eastern Europe in the Twentieth Century,* p. 52.

23. P. Berger 'The Austrian Economy, 1918–1938', pp. 270–84.

24. C. Maier 'Two Post-war Eras and the Conditions for Stability in Twentieth-Century Western Europe' *American Historical Review* LXXXVI (1981), 328.

25. B. Widdig *Culture and Inflation in Weimar Germany* (Berkeley, 2001).

26. T. Mason, *Nazism, Fascism and the Working Class* (Cambridge, 1995), p. 60.

27. A term used in 1943 by a high official in Hitler's *Reichskanzlei*, according to: Joh. Houwink ten Cate and G. Otto (eds) *Das organisierte Chaos. 'Ämterdarwinismus' und 'Gesinnungsethik' Determinanten nationalsozialistsicher Besatzungsherrschaft* (Berlin, 1999), p. 11.

28. *Journal of Modern European History. Violence and Society after the First World War* Vol I/2003, nr. 1, various contributions.

29. S. Haffner *Geschichte eines Deutschen. Die Erinnerungen 1914–1933* (Stuttgart and Munich, 2000), p. 121.

30. In early-twentieth-century Holland, much nervousness developed when Queen Wilhelmina had several miscarriages and the dynasty of Orange was in danger of extinction. Politicians started to debate the options: find another royal house, or return to the Republic. In 1909, however, the later Queen Juliana was born. During the Second World War, when Wilhelmina was in exile in London, Juliana would be sent to Ottawa, Canada, in order to 'spread the risk' and safeguard the dynasty.

31. Count G. Ciano *The Ciano Diaries, 1939–1943*, ed. by H. Gibson (Safety Harbor FL, 2001), p. 484.

32. M. Weber *The Theory of Social and Economic Organization* (New York, 1964), p. 328.

33. B. Anderson *Imagined Communities. Reflections on the Origin and Spread of Nationalism* (London and New York, revised edition, 1991), p. 85.

34. R. Pipes *A Concise History of the Russian Revolution* (New York, 2nd edn, 1996), pp. 214–17.

35. C. Fasseur *Wilhelmina. Krijgshaftig in een vormeloze jas* (Amsterdam, 2001), p. 279; N. van der Zee *Om erger te voorkomen* (Amsterdam, 1997).

36. R.J. Crampton *Eastern Europe in the Twentieth Century,* p. 200.

37. M. Mazower *Inside Hitler's Greece. The Experience of Occupation, 1941–1944* (New Haven and London, 1993).

38. M. Mazower *Dark Continent,* pp. 1–4.

39. K. Mannheim *Man and Society in an Age of Reconstruction* (London, 1940), p. 135.

40. This topic is elaborated in Chapter 5 of this book.

41. C.Z. Codreanu, 'A Few Remarks on Democracy', in S. Fischer-Galati (ed.) *Man, State, and Society in East European History* (New York, 1970), p. 329.

42. L. van Yperseele *Le Roi Albert. Histoire d'un mythe* (Ottignies, 1995).

43. I. Kershaw 'Working Towards the Führer: Reflections on the Nature of the Hitler Dictatorship' in I. Kershaw and M. Lewin (eds) *Stalinism and Nazism. Dictatorships in Comparison* (Cambridge, 1997), pp. 88–106.

44. M. Weber *Theory of Social and Economic Organization,* p. 361.

45. Strongest perhaps in G. Aly *'Final Solution'. Nazi Population Policy and the Murder of the European Jews* (London, 1995).

46. R. Ben-Ghiat *Fascist Modernities. Italy, 1922–1945* (London and Los Angeles, 2nd edn, 2004).

47. Most recently in C. Koonz *The Nazi Conscience* (Cambridge MA and London, 2003).

48. E. Fraenkel *The Dual State* (New York and Oxford, 1941).

49. J.V. Stalin *History of the Communist Party of the Soviet Union (Bolsheviks): Short Course* (New York, 1939), p. 359.

50. A.J. de Grand *Fascist Italy and Nazi Germany. The 'Fascist' Style of Rule* (London, 1995), p. 25.

51. H. Woller *Rom, 28. Oktober 1922. Die fascistische Herausforderung* (Munich, 1999), pp. 40–57.
52. R.J. Crampton, *Eastern Europe in the Twentieth Century,* p. 86.
53. P. Ayçoberry *The Social History of the Third Reich, 1933–1945* (New York, 1999), pp. 100–43.
54. J. Rothschild *East Central Europe between the Two World Wars* (Seattle, 1974), p. 24.

–3–

National Legitimacy – Ownership, Pretenders and Wars*

Legitimacy at the Level of the Central State

In the summer of 1940, German armies established Hitler's hegemony in Western Europe when they defeated France. As a result, the rulers of the Third Republic lost office and the political structure in which they had functioned was partly overturned. Marshal Philippe Pétain assumed power to lead France into a new era in European power relations. The new regime set out to accept defeat and temporarily occupation in order to remain out of the war and work for the internal regeneration of French society. Pétain and his associates took care to appropriate legitimacy for their assumption of power. They secured institutional legitimation by means of a majority vote of those representatives of both French houses of parliament present at a meeting in Vichy on July 10. This action granted the Marshal full constitutional powers and a mandate for change. Behind the apparent respect for inherited institutions, however, there was a major break with the republican constitutional order, since the legislature agreed to relinquish its powers. Thus, parliamentary rule was suspended in favour of an authoritarian system and the civil service, the legal system and the police could follow the orders of the new regime without reservations. The justification for this political rupture was the need to overcome the assumed defects of the pre-war republican political order which had led to defeat. Consequently, the new regime set out to rally as many as possible behind the person of Pétain, to discredit the pre-war system in many ways, and to exclude the old leadership held responsible for defeat. Their aim was a 'National Revolution', which in fact was a reactionary effort to regenerate France from within. The new state was no longer defined by the ideals of the Enlightenment (*égalité, liberté, fraternité*) but by the protective and conservative slogan of '*travail, famille, patrie*'. The person of the Marshal was to be the keystone of the new political edifice, the one who could guarantee continuity and national cohesiveness, the bearer and protector of legitimacy.[1]

This chapter deals with the 'ownership' of legitimacy within the institutional framework and political community of the nation-state, and in particular with the

*This chapter was written by Peter Romijn, with Martin Conway as co-author, and the assistance of Denis Peschanski.

Figure 3.1 Vichy's National Revolution promised to build order out of the former disorder. Courtesy of Archives Nationales, Paris.

question how this 'property' was contested by pretenders within the context of the European wars which occurred between 1936 and 1945. This issue is discussed as a continuous chronological process, in order to locate and analyse competition for legitimacy in an era when European states went through a rapid succession of political change. Such transformations included mobilizing for the war effort, foreign occupation and drastic regime change. At its root was a simultaneous process of redefining nationhood, the body politic, the public interest and citizenship – the very issues that were at stake in the process of the appropriation of legitimacy and the retention of it. In this respect, the French experience of regime change in 1940 as a result of military defeat is a telling example of what happened in Europe as a whole under National-Socialist and Fascist occupation. The moment of transition was defined and sanctioned by indigenous institutions and thus was attributed an image of legitimacy. The new regime called for national unity and rallying behind strong leaders, while promoting a continuity of the civil service, judiciary and police under the aegis of the central state. All these arrangements left cooperation with the occupying force and compliance with its political project for the time being unaddressed.

For the sake of clarity, we argue that during those years three different poles of legitimacy manifested themselves within Europe which competed for the ownership of legitimacy: the liberal democratic camp, the radical Right, and the radical Left. These poles are defined by their ideological position in the first place, because that was how they represented themselves in the political struggle of the time, and defined the nature of their claim for ownership of legitimacy. Thus, in the age of mass politics, all three sought to underline that their own platform was to be seen as the very expression of popular will and the general interest. The liberal democratic tendency stressed individual freedom of expression and action as the means to promote the common good; the radical Left and Right had their own interpretations. The radical Left postulated the idea of some form of the 'dictatorship of the proletariat' as a means of deciding the class struggle in the name of 'the people' while the Right promoted the dictatorship of 'the Movement' and its 'Leader' in order to transcend the dichotomy of capital and labour and safeguard the interest of the popular community.

This assumption does not mean that ideology embodied the single important line of division in political life before and during the Second World War. Economic, social and political crises forced regimes from all backgrounds to improvise and compromise in order to remain in power. As we have seen in the previous chapter, both the authoritarian Right and Left, once in power, were forced by circumstances to resort to experiments in the governance of society to stabilize their rule and claims to legitimacy. At the same time, liberal democracies transgressed ideological borders by accepting corporatist models of economic planning and on occasions outlawing strikes and other social protests. Nevertheless, in inter-war Europe, matters of legitimacy were generally framed by political groups, if not by the people in general, within ideological conceptions. In the 1930s, political agency all over Europe radically changed in character. Politicians reorganized their following as disciplined mass movements, working towards the collectivity and thinking in terms of 'community above individuality', as expressed by armbands, uniforms and flag-waving, thus promoting a 'collectivization of the mind'.[2]

During the Second World War the dynamics of legitimacy worked in several different directions. Old states and institutions collapsed or were suppressed and the political forces that had made them work were suppressed. New ones emerged and hurriedly tried to develop new means of expression and communication between the rulers and the ruled. Under the shadow of confusion and persecution, it took time before political countercultures developed. When they occurred, they were of very diverse political and ideological backgrounds, and thus legitimacy became fragmented and took different forms while the contenders tried to appropriate it. Legitimacy was in this sense a malleable but not a passive phenomenon. Rulers (and events) influenced it, but it also depended on the attitudes of the ruled, who did not necessarily accept the definitions of legitimacy presented to them by their rulers, and those who wanted to be their rulers. Thus, for example, in France, one might argue rather schematically that there were five regimes between 1936 and 1946: the Popular Front government, the Daladier-Reynaud government, the Vichy regime of the early years promoting its National Revolution, its more explicitly pro-German successor and the De Gaulle liberation regime. None of these regimes had uncontested legitimacy and experienced varying degrees of success (or failure). They sought to demonstrate their claim to legitimacy by a variety of means: law, history, the will of the people and a rather abstract sense of the national interest were invented with the aim of claiming 'ownership' of an elusive entity of legitimacy that was never entirely under their control. This chapter will discuss how, at the level of the embattled nation-state, legitimacy was at stake and contested, how it became fragmented as a result of war and occupation, how it became rearranged in the course of the occupations and, finally, at the end of the war, how it was re-established within the framework of the nation-state.

From our point of view, a clear distinction should be made between the continuous struggle for power among the different contending states and power blocs and the competition within those states for legitimacy as such. For reasons that have been addressed in the previous chapters, the appropriation of power, even of absolute power, is not identical with the construction of legitimacy as a longer term basis of a particular regime. In the era of the European wars of the mid-twentieth century, however, large-scale shifts in political power, in the form of conquest and regime change posed spectacular challenges to new rulers to appropriate (construct, maintain, and defend) legitimacy in a given political sphere. The 'war for legitimacy', therefore, had dynamics of its own, separate from those that determined the military war for power. Legitimacy was not made by military power, but war and occupation had a strong potential to provoke regime change and affect legitimacy by forcing people to reconsider their relations to authority.

In the established states in north-western Europe especially, the elites that had remained in possession of the state after the First World War based their claims to rule on legal and institutional continuity. They justified their seemingly fixed position by pointing to the principles of liberal parliamentarism. Derived from the evolutions of the nineteenth century they saw the nature of freedom as residing in a balance of the electoral principle with the constraints of the rule of law and historical or constitutional tradition. The new regimes of the radical Left and radical Right went further. While employing old forms as long as these were considered to be expedient, they sought to develop a practice of governance that could comply with their ideological principles. The new dictatorships linked all the characteristics of a strong state with a more or less declared indifference as to the continuity and viability of institutions. On the road to taking over political power, both the radical Left and the radical Right were fully prepared to make use of the electoral process. After all, they shared the ambition to represent the interest of the popular masses. When they had assumed power, however, a state of revolution was created, in which the old contract with society was supposed to be void and replaced by a new one. The popular vote was now carefully orchestrated through plebiscites in order to show off public approval of specific acts of the regime and its legitimacy in general. Thus, the National-Socialist leadership organized the March 1936 elections for the German *Reichstag* after the re-militarization of the *Rheinland* as a demonstration of public confidence in Hitler as the German *Führer*.[3] Both the radical Right *Führer*-principle (in its several national varieties) and the radical Left concept of people's democracy served the purpose of ideological justification of the position of those in power.

Seen from the ideological perspective, the three different poles mutually excluded the possibility of peaceful co-existence. Each assumed that in the long run their existence was endangered if the others remained as contestants. From their perspective, each of the contenders in the European political order was fundamentally exclusive of the others: 'us' versus 'them', phrased in rhetorical terms as democracy versus dictatorship, the international working class versus the forces of reaction or the 'folkish' and ethnic community against the internationalist threat. In the political struggle for the consolidation of power, the radical Right would incessantly and rigorously present Hitler, Mussolini, Quisling, Mussert and their many equivalents as the last bastion against the Bolshevik threat. For tactical reasons, compromise or even forms of partnership between the three poles could be considered possible. Such judgments, however, were the domain of high politics, were played out among the elites themselves and were not open for discussion among the ruled in general. Within the framework of their states, rulers tended to ideologize conflicts of all kinds in order to promote unity within their own movements and to counter contestation for power. On the other hand, the fact that both radical newcomers strongly expressed transnational ambitions gave their supporters in other states very strong mental and – if circumstances allowed – practical support to challenge their own rulers.

Consequently, administrative procedures and public rituals in the competing systems stressed polarization. In the liberal democratic states this was expressed by stressing the symbolic importance of enduring political institutions such as parliament and the monarchy, or presidency. This was reflected in the way in which elections were organized as 'the national celebration of democracy' or religious pluralism was elaborated as an expression of unity forged out of difference. Para-statal or voluntary institutions, such as welfare organizations and trade unions within civil society, were highlighted by the political classes as partner-carriers of modern civic virtues within a liberal framework. The implication was that people did not need to be told by the state how to promote their own interests. In this way, too, the 'open' character of these societies was underlined. Political dissidence was to be canalized into disagreeing within the system. Those who opted to be outsiders in the end threatened to destroy the political order. If the elites felt sufficiently strong, they managed to erect a *cordon sanitaire* around radical dissent, as for instance in the Netherlands where radicals both from the political Left and from the Right were confronted with bans on public appearance in uniform and restrictions on their employment in public office. In opposite cases, such as in Austria, power was so fragmented that even within a Right-wing authoritarian government National Socialists were tolerated while scheming towards the overthrow of the regime with the active involvement of the neighbouring German state.

What liberal democracy presented as signs of strength and viability was seen by the competing tendencies as an indication of weakness and lack of willpower. The radical Left stressed the inevitability of class struggle. In the Communist view, especially, the takeover of political power would create a new regime that would be unpolluted by remnants of the preceding class society. The will of the people was to win and the Communist Party, as its vanguard, was supposed to forge absolute unity. Political rituals and symbols were created to represent the ambition of 'power for the working people'. They represented the image of triumphant masses marching under slogans of universal liberation and protected by the force of Soviet power. The display of collective enthusiasm – flag-waving, singing, shouting slogans – set the norm for all. In the same vein, fascist and National-Socialist regimes displayed rigid unity as a symbol of what happened when the 'national' movement expressed the ambition to embody the essence of what a popular community was, or should be.

Ethnicity and 'folkish' essentialism were at the core of the radical Right's collectivist ideology. The fascist and National-Socialist ideologies essentially believed in the leader principle as the only way properly to represent the interest of the people-nation and to define its course. In contrast, the Communist Party glorified the collective 'will of the people'. Both tendencies, however, focused power within a small and closed elite and assumed the image of single-man dictatorships. Thus, the parades in front of the Communist leadership lined up on the Kremlin Wall in Moscow celebrated the collective process of 'democratic centralism' and the Nuremberg Party rallies were carefully orchestrated to present the marching masses to their one and only *Führer*, who by virtue of his supreme intuition was the embodiment of the collective will.

At least from day one (3 September 1939) onward, and possibly even before, the Second World War was a war of territorial plus ideological expansion. War, as Mussolini strongly expressed it, was essentially linked to creating opportunities for fundamental regime change. The decivilizing effects of war were instrumental to breaking up the old society's resistance to revolutionary fascism's ambition for radical change.[4] In north-western Europe, the German project was to win over the conquered societies and prepare the new subjects and their societies by means of nazification for affiliation to, or even integration in, the Third Reich. Military occupation was driven here by strategic considerations, but at the same time served the purpose of convincing the defeated by 'shock and awe' that the old order in Europe was obsolete and its days limited by its sheer lack of viability. On the contrary, military conquest in the East, beginning in Poland, was not at all about persuading the vanquished to accept National Socialism as a superior system and Nazi Germany as a guiding light. The territory was reserved for German settlement and the population was considered to be racially inferior and therefore to be reduced to slave labour. In central and south-eastern Europe, developments were initially left by Hitler to see what the lesser allies would accomplish in subcontracting to establish the sphere of influence for the radical Right regimes. Mussolini's Italy, in particular, was frantically but with growing difficulty working to dominate the Mediterranean by force.

Such broad varieties in purposes accounted for different politics of occupation and set different parameters for the power struggles under the cover of National-Socialist and fascist occupations. As was argued in Chapter 1, we hold the view that the location of political power is not identical to the location of legitimacy. Consequently, we believe that the 'ownership' of legitimacy was primarily at stake in the internal political processes within the different occupied territories, and primarily remained connected to issues of normative notions as to what constituted just and good government.

1936–40 – National Legitimacy Contested

In the years immediately preceding the outbreak of the Second World War, relations within the European state-system had become complicated, because the international and domestic political spheres became more and more entangled. From 1936 onwards, the liberal democracies were forced on the defensive against the more aggressive radical contenders for power, as a result of mounting dissatisfaction with the existing political order and the effects of the world economic crisis. Their system of rule and the preparedness to defend it were tested most seriously in Spain. The defence of the Spanish Republic against the Nationalist *coup d'état* would by nature have been a responsibility of the liberal democracies, which ostensibly were part of the same political camp. Their hesitation to support the Republic's legitimate rule was provoked by their perception of an underlying social revolution, and counterrevolution, which turned the conflict into a blazing civil war. Consequently, the United Kingdom, France and other liberal democracies essentially opted for aloofness, while Germany and Italy on one hand, and the Soviet Union on the other, involved themselves as a means of testing the water for the anticipated cataclysm.

Radical internationalism on both sides notwithstanding, their leaders were primarily tied to their national interests and had to pay attention to the preoccupations of domestic politics. As it was, neither Mussolini, nor Hitler, nor Stalin, had unlimited opportunities for adventurism in foreign politics. Stalin had explicitly drawn a line committing himself to building 'socialism in one country' until the time would come to export class struggle from a position of greater strength. In the aftermath of his Ethiopian War of 1935–6, Mussolini had discovered that – even if he had succeeded in rallying domestic support – it had seriously damaged his international reputation.[5] To make matters worse for the *Duce,* the imperial enterprise had cast serious doubt on the ability of the Italian armed forces to wage a larger scale war. Hitler, for his part, knew that he was speculating on the British and French reluctance to intervene when he reoccupied the Rhineland in March 1936. Before war broke out, he never could be completely certain that his leading generals would comply with such gambles and that the population at large would accept them.

Under those circumstances, national leaders were looking for options as to how to determine who was the 'main enemy' and how to face him: by means of confrontation or accommodation? Besides playing the diplomatic game, European political elites initially waged the domestic struggle for legitimacy by stressing polarity in legitimacy. They confronted external players as well as fundamental discontent from within. The outbreak of the Spanish Civil War ignited an already latent process of contestation of legitimacy that fundamentally affected all of Europe. From 1936 onwards, the legality of institutions and those who occupied them was radically challenged in different areas in Europe, and in many places fully denied. Spain had brought armed insurrection (on all sides) back into the practice of European politics. This radicalized political forces, and raised new possibilities such as secession (advocated by Flemish Nationalists in Belgium, or Slovak Nationalists in Czechoslovakia) or ideologically inspired insurrection against rulers (such as by the Legionaries in Romania). Justifications for the creation of new bodies of governance, the appropriation of the monopoly of violence, and socio-economic transformations, occurred along the manifold dividing lines of political representation, nationality and regionalism, socio-economic divisions, political and religious ideology and local conflict. Austria between 1934 and 1938 was a characteristic example of a state where recognition of political legitimacy became strongly fragmented, and the rulers had to give way to an even more radical Right-wing neighbour in possession of superior military force. This situation would a few years later be reflected in many areas of National-Socialist and Fascist-occupied Europe.

When both the radical Right and Left engaged in the Spanish conflict from abroad, the main contenders in the competition for domination of Europe felt forced to seek temporary allies across the ideological divides. In some states (such as Spain and France), the mounting international tension obliged a Popular Front between liberal democrats and the radical Left. In fact it did not survive the defeat of the Spanish Republic and in principle ended when the Molotov-Ribbentrop Treaty was concluded in 1939 and reversed all diplomatic and political alliances. In other states, liberal-democratic elites sought rapprochement with the extreme Right (Poland, the Baltic States, Portugal, Hungary, Greece and Romania). Elsewhere (the Low Countries, Scandinavia and Switzerland), a reluctance to choose sides resulted in the regimes keeping a distance from both radical Right and radical Left – at least for the time being. In the last category of states, however, the competition for legitimacy tended to shift from bi-polar towards a tri-polar rivalry, when the ruling elites were challenged by both the radical Left and Right. This was an ominous sign of things to come for those states that would be subjected to the rule of the conquerors of the radical Right between 1939 and 1941, leading to a more fundamental fragmentation of legitimacy.

The approaching war generated mobilization of societies. Their capacities to wage war, if necessary, within the framework of the nation-state worked in two ways: as a test of the collective will to defend the political order and the national territory, and as a rallying point for organizing support for the regimes. In the second half of the 1930s, both aspects of mobilization became omnipresent in political life. International developments were more eagerly observed by the mass of the population and debated in the public sphere. Here the media played a prominent role and in particular the new wireless transmitter brought world politics and imminent crises into people's homes. All over Europe, many listened almost in real time to reports about the Munich negotiations and its preliminary conclusion of 'peace in our time', and many private persons from different countries addressed messages of gratitude for the peaceful outcome to British Prime Minister Neville Chamberlain.[6] This also pertained to internal political life – for instance related to budget discussions in national parliaments, where socialists, in particular, were challenged to give priority to support national defence over internationalist theory and sentiment.

Foreign threat and military spending served to define the nation more strongly in geographical and spiritual terms. In young nation-states driven by irredentist ambitions, such as in Hungary, the nation was considered to be incomplete as long as large parts of the Hungarian-speaking people lived outside the state's borders. Royalty regained in part their mythical images of the King (and in Holland indeed the Queen) as the First Warrior of the nation. The Belgian King Leopold III reached back to his royal father's famous stand at the River IJzer in the First World War. He tried to rally the different parts of Belgian society behind him by assuming active, if not always uncontested, roles in foreign and defence policy. The medium of film was used to promote the image of strength of armed forces, prepared for defence and if required for attack. Dutch cinemas showed how the country's many waterways would be employed to stop the enemy, while British audiences were shown reassuring images of the new generation of battleships under construction. Public demonstrations and parades by military planes, tanks or warships served the same purpose, drawing huge crowds. Private organizations were founded, or revived since the First World War in order to raise the military mindedness of the public.

In the field of culture, European writers, journalists and historians felt stimulated to consider what defined their nations and why they were defending them. In some cases they were commissioned to do so. A semi-official organization for the promotion of citizenship in the Netherlands provided mobilized soldiers with a book called *Dutch Heritage and Responsibility*.[7] At the same time, more tangible forms of civil defence were tested: air-raid shelters were prepared, extensive drills against gas attacks were carried out and anti-aircraft guns were placed in vital places. Most governments started to prepare strategic stocks of provisions, medicine and fuel and took steps to prepare for rationing. This policy was not just a matter of preparing for contingencies as it also encompassed the wish to spread a reassuring idea of responsibility on the part of the rulers, as a promise of 'good government' if matters were to come to the worst. Thus, as a result of the mental and material mobilization of societies, the contract between rulers and the ruled was stretched and strained. When it actually came to the deployment of military power, defeat could generate a sense of new realities, and that the time had now come to break that contract.

The German *coup-de-mains* that brought *Rheinland*, Austria and the Czech borderlands into the *Reich* created such new facts without even waging war. Hitler wanted to convince the German people that bold action under his visionary leadership was their best option to regain national self-confidence. The politics of appeasement calculated the costs at stake and considered them to be too heavy a burden. De facto, this choice implied a conditional acceptance by the liberal democracies of Hitler's limited aspirations for the time being. It was followed by a step of the same kind by the USSR when it was prepared to accept the idea of the Molotov-Ribbentrop Treaty in August 1939. As each of the power blocs geared up for armed conflict, polarity in legitimacy was breaking down. The fact that a European war did not actually break out between 1936 and 1939 should not conceal the fact that the aggressive foreign policy of the radical Right (Germany in Central Europe, Italy in Ethiopia and the Mediterranean) prepared the minds of their adherents for more to come and more to claim. For the Soviet Union, on the other hand, the 1939 Treaty was an instrument to proclaim their westward ambitions in Poland and Finland.

When Germany waged an all-out war in 1939 and 1940, the strategy of *Blitzkrieg* provided a full and convincing picture of what a decisive deployment of military means could achieve politically. Until then, as Raymond Aron observed, the only thing that realistically could have stopped Hitler's regime intent upon unlimited action was a conspiracy on the part of the traditionalist conservative military.[8] In the light of Hitler's successes in Poland and the West, especially in overwhelming the old enemy France, this door remained closed for a long time to come. For many Germans, the impossible suddenly seemed to come within reach: German domination of the continent and its enemies whom it held responsible for the demise of the former *Kaiserreich* and the upheavals of the inter-war years.[9] Thus, the resort to war did not just change power-relations between and within states – it also affected how people perceived the political order and the potential of political agency. War enabled regimes to overcome mental and practical obstacles in order to make real their political ambitions. Moreover, war brought many abroad, into the conquered area, with a sense of establishing a new order and strengthening their own nation. The regime that made all of this possible succeeded in justifying itself by the decision to opt for the very tool of war.

Thus, the German domination of Central and Western Europe achieved between 1938 and 1940 (starting in Austria, ending in France) redefined internal politics in the occupied territories. The radical Right's 'New Order' was triumphant, the liberal-democratic system now defeated and its agents demoralized. Within this sphere of influence the radical Left was hardly a player as it was kept at a safe distance by the conditions of the Molotov-Ribbentrop Treaty. The legitimacy of the 'Old Order' in the occupied territories seemed to be fully destroyed, as was shown by the example of Vichy in July 1940. The first stage of the occupations was characterized by the effort of the occupying forces to seek the active involvement of the indigenous elites, often at the expense of the local pro-Nazis and fascist groups. As the former administrative elites remained in place, the state was brought under the control of foreign rulers. As conquerors, they took care to take the monopoly of violence away from the defeated states, by assuming control over police and armed forces. Military officers taken as prisoners of war were released on condition that they would swear an oath never to take up arms against Germany.

Thus, the Old Order when defeated in 1940 lost its agency and many of its claims to legitimacy. Accommodation to, or collaboration with, the newly established regime was made easier for the old elites, as it seemed either logical or desirable in the name of the greater national good. Those who took care of the administration and economic life stressed their inherited legitimacy of occupying their positions before the war. Their promise was to normalize daily life by taking care of the economy and administration at large. Increasingly, they had to justify their opting for 'the lesser evil' (as the Belgian elite phrased it in the aftermath of defeat in 1940) by pointing at their role of mediators between the occupying force and the indigenous society.[10] In order to maintain such a position, they had to appeal to the populations to refrain from 'irresponsible acts' of resistance – from symbolic action to violence. Throughout occupied north-western Europe, the first year or so of occupation saw proclamations in which authorities from the Old Order called upon their compatriots not to disturb law and order, abide by the new rulers and not to evade rationing. Interestingly enough, the exiled governments initially took the same point of view in their radio broadcasts to the occupied territories. Calls for active resistance were taken up first by scattered patriotic activists, supported by a clandestine press that only significantly started to develop in the course of 1941.

A closer look at what actually happened when regimes of occupation were established in the early stage of the Second World War in north-western Europe helps to explain which instruments the occupying powers sought to apply and how they worked towards the purpose of appropriating legitimacy. With hindsight, it may seem strange that invading neighbouring states and overthrowing their regimes by brute force hardly caused trouble in terms of establishing workable relationships with the conquered peoples and their elites. This is even more the case when one considers that the justifications that were first made public were in fact ones of German strategic interest. Their efforts to demonstrate that the British and French governments were to blame for the war in the first place, and for the consequent misfortunes of the populations of Scandinavia, the Low Countries and their own states, were not quite convincing. Still, after defeat, such arguments proved at least to be comprehensible. One need not fully accept such an explanation in order to understand why the German regime had acted in this way, especially if it was seen in the light of longer standing frustrations about the Versailles Treaty.

As soon as they had established themselves, justifications for conquest moved towards pointing to the need to understand the nature of the times. German domination of continental Europe – and probably more to come! – was presented as an effort to create new perspectives for those who were seen as fit and able to belong to the 'New Order'. Nazi propaganda announced a glorious future at different levels: jobs and prosperity; working for progress and the common good instead of for the interest of the happy few; the cleansing of supposedly 'alien elements' from the body politic; and the end of liberal individualism, to be replaced by the 'popular community'. There are many indications that this propaganda was working, not just because of the shock of military defeat, but also as a continuation of those critical voices, who in the 1930s had challenged the legitimacy of the traditional elites. Now German dominance was seen as an established fact, industry and labour alike were ready to produce for the German war effort, in shipbuilding, construction, producing provisions and equipment for the armies of occupation to mention only a few crucial activities. This was partly caused by the need to reorient economies, but the basic wisdom was expressed by Marshal Pétain. After meeting Hitler in October 1940, he spoke the famous words broadcast by wireless that 'j'entre aujourd'hui dans la voie de la collaboration'.[11] In occupied Holland, the Germans started to construct military airfields to prepare for the Battle of Britain. Provincial governors intervened in order to make sure that the contractors would not be required to employ solely members of the Dutch Nazi Party – soon 40,000 Dutch, many of them out of work for years, were building runways and shelters for the *Luftwaffe*.[12]

Swift and utter defeat produced much soul searching among the traditional elites and political parties in the occupied territories. The establishment of the 'New Order' facilitated a turn towards indigenous Right-wing authoritarianism. What helped to catalyse this process was that in many conquered territories, the state and its institutions lost significance as a focus for rallying people. It was replaced by active promotion of the more idealistic concepts of the Nation, the Fatherland, and the National Community. These were the very essentialist and anti-internationalist concepts of the body politic that offered common ground to both movements of national unity and the radical Right. For the time being, the Vichy regime, the *Nederlandse Unie*, and the Slovak People's Party, among others, could pretend to speak the same political language as their German counterparts who controlled them. The idea of 'earning the respect' of the National-Socialist occupiers by means of a display of national unity, regeneration, and reconstruction was widespread in Europe in 1940–1, and served to keep legitimacy largely in the hands of the national elites engaging in these projects. This was an uncertain ownership of legitimacy, partly by default of a viable alternative, and contingent on success. At the same time, it was evident that the drive to continue working and living under the new circumstances determined the attitude of the ruled and the rulers alike.

At the same time, departing from strategic considerations, the authorities of occupation in north-western Europe were inclined to bet on the traditional elites first. Joseph Terboven, Hitler's *Reichskommissar* for Norway, was extremely upset about the seizure of power by Vidkun Quisling, the leader of the country's extreme-Right grouping, the *Nasjonal Samling*. On the day of the German invasion of Norway, when King Haakon's government had withdrawn from the capital of Oslo, Quisling addressed the nation over the radio and declared himself Prime Minister. Quisling's coup – although initially welcomed by Hitler – soon proved to be unproductive for the German military advance. After six days, he was dismissed, a period long enough to saddle him with the widespread reputation as a traitor. His name was used by Churchill to brandish political treason, when the British Prime Minister spoke on the radio of 'the vile race of Quislings ... which will carry the scorn of mankind down the centuries'. Terboven returned Quisling to a position of power in September 1940 but he turned out to be no asset at all as he represented an absolute deficit in terms of legitimacy.[13]

Elsewhere along the North Sea, German occupiers tried to construct arrangements with the ruling elites of the Old Order. Dutch Nazi-leader Anton Mussert was extremely disappointed that he was not immediately installed in power or even allowed to address the Dutch people via the radio. In this respect, *Reichskommissar* Arthur Seyss-Inquart in The Hague had drawn lessons from the Quisling experience. In Holland, Belgium, and France, the highest ranking civil servants decided to remain in office. In the first two states, now the governments had fallen apart and left the country, they based their legal position on international law. The 1907 Hague Convention in particular had stipulated the rights of both the occupier and those in the occupied territory. On this basis, the highest ranking civil servants accepted an arrangement to remain in place after the own government had left for exile. Despite all the hopes of the elites that they would be able to resort to this legal protection in case of trouble, the one thing that the National Socialist regime did not want to honour as a matter of principle was the precedent of supranational law over the *Führer's* will. Therefore, these arrangements acquired the character of a fundamental statement of intention to work together but without having a legally binding character.[14] In Denmark and France, the defeated governments were negotiating to remain in place. In Denmark they claimed that constitutional normalcy remained in operation in internal matters, even to the point of organizing and holding parliamentary and municipal elections. In France, the constitutional order was changed in order to facilitate Pétain's reactionary and authoritarian project.

Significant differences can be seen between these occupied states. Denmark, Vichy France, Finland, Croatia and Slovakia were treated as (subjected) allies, although the line between them and the protectorates (the Czech Lands under German rule, Albania under Italian tutelage) remained very thin. The Netherlands, Norway, the Ukraine during part of the occupation and territories in Lithuania and the former Baltic states functioned as *Reichskommissariate*. Belgium, the German and Italian-occupied parts of France, the British Channel Islands, parts of the Soviet Union, parts of Yugoslavia, and Greece were all under Axis military rule. Annexed territories included Austria, Luxembourg, Nizza-Nice, Alsace and Lorraine, as well as parts of former Poland and the Baltic states. Historians have given much attention to the different ways in which these occupations were organized.[15] Much has been made of the differences between military and civilian rule and it has, for instance, become common wisdom to make much of the difference between military rule in Belgium and civilian rule in the neighbouring Netherlands.

In fact, the decisions that the occupiers took about the status of occupied territories could in some cases indicate their intentions and ambitions, whether they were explicitly formulated or not. Annexation had to do with frustration about *irredenta* or the ambition to create *Lebensraum* for the own population. Long-term strategic considerations could account for the introduction of civilian rule. In a *Reichskommissariat*, a personal representative of the *Führer* could work for the nazification of the relevant societies to create the preconditions for a possible future integration into the Third Reich. On the other hand, there are many inconsistencies in such a deterministic approach. Holland and Norway, for instance, had populations considered to be 'Germanic' and thus were envisaged for future annexation. But the situation in the eastern *Reichskommissariate* was much more ambiguous from this perspective. Belgium and France were both under military rule – both northernmost *départements* of France even came directly under the German commander in Brussels – but occupation politics took quite different directions, as Chapter 4 will show. Moreover, the Netherlands had a civilian administration but, especially in times of trouble, the highest military authorities took over. In contrast, Berlin regarded eastern Europe principally as an area of *Lebensraum*, and therefore was much less interested in reaching out to the indigenous elites.

Essentially, the authorities of occupation searched for collaboration at a level that reflected their purposes. Their interest in betting on the traditional elites, as sociologist Cor Lammers has argued, was to make maximal use of their command of the institutions of the state and civil society.[16] Thus, the occupiers could be expected to cause the least possible disruption in areas where political and administrative arrangements were forged to maintain 'business as usual' – still under strict parameters as prescribed by Berlin. In doing so, they combined the colonial concept of indirect rule with the freedom to intervene more directly. The term *Aufsichtsverwaltung* ('supervisory administration') was deceptively misleading as a result of the strong will of the leadership in Berlin who were determined to promote their policies by all means at their disposal: safeguarding the German strategic position, economic exploitation of the occupied territories, persecution of Jews and other minorities considered to be inferior, promoting nazification and suppressing dissidence.[17]

For the time being at least, forms of accommodation flourished. In the newly divided territories of the former Czechoslovak state, the Protectorate of Bohemia and Moravia and the new Slovak State were integrated within the German political and economic spheres of interest. Czech industry was providing jobs and livelihood for the working class, while Slovakia was allowed to develop a new national identity in line with the 'new order'. Hungary, Romania and Bulgaria were treated as junior allies, where the more traditional authoritarian Right could be left in place as long as the German interest was not threatened. Prior to the German invasion in 1944, Hungary's position was ambiguous; a stance that reflected deep splits within the governing elites. Horthy's regime enjoyed partial legitimacy that it drew from the demand for territorial revision especially related to Transylvania, a strong anti-communism (in which it branded socialism as 'unpatriotic') and anti-semitism. At the same time, the ruling elites were divided as to how far, and at what cost, to choose the German side. Thus, Horthy managed to remain in power while obstructing the radical Right from sharing power.[18] Likewise, in Romania, Marshal Antonescu eliminated the radical Right from an earlier coalition government after an abortive putsch in January 1941. In the Italian-occupied territories, in 1940 Mussolini continued working towards Italianizing political, social and cultural life as had been the practice for many years in for instance Slovenia.

When considering forms of accommodation, it should be noted that when indigenous elites at the level of the central state for tactical reasons of their own actively opted for allying themselves with Germany, they opted for the position of (junior) ally. The higher the connections of the occupying regime with the indigenous administration, institutions and civil society, the more favourable were the prospects for the relevant elites, and for the occupier. Thus, politicians, civil servants, Church leaders, trade unionists, or figures from the media could be instrumental in making the new rulers acceptable and bestow degrees of legitimacy on them that could not be derived from inherited positions. Significantly, Roman Catholic clerics were prominent in the regimes of the satellite states of Croatia and Slovakia, whereas the prelate of France opted clearly for Vichy in a statement in November 1940: 'Pétain is France, and France today is Pétain'.[19] On the Protestant side, an influential group in the German Evangelical Church had supported the consolidation of Hitler's regime and participated in it. In Norway in 1940, the Lutheran Bishops supported the idea of a compromise with the occupying forces.

The German conquest of much of mainland Europe had created, in the eyes of millions all over the continent, a new reality that was destined to be durable. Interestingly, people even started to describe the time in which they were living as 'post-war'. There was a collective urge to opt out of the war and to take care of the necessities of life.[20] The bottom line was that it was up to all to adapt to the new realities. Despite this, a major war was still going on and all rulers, both indigenous and foreign, had to bear in mind that their possession of legitimacy could be threatened if they were no longer able to provide the minima of security and livelihood. 'British pilots have no mercy!' was the slogan on German placards on the continent in order to blame the enemy for causing loss of life during bombing raids.

Likewise, the British navy was blamed once again for blockading the Continent and provoking shortages of food and other essential products.

Like the German and Italian rulers, the elites in the non-defeated states (the United Kingdom, the remaining neutrals, and Finland after the 'Winter War') maintained their own appropriation of legitimacy, although they never could be completely certain whether setbacks and hardship might lead to opposition. On the whole, the capacity to wage war was an important property of legitimacy in the contending states, just as the capacity to evade war was in the neutral states. Rulers in the neutral states were not obliged to seek accommodation with occupiers but they had to maintain forms of co-existence with the belligerents whom they wanted to keep out. In doing so, they had to keep a keen eye on relations of military force and to decide how far they could go in adapting to those who posed the largest threat. Thus, Social Democrat-ruled Sweden allowed Germany to acquire essential raw materials for its armament industry in order to avoid occupation. Similarly, the authoritarian Right-wing dictator Salazar in Portugal had to take account of the need to appease Britain and the United States in order to safeguard Portugal's colonial empire and, step by step, he facilitated their use of the Azores, indispensable as they were for transatlantic transport lines. This is not to argue that neutrality was a mission impossible because that is self-evident. The important point is that rulers in neutral states were obliged to balance considerations of domestic credibility with *Realpolitik* in their international relations, and that they would be judged according to their degree of success or failure.

In the non-occupied belligerent states the rulers had to take into account that the war might strongly affect their relationship with the ruled. All remembered what had happened at the end of the First World War, when governments that had been defeated were overthrown as a result of lost confidence and popular uprisings. Moreover, the memory of the massive killing in the Great War gave rise to prolonged war weariness and waves of pacifist-inclined sentiment. When war came, in fact, the masses proved much better able than expected to absorb the effects of warfare and destruction on their personal lives. Massive shelling or bombing from the air did immense damage to civil populations and caused great personal suffering and tragedy. Nevertheless, for the time being, these phenomena did not disrupt social life to such an extent as to produce large amounts of anger at their own rulers and undermine the latter's legitimacy. The challenge for those in charge was to show that they were able to take as much care as possible to minimize the damage done by the enemy, and to explain convincingly what the purpose was of the suffering and sacrifice. For this reason, and very early in the conflict, the British authorities promoted in their propaganda towards the 'Home Front' a myth of the Blitz. Brits were supposed to remain stoic when bombed from the air and, most of all, resolved to continue stubbornly with daily life as part of the collective effort to win the war. As was the case all over Europe, bombed-out town dwellers tended to spread into the surrounding areas for temporary shelter. Of course a risk existed that they would thus spread dissatisfaction with their government. In fact, especially during the first years of the war, the effort to rescue and reconstruct was more often than not a shared effort by fellow citizens and rulers alike, and therefore had a significant and politically stabilizing rallying effect.

Thus, in the years before the Second World War actually broke out, relationships between rulers and the ruled all over Europe grew tenser. Legitimacy was increasingly contested, both from outside, by other regimes, as well as from the inside, by protagonists of other regimes. War and occupation by the National-Socialist and fascist regimes caused profound political changes at the level of the central state. In states that had lost the war, the rulers were removed or became dependent upon the occupying powers. In occupied north-western Europe, the German conquerors tested the waters to see how far the national elites would be prepared to accept the new rulers, their ideologies and purposes. In the occupied territories, notably in the east, polarity was radically turned around: the former rulers of the central state were 'them' now, and those who had been the contestants from the outside were now in charge. This clear-cut division was to come to an end, however, once again because of a military campaign: the German invasion of the Soviet Union. The German authorities tried to maximize European support for this endeavour under the slogan 'who is not with us, is against us'.[21] As a matter of fact, this stance had the opposite effect from that intended and caused a fragmentation of legitimacy. As legitimacy deserted the occupation regimes, it did not necessarily go anywhere else. A variety of contenders for power competed, none of whom possessed a clear legitimacy.

1941–3 A Fragmentation of Legitimacy

Until June 1941, Hitler's Germany and its allies had fought a largely conventional war for domination of its enemies in the West – although from Hitler's perspective, domination implied that inevitably, the time would come to subject the ruled to the National-Socialist redefinition of the relationship between state and society. Only the conduct of German armed forces in Poland gave an impression of the destructive character that the war in the east would assume when the Soviet Union was invaded. That self-proclaimed *Weltanschauungskrieg* displayed no concern at all with constructing legitimacy among indigenous elites for Nazi domination. In many places, starting in Poland, intellectuals, clergy, and administrators were killed. From the German perspective, their rule over a population that was considered to be racially inferior and the ultimate colonization of their living space could only be hampered by local elites who might wish to play a role of their own. Therefore, initial offers of collaboration in the Ukraine and Belarus were turned down and only at the lowest level accepted in the form of *Hilfswilligen* ('those prepared to help'). Legitimacy lost relevance in the occupied territories in the east through a lack of contenders. The Nazis simply were not interested and the local elites were reduced to a position of insignificance.[22]

In the German-occupied territories in western and central Europe, legitimacy became utterly scattered between 1941 and 1943, when it moved away from the level of the central authorities, whoever they were. At the outset of their rule, the occupation authorities had tried to find out how they effectively could tie indigenous elites to their regimes. In general, however, after the first year of occupation, the 'attentism' of these elites and their propensity for accommodation with the new rulers proved to have limitations. The 'other side of resilience' was that authorities of the old order who still remained in place took care to manoeuvre carefully in order not to become contaminated politically through their close association with the occupying authority. The policy of nazification of state and society became an essential part of the dynamics of National Socialist rule. This was initiated in some countries earlier than in others, but in essence the German authorities required that the administration, the media and cultural life would be reoriented towards supporting their purposes in the occupied territories. Working by means of the carrot and the stick, they were not content with suppression of dissidence alone, but required active involvement in what can be called – with reference to British historian Ian Kershaw – 'working towards the *Führer*' from the Reich's dependencies.[23]

As a rule, indigenous authorities were cautious to show visible support for the occupying forces' own political purposes. They took care not to be present at triumphant political rallies, not to socialize too much and to abstain from all kinds of symbolic acts that would imply sympathy for the occupying force and its ideology. Non-Nazi civil servants in Belgium or the Netherlands had a silent understanding not to be voluntarily present at New Order propaganda rallies such as communal stew meals (*Eintopfessen*), military parades and the like. Such behaviour indicated that their collaboration, however substantial it might be, was conditional and orientated towards maintaining their own grip on legitimacy. How far this was a viable option remained to be seen. The leading circles in the occupied societies had remained in their place with the aspiration of providing a shield for the occupied society as a whole.[24] Therefore, their main aim was to avoid their replacement by members or sympathizers of the indigenous Nazi and fascist movements. *Esprit de corps* and a sense that they were the main pillars of a society in a time of crisis led them to attach the highest importance to remaining in their posts and thus preventing any takeover by the contenders from the other side. They counted on public understanding and support while accepting the need to execute policies that were required by the occupiers, even in case of necessity to accomplish specific harsh measures. In the end 'the lesser evil' is an utterly paternalist policy that can only work when the ruled let the rulers act in their interest. In the second and third years of the war, much legitimacy flowed away from the national authorities of the Old Order, as more and more of the population came to experience that the shield provided by their rulers was not effective anymore. Those affected by material need, persecution, and compulsory labour started to look elsewhere for protection.[25]

One place they could look was to the explicitly collaborationist regimes that had gained power in 1940. These collaborationist governments had hoped to build their legitimacy after defeat by redefining the political space in which they could rule. From the perspective of legitimacy, the crucial issue was whether they could be recognized as authentic representatives of the nation. In France, Greece, Slovakia and Croatia, government collaboration kept legitimacy on the central level, often relying on their heads of state as unifying national symbols – as in Belgium, where King Leopold III had remained in the country and thus broke with his government, which had fled the German armies and ultimately departed for London. When German occupation policies became harsher, the political space for the collaborationist governments became consequently smaller. Thus it was now impossible, if it had ever been possible, for collaborationist regimes to appear as legitimate defenders of the national interests in the eyes of their people. On the contrary they were seen as agents of foreign and alien power and this brought about a contestation of their authority. As chunks of legitimacy fell off of their regimes, so New-Order bureaucrats sought to seize them by force, but were simultaneously opposed in their arbitrary actions by the increasingly active resistance movements.

The first efforts of National-Socialist leaders such as Quisling in Norway, Mussert in the Netherlands, or Clausen in Denmark to acquire governmental power had met with considerable reluctance from the German authorities. When Quisling in February 1942 was thus finally named as prime minister of a collaborationist government, the news caused upheaval in occupied Holland. Here, in late 1941 Seyss-Inquart had declared Mussert's *Nationaal Socialistische Beweging* to be the only political party that was allowed to represent the political will of the Dutch people, while Mussert himself was recognized by Hitler as 'Leader of the Dutch People.'[26] In the first months of 1942, the nomination of Quisling in Norway caused many to think that Mussert would also be promoted to be prime minister. Radical Left elements of the resistance set out to liquidate some prominent members of Mussert's movement, who were thought to be possible candidates for positions in a collaborationist government. Thus, it became obvious that, because of the complete lack of legitimacy, a formal NSB government would provoke fierce resistance and permanent unrest. Mussert had to content himself with a vague, and in fact empty, advisory role. Much the same process was evident in francophone Belgium, where by 1942 the German authorities began a policy of appointing members of the collaborationist Rexist movement led by Léon Degrelle to positions of local power, prompting often violent responses from the population.[27]

Nevertheless, although the occupying authorities understood very well that the political impact of their collaborationist allies would be counterproductive, they were increasingly obliged to employ, through a lack of alternatives, indigenous Nazis in order to direct state and societal institutions towards the New Order. This happened in state bureaucracies, especially in sensitive, policy-oriented areas such as the police, the judiciary and the field of culture and communication, as well as in services regulating employment (more and more located in Germany) and in local government. The New Order officials who took over were generally seen as usurpers of power in the first place. With a very few exceptions, they generally lacked a popular mandate from election, or an appointment on the basis of pre-war selection norms. Seyss-Inquart bluntly stated that the Dutch Nazi party was 'indispensible for the nazification of Holland, and therefore tolerated.'[28] Thus, the recruitment of indigenous Nazis worked to move legitimacy away from the central level and from the state institutions in general. Nevertheless, at the lower levels, New Order officials were sometimes able to keep their distance from their movement's political leadership and deliver a hint of 'good government'. In those cases, they could in fact appropriate fragments of legitimacy that had disappeared from the central level. Thus, they might perform roles similar to the representatives of the Old Order on the same level if they could successfully act as 'middle-men' between the population and the regime.

In the aftermath of the attack on the Soviet Union in June 1941, the Germans started a drive to mobilize their occupied territories and their productive capacities in support of the intensified war effort. In the course of the two years following the invasion these economies were integrated into the economic system of the Third Reich. Initially, German domination produced an economic upsurge in most occupied territories and dramatically diminished unemployment. This was a most significant asset in the National-Socialist claim to legitimacy in the occupied territories, in the same way as the *Autobahn* construction in the 1930s had been instrumental for promotion of the New Germany. The momentum could not be maintained, however, and had the opposite effect when the German war effort was in fact perceived to exploit and impoverish the occupied economies.

The attack on the Soviet Union was also the major stimulus for the fulfilment of Hitler's promise to eliminate European Jewry.[29] The catastrophe of the *Shoah* largely and rightfully determines the memory of the Second World War and National Socialism. In this context, however, we are concerned with how far it affected the issue of legitimacy. At the core of National Socialism and fascism were policies to target specific minorities for persecution, declaring them to be outsiders from the national community, and putting them under threat of exclusion, and even physical elimination. When National-Socialist and fascist rule expanded over Europe, the Jewish population was segregated with disturbing rapidity from existing societies as a first stage in their persecution and extermination. Much has been debated in the historiography about the nature of this eliminationist streak of the radical Right. Debates have focused on issues of ideology and the question as to whether German National Socialism should be recognized as having been fundamentally different from fascism elsewhere.[30] Seen from the perspective of the policies conducted under the rule of the radical Right, both in their homelands and in occupied territories, it seems clear that the ultimate radicalization towards persecution and genocide was developed by Nazi Germany. Nevertheless, it is beyond question that Mussolini involved Italy in the exclusion and persecution of Jews.

If misgivings might exist in the occupied territories about the fate of individual Jews, it did not prove too difficult to imagine the body politic without its Jewish citizens. In some of the occupied territories, there was no precedent at all for stripping Jewish citizens and subjects of their legal rights and persecuting them. Indigenous authorities felt uneasy about their involvement in preparing and enforcing the relevant coercive measures, and were concerned to take as little formal responsibility as possible for them. Their fear of loss of legitimacy generally remained limited to the extent of their involvement in persecution of 'their own' former citizens. As a rule, the legitimacy of those who remained in office as administrators or police was not challenged as long as they did not stand out as particularly fanatical or cruel. Collaborationist authorities maintained that it was legitimate for the persecutors to single out the Jews in general as enemies. Nazi ideology had established this as a fact and now that a war was going on ('a struggle of life and death'), international law allowed the internment of the members of the enemy within their own sphere. Such eclectic references to international law in support of measures of cleansing the popular community prepared minds for reformulating the nation-state in exclusive terms.

Crucial questions in this respect are how the Nazis managed to spread their radical racist persecutions throughout occupied Europe, how rulers used them to justify their rule and how far their ambitions on this issue converged with those of the ruled. In some cases, rulers felt that they could appropriate legitimacy if they could narrow down the national community by applying ethnic standards. In some pre-war states, such as Poland and Romania, anti-Jewish laws had been passed. In most of the occupied territories collaborationist authorities made themselves at least guilty of complicity in the persecution. In several places (the Netherlands, Vichy France) they decided to take some steps even before German pressure was put upon them. Under Mussolini's leadership, Italy – traditionally seen as not inclined towards racist policies – decided on a series of anti-Jewish measures that would finally result in deportation and mass murder of Italian Jewry.[31]

Interpretations of the role that the persecution played in justification of the regimes vary greatly. Daniel Goldhagen's analysis about the genocidal mentality of German society suggests that Hitler's regime was doing no more than enacting the secret wish of many of its subjects. As soon as the unthinkable became reality, he argues, many participated.[32] Goetz Aly has pointed to other reasons to join the persecution, arguing that confiscation of Jewish property was employed by the regime in order to provide its own population with the spoils and thus offered them relative prosperity.[33] Earlier authors, such as Michael Burleigh and Wolfgang Wippermann have, however, pointed to – among other things – the need to understand racist policies and persecution in a larger context of schemes for the management of social and demographic issues – such as racial hygiene, forced settlement and resettlement and discrimination. In Germany, they argue, Hitler's regime sought to redefine social frontiers by prioritizing racial distinctions over those of social class.[34] Nevertheless, the German leaders managed to gain support for their purposes and policies. This support may have been half-hearted, given for tactical reasons, or simply out of fear, but it was largely effective anyway. It was strongly connected to more general European attitudes towards 'other races' – from the colonial experience, and now directed towards Jews and Slavs.

Justification for the persecution tended to be formulated in offensive terms if given by convinced Nazis. 'True believers' formulated the purpose entirely positively: working towards an ethnically cleansed, and therefore morally 'cleaner' future nation. Even if they addressed human costs, they stressed the need not to compromise over what was seen by them as a historic necessity. Showing no mercy might be depressing, but was presented as the only means of proceeding.[35] Those who were involved as 'non-believing' accomplices would justify their behaviour in more defensive ways, pointing to the fact that the occupier had defined a 'Jewish problem' and was entitled to act on that premiss, that the needs of the times compelled them to cooperate and that it would be better anyway for the Jews if their own authorities and police would deal with them. As a rule, Jewish refugees and other non-citizens were given up first, but no effective barriers were established against the discrimination and deportation of their own Jewish citizens when it came to that. Despite all such considerations, alongside self-centredness and outright cynicism, there was moral outrage, and a propensity among populations in occupied territories to protest about discrimination and persecutions. Church leaders protested, clandestine newspapers wrote in outrage and the resistance took action to help the persecuted to evade or hide. The visible first stages of the *Shoah* – discrimination, spoliation, isolation and deportation – showed the true face of the occupation regime. It compromised collaborationist rulers but in general it did not take away legitimacy from them in large degrees, indeed not to the degrees that might have been supposed on the basis of post-war moral outrage.

Most important in determining popular attitudes to the occupation authorities, however, was the rapidly accelerating determination of the leadership in Berlin to draw the workforce increasingly to the *Reich* from the occupied territories. By way of conscription and coercion, hundreds of thousands of Europeans were obliged to leave their homes and families and work in Germany. Moreover, the German authorities could not hope to organize this labour draft without assistance from the indigenous administration, from the highest ranking officials to the local staff of the labour exchanges. Initial enthusiasm about better chances of employment withered away and turned into hostility when the conditions of working in Germany progressively deteriorated. The use of force, the dangers of working in places under ever growing threat of aerial bombardment, and the working conditions themselves were reasons why working in Germany provoked ever growing amounts of evasion and resistance. It may very well be that forced labour in its full extent was the single most important factor in radically estranging the subjugated peoples from the regimes of occupation and from their own authorities which were involved in the policy. Until forced labour became a fact, individuals could hope that they would be left alone, as long as they did not belong to a category of people liable for persecution, such as Jews or Communists. Now, the regime stretched its activities to all individuals, and hardly any category was safe. Thus, repression accelerated and discontent led to actions that showed fundamental opposition towards the occupation regime: spontaneous strikes, the clandestine resistance press, and acts of sabotage. Thus, the process of evaporation of legitimacy from the level of the central state, including those remaining officials from the Old Order, was strongly reinforced.

A second factor that caused the fragmentation of legitimacy was the political implication of the invasion of the Soviet Union itself. Now all three power blocs in Europe were involved in the war and thus all three poles of legitimacy were actively engaged. The 'Fatherland of All Workers' was under attack and a coalition between the radical Left and liberal democracy was forged. This went much further than the pre-1939 Popular Front concept, because a formal alliance between states – and not between political movements of the (bourgeois and radical) Left – took shape. Nevertheless the alliance took time to materialize, whereas it did not end the competition and fundamental differences between the new allies, who were more united by a common enemy than by a common cause. All in all, the radicalization of the politics of occupation and the involvement of the Soviet Union in the war were the combined causes of a process of fragmentation of legitimacy. The Nazis could no longer be sure where it was located and how to get hold of it. Thus, as they had to rely increasingly on compulsion and the use of sheer force, legitimacy largely disappeared from the central level of the occupied political entities.

The other contenders, for their part, were in a similar position. The protagonists of the Old Order had to overcome utter defeat and search for options: where to start to reconstruct legitimacy for their cause? The central level was immensely problematic as the administrative and economic elites grew increasingly contaminated by collaboration. Those in the lower levels could only hope to be recognized by their actions as protectors of the population, rather than as enforcers of the occupying powers' policies. The radical Left, from their perspective, had to build an alternative from the bottom up, turning dissatisfaction into politically inspired resistance. The Communists, in particular, needed to overcome the damage done to their image by the Molotov-Ribbentrop Pact. Moreover, civil societies in the occupied territories and their leadership had major difficulties in determining their positions. Church leaders from the different denominations had opted for preservation of their own organizations and institutional infrastructure in the first place. Given the fact that they existed now under a militantly pagan state, they wanted in the first place to maintain their distance and some freedom to manoeuvre. While they strove to exert moral authority, only persecution of the Church and of individual believers could turn resentment into resistance.

Thus, the events of 1941, when Germany seemed to be overwhelmingly successful on the Eastern Front, contributed to a further fragmentation of legitimacy in the occupied territories. The radical Right, although firmly in power, started to lose it. Their hold on legitimacy was weakened, in the first place because the contenders were brought together in an alliance with the purpose of defeating National-Socialist and fascist rule as the common enemy. In the second place, the growing stress caused by the system worked to undermine their legitimacy. Nazi Germany and its allies in 1941 and 1942 gave every impression of being triumphant on the battlefields and yet it became clear that they would increasingly have to rely on sheer force in order to dominate the occupied territories. The Japanese entry in the war opened in December 1941 with the attack on Pearl Harbor, causing an immense blow to the United States. The latter's entry into the war however, provided another strong impulse to change radically expectations about the outcome of the war. Now a compromise peace, which would force the occupied peoples to adapt to the ambitions of Nazi Germany and its allies, became less and less probable. Thus, the birth of resistance as a movement of political significance took shape.

Resistance movements were extremely manifold and elusive by nature. Some of them did not consider themselves to be engaged in resistance, and some did not wish to see others in that perspective. Activities included production of clandestine newspapers; spontaneous or organized strikes; assistance to people in hiding or to military personnel trying to escape; individual protests, armed action and sabotage; preparations for maintaining public order after the enemy's surrender, and many more actions that as a whole indicated the formation of an 'underground' society. Political backgrounds and the purposes of those activities could differ along the entire political spectrum, from the authoritarian Right to the radical Left. Nevertheless, in order to have a political impact, resistance required a platform that aimed at having an influence at the level of the central state. No individual realized this as soon, and worked so hard for it, as the Free French leader in exile, General Charles de Gaulle. In September 1941, he announced the birth of the French National Committee (CNF), renouncing the legality of Vichy's coming to power and placing himself in the lineage of the French Revolution. His argument was that the constitution of the Third Republic prohibited a change of the constitutional order.[36]

De Gaulle strengthened his alliance with the internal resistance by meeting with Jean Moulin, who significantly had been dismissed as a Prefect in Vichy France, and who became a national leader of the internal resistance movement. As Denis Peschanski has pointed out, men who initially served as officials under Vichy were quite prominent among the first generation of resisters in France. This was produced by a drive on the part of Pétain and his entourage to tighten central control over the high-ranking civil servants and demand their complete loyalty to the cause of the Vichy government.[37] When the competition for legality between Vichy and De Gaulle developed fully, the Communist resistance opted for an offensive strategy, by mounting armed attacks against the German military. This was intended to provoke the occupier – and its French collaborators – into showing their true nature. And, indeed, in October 1941, the retributive killings of hostages taken by the Germans raised enormous indignation.

The French example stands out because of the clarity of the political divisions, which tainted the struggle for the possession of legitimacy on a national level. The struggle was waged by three main contenders. The first was Vichy, which started to radicalize and grew contaminated through its close association with the German authorities in Paris, the internal contradictions that it could not solve, its inability to protect the overseas possessions of France and the deteriorating standard of living. The second was De Gaulle, who was absent physically but worked as a rallying figure for a developing national opposition to Pétain, willing to dedicate itself to the idea of a free and liberated France. De Gaulle gave ample evidence of a commanding personality, mainly by means of his compelling radio speeches. Moreover, he was a strong- and single-minded person, who was resolute in his desire to embody personally French republicanism and in no way to compromise to reach his goal. The third party was the French radical Left, most notably the Communists, who were eager to engage in the underground battle to put the Nazis and their French collaborators on the defensive and gain – as the *'parti des fusillés'* – a reputation as the true defenders of the Republican and socialist France.

In many ways, the Communists and the Gaullists reinforced each other's claims to legitimacy, while not really sharing it – ownership was to be contended for in the last stage of the war and the subsequent regime transition. This issue was especially urgent for the underground movement in states the post-war status of which remained unclear, as was often the case in Eastern Europe. Divergences between the liberal democrats and the radical Left were, however, latent everywhere, in France just as much as in underground Poland. In many occupied states, the Communists stepped forward from relatively marginal positions before the war. War, occupation and discontent created space for violent activism. At the same time, as political outsiders within their own societies and as declared enemies of National Socialism, they were the first to be persecuted by the German police and their indigenous collaborators. The truce between Moscow and Berlin did not prevent such persecution at all. Communist parties had underground experience, and were able to develop strategies and actions of their own. They expanded their networks, tested the water for organizing strikes, such as in February 1941 in Amsterdam, and educated young members in sabotage and armed action. All over Europe, the Communist resistance gained a reputation as the ones who were prepared to make sacrifices and do the 'dirty jobs'.[38]

The very fact that they were violently persecuted strengthened their appeal to those who wanted to become involved in action, and at the same time provoked an influx of a younger leadership, more independent from Moscow and more nationally minded. Thus, even within the radical Left, legitimacy did not take a single form. Moscow adapted to this situation in the hope of turning it to its longer-term

Figure 3.2 The French collaborationist militia, the Milice, presented itself as the only defence against the internal and external threat posed by Communism. Courtesy of Archives Nationales, Paris.

advantage, when it made known in 1943 that the Communist International was dissolved. Communist resistance could now express its commitment to national liberation on progressive platforms. By nature of the resistance movements, in most states the appropriation of legitimacy was characterized by the provisional character of the movements. In states where civil societies and pre-war institutions at least partly managed to survive, resistance could become a powerful influence in the contestation and appropriation of legitimacy. Whereas in those occupied territories where the occupier had destroyed indigenous social and administrative structures, as in Poland or Yugoslavia, resistance groups could develop the comprehensive ambition of representing and actually replacing the central state.

1943–5 Legitimacy Re-arranged

From the perspective of Grand Strategy, in early 1943 the expectations about which alliance would win the war were turned over. The German-led armies discovered in northern Africa and at Stalingrad that their ambitions had overstretched their means and they were defeated there. The Italian armed forces and dissident Fascists opted out of the war in July 1943. Before that happened, the Allies had definitively decided at Casablanca in January 1943 to pursue a policy of unconditional surrender. All this caused a wave of premature optimism in the occupied territories that the war was about to end in an Allied victory. Thus, all minds were directed to thinking about the imminent regime change and the fundamental question of who was to fill the vacuum left by the occupiers. In fact, the fall of Mussolini in Italy demonstrated how both the Allies and the Germans were now establishing their own military control. They divided the country by a new military front line and had to search for new allies in the nation they brought under their subjection in order to provide a collaborationist platform for their rule. In the two subsequent years, the political map of Italy became even more complicated than the military one, when an indigenous, multi-faceted and extremely violent struggle for power originated under the surface of the slow Allied advance and the determined German defence of its Italian territory. The Fascist regime tried to re-invent itself and rally its most radical supporters by proclaiming the 'social' Republic of Salo. The apostates of the former Fascist regime and the resistance of the Left started to focus on a modernized and democratized nation-state. Thus, from the perspective of legitimacy, the Italian experience showed how the endgame redirected attention once again to the central level.[39]

Vichy France, on the other hand, lost in late 1942 its strongest assets in its claim of self-evident legitimacy for Pétain's state and regime: its north African territories were lost as a result of the Allied invasions of Morocco and Tunisia; the French Navy scuttled its inactive fleet, and Hitler decided to occupy the 'Free Zone' of southern France. After the Allied landings in north Africa, the French *de facto* rulers there, first Darlan and then Giraud, offered the Allies their cooperation, aspiring to link up anti-German feelings at home with continuation of Pétain's National Revolution and expecting to bet on the winning horse.[40] American President Roosevelt and British Prime Minister Churchill were inclined to accept this offer of collaboration, just as they believed they would benefit from the regime change instigated in Italy by Badoglio and the other leading representatives of the Fascist state who had opted out of their military alliance with Germany. Roosevelt told the Vichyite Darlan that he could consider himself 'faithful to the Marshal in carrying out my orders'.[41] He and Churchill had many misgivings about De Gaulle and did not formally recognize his exiled committee as the government of France.

De Gaulle for his part, moved to appropriate all of the legitimacy that had flown from the Vichy regime, in the first place by his decision to move his French Committee for National Liberation (CFLN) from London to French territory in Algiers in 1943 as soon as the military circumstances permitted and the Allies had adapted their policy after Darlan's assassination in December 1942. Moreover, he strengthened his grip over the French state and patriotic resistance in metropolitan France, and by doing so also set out the political margins for the Communist resistance. De Gaulle had perhaps the strongest sense of all European political leaders working towards regime transition in this phase as to what constituted legitimacy, and directed all his effort to winning it.

After Stalingrad, power relations in occupied Europe did not change immediately. On the contrary, in many territories repression radicalized, exactly because the occupier lost any interest in indigenous attitudes. When the occupying regimes decided to rule by means of terror, they demonstrated a fundamental lack of interest in legitimacy, and their abandonment of efforts to nazify societies reinforced this reliance on what they had by way of brute power. At the same time, from the perspective of regime change, representatives of civil society, parts of the state apparatus, and different tendencies in the resistance now started to manoeuvre in order to be involved in a regime change and needed to found their claim to legitimacy on such a move. The prime manifestation of this development was the redefinition of resistance as national resistance, and in connection with this, the claim of such national resistance movements to being the rightful owners of legitimacy in succession to the pre-war regimes.

Thus, while in the middle years of the war, there had been a fragmentation of legitimacy, now the issue was how to forge these chunks of legitimacy together as a pre-condition for the recovery of legitimacy for post-war rulers. As A.J. De Grand points out with regard to Italy in 1943, the two decades of Fascist rule and the war itself had not deprived the possibility for the conservative elites, including the Catholic hierarchy and parts of the armed forces, who had supported the regime for their own purposes, to disengage themselves and seek out different options: 'When the regime dissolved, each constituent element had preserved something in its original base which it could use as a springboard to the post-Fascist era.'[42] The radical Fascist experiment, which took shape as the Republic of Salo, demonstrated that the movement could still rally loyalty among its unconditional supporters. The stressing of the 'social' element in its title was explicitly intended to foster the ambition to continue, even under siege and in the middle of a raging civil war, where pre-1943 Fascism had left off. In Germany, on the other hand, as the case of the 20 July 1944 attempt to kill Hitler showed, it was much more difficult for conservative opponents to transgress the psychological line of violating the oath of allegiance to Hitler as German *Führer* and work for regime change. The Allies' commitment to unconditional surrender implied nothing less than the intention to tear down the enemy state and its institutions, in order to replace it with structures modelled on those of the winners. Paradoxically, this principle probably fostered more loyalty than had been expected to Hitler's state.

Perhaps rather remarkably, in the occupied territories recovery of the nation-state became the central issue. The former – now occupied – European states had held legitimacy by virtue of their very existence. From the nineteenth century onward, their legitimacy had been built up gradually and transferred from generation to generation. Education in schools and churches, and the establishment of all kinds of civic ritual had contributed to an accumulation of legitimacy which in 1940 was taken away by military defeat and the failure of the elites. The former states were occupied territories now, forged into ideologically driven transnational communities, or broken up and colonized. With a fresh memory of the collapse that had followed the *Blitzkrieg* in 1940, the nation-state remained a problematic goal to fight for. Moreover, both the radical Right and the radical Left had theoretically steered away from it, respectively stressing the ethnic and the popular basis of their own statehood. When it seemed that the radical Right was actually losing the war, the recovery of the subjected nation state re-surfaced as a unifying purpose. As the crisis of liberal democracy in the 1930s had not been forgotten, this could only be rendered attractive if common ground could be found to redefine the post-war nation-state as a 'safe haven' for its citizens.

The new legitimacy was constructed on the middle ground that existed between the liberal democratic and radical Left political platforms. The governments in exile played a significant but belated role in this process. During the early 1940s these regimes, with the exception of De Gaulle, had been something of an irrelevance, often mired in internal dispute and divorced from the realities of occupied Europe. But in the spring of 1944, military liberation became more imminent and so they could revive their claims to return to rule, albeit through reaching agreements with internal forces such as the burgeoning resistance groups. These had originated during the first phase of the war, but only gained size and influence in the second. Both tendencies directed themselves towards recovery of nationhood, national independence and national pride. Many clandestine newspapers pointed by their name to recovery of the nation state (*Libre Belgique* and others) or to higher moral ground (*Trouw*, *Humanité* and others). Such publications were explicitly intended to demonstrate in public that the New Order monopoly of political expression could be challenged. Even scratchy bulletins of war news without much of a political message served this purpose. In the second phase of the war, the resistance press developed a pluralist forum that worked to prepare public opinion for regime change and political life afterwards.

Deprivation of the freedoms of association and expression was a powerful motive to act clandestinely against the regime. The New Order tried to control what was said and done in classrooms, attacked religious freedoms, sent spies to cinemas, dictated the content of newspapers and appropriated free trade unions while exposing the masses to forced labour, all under threat of prisons, concentration camps and death penalties. Such a regime threatened to destroy everything for which the previous generations had fought, exposed itself as evil, and provoked resistance. For these reasons, people went underground and risked their lives. Their purpose was to expose the nature of the regime and its collaborators and take away its claims to legitimacy.

In the second phase of the war, the New Order's monopoly of violence was fundamentally challenged. What mattered in most cases was not the illusion that the occupying military forces could be thrown out by means of internal armed revolt. Even in the most celebrated examples of Partisan activity (Yugoslavia, Greece, Albania, western parts of the Soviet Union), armed insurrection at best created a no-man's land where both parties had to be extremely careful while they were pursuing each other. In most occupied territories, armed resistance came into existence as an effort to give a certain degree of protection to the population against specific repressive measures. Identification papers and rationing cards were seized through armed hold-ups, political prisoners were liberated and supposedly dangerous administrators and police-officials were kidnapped or killed. Thus, the armed resistance took over the function of 'the strong arm' of the now powerless former state. Its representatives who had remained in office meanwhile had to make their final choice: would they belong to the enemy camp, or were they prepared to support the resistance from within their functions?[43]

Armed resistance existed in parallel and initially in mostly separate spheres, the first as outposts of the British and Soviet secret operations in occupied Europe, organized without much knowledge of the exiled rulers. The second one was the armed branch of the various resistance groups, improvised organizations for self-defence and offensive action. The third was the model of the 'Homefront', *Armia Krajova* (Poland), *Hjemmefront* (Norway) or *Binnenlandse Strijdkrachten* (the Netherlands). They were conceived during the last stages of the occupation as the underground army of the exiled governments. Their personnel were from the resistance but they were not supposed to act autonomously. The exiled governments took formal responsibility for them and commissioned these forces with a dual mission: to take part in operations behind the front line, but also to safeguard their ruler's interest in the period of regime transition. Enlisting for these activities, however, was a vital new source of citizenship, both for newcomers and for the youngest generation. Working-class uniforms of overalls and arm-bands worked as social equalizers and created a new glamour for those who tied their fate to that of the Allies. After the liberation, they would be issued with standard Allied battle dress and thus would be publicly visible as part of the Victorious Alliance. This also implied that they sought a major role in transition politics.

While fighting the oppressors, many in the different resistance movements felt that return to peace and the rule of law within the old state would not be enough. Those on the liberal-democratic side asked themselves why so many citizens in the 1930s had been vulnerable to the messages of the radical Right. For obvious reasons, the perceived failure of the pre-war political order had to be averted in the post-war era. Political programmes were formulated for constructing new societies that would

Figure 3.3 Belgian resistance fighters mobilize at Fosse-la-Ville during the Allied liberation of September 1944. Courtesy of CEGES-SOMA, Brussels

not be affected by the failure of the old ones. These platforms included a radical purge of all those who had been contaminated by collaboration, as well as social reform, including greater opportunities for political participation by the masses and recovery of public morale after the Nazi and fascist perversion. The alliance between the Western powers and the Soviet Union was a fact now. Both the sacrifices and successes of the Red Army and Communist resistance movements added greatly to the prestige of the radical Left. Moreover, a more 'national' idea of Communism seemed viable. There was an influx of many talented newcomers, who in the course of the war managed to create a bridge from the radical Left to the establishment, which had hardly been conceivable before the war.

The final years of the war were therefore characterized by a reconfiguration of legitimacy. Chunks of it remained lower in the administration and in the civil society. Crucial in the appropriation of legitimacy was now the question as to whether these owners could establish themselves as protectors of people's interests, both materially and immaterially. Thus, church leaders – bishops and village clergy alike – were often, though not always, acknowledged for providing guidance, safe havens and the relief goods they could commandeer. 'Good officials' in the administration were recognized for keeping oppressors at a distance by acting as middle men between the population and the regime, or for procuring and fairly distributing food, employment and justice. Professional classes such as medical doctors kept their professional values and social prestige intact, from which they could create moral space beyond the reach of the enemy to help people. The Red Cross could even formally claim such a space on the basis of its position in international law. All such institutions and representatives would come together in the final stages of the war, and connect with resistance leadership, in order to manage parts of the atomized society, for reasons of local crisis management and in order to take care of relief. Thus, while war raged and the central level of society pursued strong efforts for total mobilization, at the bottom an effort was going on to keep the fabric of society intact as far as possible.

The alternative offered by notables and resistance leaders offered a provisional regime only. Although their involvement evidently fostered local and regional self-consciousness, the mental framework for political agency was, and remained, the nation-state. During the final phase of the war, several sides organized concerted efforts to bring the different 'containers of legitimacy' together and forge them in the shape of a comprehensive authority. From the bottom, new branches of an amalgamated shadow executive took shape that sought to take care of the needs of society and intended to prepare for transition and reconstruction. National Councils of the resistance were formed to assure the coordination of the movement and at the same time work as parliaments. Their assumption of this dual function underlined their claims to represent the essence of nationhood. From this point of view, they shared the move to restore legitimacy at the central level with the resurgent governments in exile. The latter tried to re-establish relationships with the underground societies and their partly renewed leadership, appointed representatives and tried to coordinate in order to prepare for actual regime change.

What gave European resistance movements a head start was their moral authority and self-sacrificing ethos. They often developed a rather critical edge to their attitude towards the old-fashioned and self-interested party politics, parliamentarians and officials, as opposed to the resistance's truly national and patriotic *élan*. In almost every sense the resistance considered itself to be the carrier of a new level of legitimacy. In Denmark, Norway, and the Netherlands, prominent members of the resistance wanted to do away with party politics altogether after the war and rejected the politicians and administrators of 1940 as compromised by collaboration.[44] In those three states, there was an appeal from the resistance to form extra-parliamentary transition governments in which mainly resistance leaders would hold office, and would prepare parliamentary elections. In an effort to strengthen her own role in the post-war political system, the Dutch Queen Wilhelmina more or less abandoned her own cabinet in exile in order to link up with these political ambitions of the resistance. Free French leader Charles de Gaulle, on the other hand, moved along institutional lines when he nominated and sent his representatives to all regional and departmental prefectures.

The Allies had a clear interest of their own in controlling, and to that end unifying, the armed wings of the resistance. SOE's half-failed scheme of the first part of the war of 'setting (Western) Europe ablaze' was now continued on a larger scale by means of deliveries of arms to those resistance groups that were willing to comply with the Allied supreme command. They prepared for military government in the transition period, and had to decide how far they would involve the indigenous rulers in these schemes. On the French side, De Gaulle made it unambivalently clear to the Allies that the Provisional Government under his leadership embodied an absolute continuity of the French Republic and was the only authority legally and morally qualified to lead the French nation. Right up until the eve of the Allied invasion of Normandy, De Gaulle negotiated with Roosevelt and Churchill to limit the role of Allied military administration. General Eisenhower provided him with the necessary backing – he was primarily interested in safeguarding the rear of his military operations and in the maintenance of public order.[45] This was the basis of a number of legal agreements with exiled governments in north-western Europe, facilitating their return and re-assumption of responsibilities under the umbrella of Eisenhower's Supreme Allied Headquarters.

On the eastern side of the Front against Nazi Germany, the Soviet Union likewise prepared and established military rule for the territories to be occupied by the Red Army. For the states other than Germany, it had started to prepare Communist nationals for future government. Poland proved to be the most telling example of the tough stance that Moscow took in order to secure its domination. The patriotic government in British exile was outmanoeuvred by Stalin, who in July 1944 abruptly bestowed authority upon the 'Lublin Committee', most of whom, as Communists, had been exiled in the Soviet Union.[46] Thus, the Allies worked to restore the monopoly of violence in name and in practice at the central level. All of these developments contributed to forging together the fragmented containers of legitimacy and appropriating them once again to facilitate the re-emerging nation-states.

Accordingly, attention shifted towards political transition, including purges and transitional justice, and political platforms for post-war reconstruction. In this respect, the political space for resistance movements in the East and the West would be different. In north-western Europe, in the sphere of influence of the Western allies, the state was gradually restored to the indigenous political classes. In the East, the Soviet Union moved to a closer supervised and strongly enforced system of domination. In both spheres, the ambition to purge the national community and the body politic of the stain of collaboration was an effort to be coordinated by the central state. The question as to how far political purges and transitional justice were started as multi-purpose, bottom-up processes, beyond the reach of the central states will be dealt with in Chapter 6. Here, it is relevant to note that the debate about which directions the purges and punishment of collaborators *should* take reconfirmed the moral stature of the resistance. At the same time, this was a powerful appeal to the authorities who were to take over the central state after the German collapse. If the rulers-to-be failed to do so, summary justice by the resistance would be a serious threat to their legitimacy. Exactly for this reason, most Allied governments in exile had set out relatively early, in 1942 and 1943, to prepare legislation and other measures for post-war political purges and transitional justice.

Resistance movements paved the way for moral and ideological exclusion from the national communities of all those who had been compromised by collaborationist behaviour and policies. Consequently, the political battle for the purges was not limited to collaborators at the summit, such as civil servants, bishops, bankers and contractors. The search for those who had behaved anti-patriotically was also directed to one's neighbours: bakers who had provided their bread to the occupying forces, schoolteachers who had spread their propaganda and members of the local collaborationist movement who by means of their simple membership had undermined the national community. In Belgium, Norway and in the Netherlands, simply being a member of such an organization was declared by law to be a reason for criminal persecution after the war. During the war, the resistance had sought to deter these enemy sympathizers from acts of treason. As the conflict escalated, the resistance had been violently persecuted and therefore had taken responsibility for 'liquidating' enemies, who had previously been fellow-citizens.

Purging the direct agents of collaboration, such as intellectuals who spread Nazi slogans or men who donned German uniforms was relatively straightforward. Much more difficult was to punish those whose actions were more ambivalent but also perhaps more significant. In north-western Europe, economic collaboration as a result of producing and working for the enemy by business leaders and workers alike, proved to be difficult to prosecute, because so many were involved and the economy as a whole would be affected. In this specific field, the resistance in Eastern Europe connected to the Soviet Union tended to be ambivalent as well. Calls for the nationalization or socialization of key industries were strongly voiced, but it was also realized that the Germans had commandeered large amounts of the workforce. Therefore, raising the issue of economic collaboration in a broader perspective could only be politically unproductive.

With the 'national perspective' on legitimacy restored, the coalitions between liberal democrats and the radical Left were put to the test everywhere. The stakes differed as did the national contexts, but all in all the struggle for legitimacy was transferred to the central level once again, and its bipolarity restored along the 'us' versus 'them' line. In Western Europe, distrust remained – and grew stronger – of the Communist resistance movements and their ambitions in post-war politics. Almost everywhere the Communists had gained considerable support. Their grip on legitimacy had proportionally grown as a result of their active resistance, promises of radical socio-political reform and connection to the now victorious Red Army. The Western Allies and governments in exile monitored Communist ambitions with concern, fearing a resurgence of the political radicalization at the end of the First World War. In Central and Eastern Europe, the Soviet Union stimulated Communist resistance and exiles to present themselves as progressive national movements, in order to contest the legitimacy of the 'reactionary nationalist movements' connected to the pre-war Old Order. Moreover, issues of political participation and social reform, especially related to labour relations and land ownership, were even more urgent in Central and Eastern Europe than in most of the West. Thus, the radical Left addressed the masses through a platform of radical reform and purge, phrased in words that closely resembled what the resisters of the liberal democratic tendency propagated as well. In general, transitional justice is the struggle for political legality transferred to the courts. In the competition for power in Eastern Europe especially, it would prove expedient to brand political contenders and adversaries as fascists and collaborators and morally – and in the end physically – eliminate them.

Before the war ended, governments in exile managed to re-establish their grip on legitimacy, as they generally stood for legal continuity with the pre-war situation. On its own, this was a rather thin and risky basis for their claim. Therefore, they had to connect with resistance at home and find a common platform for post-war reform. At the same time, such moves were part of re-establishing their authority over resistance movements and society at large in the occupied territory. General De Gaulle did so in France while confronting the Allies; the exiled governments of the smaller nations present in London were highly dependent on the American and British preparations for how to rule liberated Europe. Both sides of the story show that, when facing the prospect of regime transition, the Allied command and the exiled rulers were in need of each other. This stimulated a return towards bipolarity in legitimacy. The 'they-against-us' competition for legitimacy grew to be the main division during the second part of the war. National coalitions were forged now, which had a dual purpose: to be endorsed by the Allies and benefit from their military effort as well as sharing or assuming political power as a basis of the legitimacy they had appropriated as an alternative to both the Old and the New Order.

This return to bipolarity in legitimacy should not hide the fact that, politically, many power struggles were taking place and that, under the circumstances prevailing in 1944 and 1945, the outcome was not in any sense predictable. With hindsight, we know that the final settlements for the outcome of the war that the Allies decided upon in 1945 were decisive for post-war politics in Europe, both from the internal and international perspectives. The subsequent Cold War firmly established political relations for decades to come, and promoted a gradual recovery. Thus, bipolarity in legitimacy between liberal democracy and the radical Left seemed completely dominant. Nevertheless, the outcome of the struggle for legitimacy in the different European states also was tied to what happened within the internal framework of the nation-state.

In Western Europe, the formal restoration of the pre-1940 nation-states hid the fact that rulers experienced many difficulties in getting a grip on legitimacy. Wherever the political order was recreated around the pre-1940 regimes, the rulers took care to present their governments as a continuation of these regimes. General De Gaulle was more than exemplary when he demonstrated this principle by establishing himself in his pre-1940 office at the War Ministry in Paris on the day of Liberation. He involved the resistance leadership marginally in his public triumph, to indicate that France as a whole was supposed to be resisting.[47] In general, as new policies were promised, old structures were reconstructed. Transitional governments paid homage to the principle of resistance but had difficulty offering the resistance any crucial posts. Returning rulers conceived and represented war and occupation as severe tests of the strength of the nation, as tests that in the end had been passed with honour, by virtue of a general spirit of resistance (not necessarily 'the' resistance).

The power struggle during the transition in the Netherlands, Norway and Denmark turned out to be a compromise between old and new politics. Restoration of pre-war national institutions and symbols under a programme of reform and renewal was relatively easy in Norway and the Netherlands. In Norway, the King, and in the Netherlands the Queen presided over a compromise of resistance and government. The Dutch Queen, who had expressed ambitions to rejuvenate the political system by means of more personal rule, gave away the momentum – if it ever existed – when she invited two Labour politicians to form a new Cabinet. One promoted a more idealistic concept of reform; the other one a more realistic version. In Denmark, the compromise had already been negotiated in 1944 between the Resistance's 'Freedom Council' and the official political parties. The (post-war) Beneš government reinstated Czech and Slovak common statehood at the cost of the German minority. Thus, Munich was undone and avenged. In other states, rulers had more difficulty in regaining their grip on legitimacy. The Dutch government postponed elections for a year in order to forge a so-called synthesis between non-Nazi-collaboration and the resistance. Subsequently it had difficulties in maintaining its position, owing to political upheaval over how to deal with the prolonged crisis over decolonization of the East Indies. In France, the state was stronger but divisions remained even more profound. The way in which General De Gaulle withdrew from the political scene in 1946 was a clear indicator that legitimacy remained fractured. The restoration of the nation-state was very difficult in Belgium, where the restoration of the pre-war political regime became embroiled in a bitter constitutional conflict between King Leopold and the non-Catholic political parties. Another difficult case was Greece, where a disruptive civil war raging during and after the war could only be decided when British forces and subsequently American assistance brought victory to the royalist side. In Italy, on the contrary, reconstruction of the nation-state was remarkably successful.

In debates about the post-war recovery of nation-states, complex issues arose about who actually belonged to the body politic. This was discussed in political terms, especially relating to collaborationists who were to be purged. But the issue was also addressed in ethnic terms, as the end of the war and regime transition opened up a window of opportunity for ethnic cleansing. The impact of the anti-semitic exclusionist discourse during the persecution cast its shadow over these debates. Restoration of full citizenship for Jews was not guaranteed in all cases, as became clear in disputes over their regaining legal and property rights. In many occupied countries the public mood remained suspicious of 'the Jews' regaining 'too much influence in society'. From a more general perspective, the definition of citizenship and ethnicity as related to the reconstruction of the nation-state became more exclusivist than before. As an outcome of the war, many borders were changed, especially in Central and Eastern Europe. Under those circumstances new rulers engaged in processes of ethnic engineering and cleansing, within their own borders, or outside.

Germany and its allies lost much territory but were burdened with many newcomers who, as 'ethnic Germans', were removed from the states where they had lived before. The wholesale expulsion of Germans from former Prussia, Poland and Czechoslovakia, expressed an effort on the part of the new rulers to establish their legitimacy as cleansers of the nation-state. In the decades that followed the war, ethnic exclusiveness remained a sensitive issue, while attention shifted towards immigration, especially from (former) colonies. In the meantime, the presence of the expellees in Germany was to pose a strong challenge to the legitimacy of the rulers, primarily of the Federal Republic. The post-war German governments had to be careful to find a delicate equilibrium between reintegration in the international community and dealing with the longer term grievances of the *Heimatvertriebenen*.

In north-western Europe, the overwhelming presence of the liberating Allied armies enabled the return of an old regime that had to compromise with the resistance. Socio-political reconstruction of the old would not suffice to retain legitimacy: a more modern political culture and the increased responsibility of the state for the provision of social welfare were required. In central and eastern Europe, Communism under the protection of the conquering Red Army appeared as leading a progressive national movement, seizing the opportunity to forge unity with other 'progressive forces' in order to gain a majority and thereby dominance. In Yugoslavia and Albania alone, the partisan resistance movements were sufficiently strong to establish themselves independently as revolutionary reinventions of the former nation-states, and actually strengthen them. In general in Central and Eastern Europe, longer-running territorial conflicts needed to be solved under the guise of 'proletarian internationalism' – if they were not to risk the legitimacy of the regimes of the radical Left. Mass expulsion of Germans was an outlet that neutralized this threat in the first vulnerable years of the regimes. Liberal-democratic Czechoslovakia (at the time) posed a telling example.[48] In Western Europe, American domination facilitated a return to a reformed version of the liberal-democratic principles, aiming at enlargement of political space and establishment of the welfare state. The radical Left was allowed to play a role in the transition, although how long the transition lasted may be disputed. In France and Italy especially, the Communist parties were a power that had to be taken into account, as long as they decided to stay in the newly established political order. But they lost the initiative to the forces of moderate reformism, social democracy and Christian democracy, in some cases supported by progressive liberalism.

Of the former National-Socialist and fascist states, Italian rulers managed to appropriate much more legitimacy than they had done so in the pre-Fascist kingdom.

The outcome of a 1946 referendum obliged the House of Savoy to abdicate and it was subsequently banished from the country. The republic built enough enthusiasm in order to make a fresh start on a basis of a programme of moderate reform and a return to the modern western world. The latter was far from being a practical possibility in the 'neutral dictatorships': Franco's Spain and Salazar's Portugal. They would only slip into the Western camp owing to the formation of the strategic blocs in the Cold War. Austria presented itself as 'Hitler's first victim' and managed to re-establish itself as a neutral nation with a recognizable national identity. Finland chose the same option, under even stronger Soviet influence. Defeated Germany was a special case. Unconditional surrender broke up German statehood and divided it among the victors, just as had happened at the beginning of the war in German-occupied Poland and Yugoslavia. In the East, German territories were annexed – the small annexations in the West are hardly worth mentioning and did not last – and the remainder was ruled under strong Allied supervision.

After the titanic clash with the Third Reich, no German nation-state survived. The German population assumed the same attentist attitude towards their respective rulers as the French had done in 1940. In their zones of occupation, the Allies installed German rulers who lacked full authority and only decades later were both the German states then in existence granted full sovereignty. In 1949 the *Bundesrepublik Deutschland* and the *Deutsche Demokratische Republik* were founded. Their elites based their claim to legitimacy primarily on the ability of their respective allies to shield 'their' Germans against 'the others' and, secondly, on economic reconstruction and performance versus the heritage of (Communist) resistance. It may very well be that a certain lack of contestation of legitimacy within these new states was stimulated by a fundamental resignation about involvement in politics at all, after the experience of a totally politicized life in Hitler's state. In the end, what was true for Germany applied to all European states: the short-term changes in regime brought about by force of arms or diplomatic agreements only gradually came to reflect slower and more difficult evolutions of legitimacy within the population.

Notes

1. D. Peschanski 'Legitimacy/Legitimation/Delegitimation: France in the Dark Years, a Textbook Case' *Contemporary European History* XIII (2004), 411.
2. See, for example, M. Reynebeau 'L'homme sans qualités' in *Les années trente en Belgique* (Brussels, 1994), pp. 12–73.
3. I. Kershaw *Hitler 1936–1945 Nemesis* (London, 2000), p. xxxii.
4. M. Knox 'Fascist Regime and Territorial Expansion: Italy and Germany', reprinted in A.A. Kallis (ed.) *The Fascism Reader* (London, 2003), p. 302.

5. For discussion of this issue: R.J.B. Bosworth *The Italian Dictatorship: Problems and Perspectives in the Interpretation of Mussolini and Fascism* (London, 1998), pp. 75–6.

6. There are many examples of public praise for Chamberlain in the Netherlands in L. de Jong *Het Koninkrijk der Nederlanden in de Tweede Wereldoorlog* Vol. 1 *Voorspel* (The Hague, 1969), p. 620.

7. J. van Gelderen, P. Geyl, H. Kraemer, F. Sassen and A.A. van Schelven *Nederland Erfdeel en Taak* (Amsterdam, 1940).

8. R. Aron *The Dawn of Universal History* (New York, 2002), p. 95.

9. R. Gellately *Backing Hitler: Consent and Coercion in Nazi Germany* (Oxford, 2001), pp. 70–5.

10. E. Verhoeyen *La Belgique occupée* (Brussels, 1994), pp. 51–211.

11. P. Pétain *Actes et écrits* (ed. J. Isorni, Paris, 1974), pp. 549–50.

12. P. Romijn *Burgemeesters in oorlogstijd. Besturen onder Duitse bezetting* (Amsterdam, 2006), p. 196.

13. H.F. Dahl *Quisling. A Study in Treachery* (Cambridge, 1999), pp. 207–12.

14. P. Romijn *Burgemeesters in oorlogstijd*, pp. 127–9.

15. The most extensive survey is B.R. Kroener, R-D Müller and H. Umbreit *Das deutsche Reich und der zweite Weltkrieg* Vol. 5: *Organisation und Mobilisierung des deutschen Machtbereichs* Part One: *Kriegsverwaltung, Wirtschaft und Personelle Ressourcen 1939–1941* (Stuttgart, 1988). See also the debate on different occupied areas in J. Bähr and R. Banken (eds) *Das Europa des 'Dritten Reichs' Recht, Wirtschaft, Besatzung* (Frankfurt a/M, 2005).

16. C.J. Lammers 'Levels of Collaboration. A Comparative Study of German Occupation Regimes during the Second World War', *The Netherlands Journal of Social Sciences* XXXIII (1995), 3–31.

17. W. Best *Die deutsche Aufsichtsverwaltungen in Frankreich, Belgien, die Niederlande, Dänemark und im Protektorat Böhmen und Mähren* (Paris, 1941).

18. M. Pittaway *Eastern Europe 1939–2000* (London, 2004), p. 18.

19. J. Duquesne *Les catholiques français sous l'occupation* (Paris, 1966), p. 49. See also É. Fouilloux *Les chrétiens français entre crise et libération 1937–1947* (Paris, 1997).

20. J. Gérard-Libois and J. Gotovitch *L'an '40: la Belgique occupée* (Brussels, 1971), pp. 346–51.

21. Words of the German *Reichskommissar* in the occupied Netherlands, A. Seyss-Inquart, already voiced after the suppression of the February 1941 strike in Amsterdam: L. De Jong *Het Koninkrijk* Vol. 4 *Mei '40 – maart '41*, (The Hague, 1972), p. 935.

22. For example, J.T. Gross *Polish Society under German Occupation: The Generalgouvernement, 1939–1944* (Princeton, 1979); K.C. Berkhoff *Harvest of Despair: Life and Death in Ukraine under Nazi Rule* (Cambridge MA, 2004).

23. I. Kershaw '"Working towards the Führer": reflections on the nature of the Hitler Dictatorship' in I. Kershaw and M. Lewin (eds) *Stalinism and Nazism. Dictatorships in Comparison* (Cambridge, 1997), pp. 88–106.

24. The paternalistic rhetoric of acting as a shield to protect France was used repeatedly by Pétain, who declared on 17 June 1940, on assuming power, that 'je fais à la France le don de ma personne': P. Pétain *Actes et écrits*, p. 449.

25. This process was very clear in France, see P. Laborie *L'opinion française sous Vichy* (Paris, 1990), pp. 262–81.

26. G. Hirschfeld *Fremdherrschaft und Kollaboration. Die Niederlande unter deutscher Besatzung 1940–1945* (Stuttgart, 1984), p. 188.

27. M. Conway *Collaboration in Belgium: Léon Degrelle and the Rexist Movement 1940–1944* (New Haven and London, 1993), pp. 153–7.

28. A. Seyss-Inquart 'Erster Bericht des Reichskommissars über die Lage und die Entwicklung in den besetzten Niederlanden, 29. Mai – 19. Juli 1940' in J.J. van Bolhuis (ed.) *Onderdrukking en Verzet. Nederland in Oorlogstijd* Vol. 1 (Amsterdam and Arnhem, 1950), p. 335.

29. C. Browning (with a contribution by J. Matthäus) *The Origins of the Final Solution. The Evolution of Nazi Jewish Policy 1939–1942* (London, 2005).

30. For a balanced overview of recent scholarship, see the bibliographical essay in J. Herf *The Jewish Enemy. Nazi Ideology and Propaganda during World War II and the Holocaust* (Cambridge MA, 2006), pp. 365–74.

31. R.J.B. Bosworth *Italian Dictatorship*, pp. 101–5.

32. D.J. Goldhagen *Hitler's Willing Executioners. Ordinary Germans and the Holocaust* (New York, 1996).

33. G. Aly *Hitler's Volksstaat. Raub, Rassenkrieg und nationaler Sozialismus* (Frankfurt a/M., 2005).

34. M. Burleigh and W. Wippermann *The Racial State: Germany 1933–1945* (Cambridge, 1991).

35. H. Welzer *Täter. Wie aus ganz normalen Menschen Massenmörder werden* (Frankfurt a/M., 2005).

36. D. Peschanski, 'Legitimacy/Legitimation/Delegitimation', 415.

37. D. Peschanski, 'Legitimacy/Legitimation/Delegitimation', 416–17.

38. J. Semelin *Sans armes face à Hitler* (Paris, 1998), p. 166.

39. D. Ellwood *Italy 1943–1945* (Leicester, 1985).

40. D. Peschanksi 'Legitimacy/Legitimation/Delegitimation', 417.

41. J.G. Hurstfield *America and the French Nation 1939–1945* (Chapel Hill and London, 1986), pp. 198–9.

42. A.J. de Grand *Fascist Italy and Nazi Germany. The 'Fascist' Style of Rule* (London and New York, 1995), p. 80.

43. See the testimony of a Vichy prefect: B. Lecornu, *Un Préfet sous l'Occupation allemande* (Paris, 1997).

44. B. Moore (ed.) *Resistance in Western Europe* (Oxford, 2000).

45. D. Peschanksi 'Legitimacy/Legitimation/Delegitimation', 419–20.
46. N. Davies *God's Playground* Vol. 2 (Oxford, 1981), p. 472.
47. This is the argument in the forthcoming PhD Thesis of Nele Beyens, University of Amsterdam.
48. B. Frommer *National Cleansing: Retribution Against Nazi Collaborators in Postwar Czechoslovakia* (Cambridge, 2005).

−4−

The War for Legitimacy at the Local Level*

Introduction

The local level was a crucial stage in the war for legitimacy. Both in its strict administrative sense as in its broader definition of civil society, the local level is crucial when studying the legitimacy of national rulers and regimes. Central rulers planning and organizing a variety of actions intended to convince the ruled of their legitimacy will find their plans fundamentally influenced by the way they are (un)able to execute them at the local level. State propaganda – however well designed, efficiently organized through local networks or universally present – remains nothing more than a set of virtual ideas if it doesn't achieve actual effects in the way in which local communities think about and react to government. As is argued throughout this book, local populations are not passive recipients of central legitimation projects. Local populations can respond in a variety of complex ways, determining their own relationship with external authorities. The way in which legitimizing actions of central rulers are perceived and the reactions or effects they provoke are strongly determined by ideas, values and convictions about legitimate rule that are already present at the local level, ideas that because they are so close to everyday life can evolve and adapt very rapidly.

The legitimacy of local government in Europe prior to the upheavals of the mid-century years was relatively stable. It rested on a number of deeply rooted props. One was the continuous historical development of local government from the *Ancien Régime* to modern times. The war for legitimacy on the local level between the 1930s and 1950s was founded on the way that the nineteenth-century nation-building process had integrated pre-modern communities, cities, counties, townships, boroughs and villages in the state framework by organizing miniature pendants of the central state apparatus and administration on subordinate levels such as provinces and municipalities. The success of many European nation-states in gradually building their national legitimacy was determined by the way existing local pre-modern and *ancien régime* traditions, conventions and structures were transformed into modern local-regional administrations which worked to strengthen the structures of the central state.[1]

*This chapter was written by Nico Wouters, with Niels Wium Olesen and Martin Conway as co-authors.

Another prop was the dominant and highly visible involvement of local governments in tasks that were perceived as essential by populations. Local government largely recruited their political and administrative personnel from within local populations, strengthening the direct involvement of these populations in their actions. With the full emergence of mass democracy after 1918 local government with a high level of democratic participation and a high level of autonomy and self-government became the norm in these countries.[2] Although obviously not 'democratic' by contemporary standards, the interwar period witnessed a fairly high democratic level in local government in many European countries.[3] Populations could directly observe local decision making and hold individual leaders accountable, they could send local leaders to parliament and most importantly they could participate directly through municipal elections and local civil society. A large majority of (mostly male) European populations could take part in municipal and regional elections. A continuing and evolving tradition of democratic decentralized government during the nineteenth century in countries such as Belgium, France, the Netherlands, Denmark and Norway gradually gave rise to a deeply rooted municipal culture that strongly determined people's ideas about how legitimate government should work. The legitimacy of central authority and regimes was therefore closely connected with the question of what exactly local populations expected from their local leaders. The success or failure of legitimation at the local level, was determined by these (changing) expectations, often tied to very concrete topics.

The legal and institutional structures of local government varied greatly across different European states.[4] To provide an encyclopaedic account would be beyond the scope of this chapter. The key factor determining these structures always revolved around the relationship between the local and the national level. This relationship determined the amount of local financial autonomy, of self-government concerning local powers and competences and of local autonomy when electing or appointing political and administrative personnel as well as the level of administrative decentralization or central control. In Belgium and France, municipal government had fairly comparable administrative-legal structures, although the role of the prefects and departmental level weighed much heavier in France than did the Belgian provincial governor and provincial administration.[5] Dutch local autonomy was strongly limited by the position of the mayor, who was a centrally appointed civil servant. The Scandinavian countries had a level of local autonomy and self-government that was far stronger than France, Belgium or the Netherlands. Norwegian and Danish municipalities possessed large powers in socio-economic fields with the necessary substantial financial autonomy.[6] Generally speaking, however, all these regimes possessed relatively high levels of (local) legitimacy.

The purpose of this chapter is therefore to trace the ways in which these rooted structures of local government responded to the challenges and changes of national regime during the mid-century years. If, as we are inclined to argue, the legitimacy of local government was in many states higher than that of the national government on the eve of these upheavals, it is clear that the local level was of central importance to the outcome of the subsequent struggle for legitimacy. As national regimes collapsed, so legitimacy migrated in part to the local level; and, as the various pretenders to national power (New Order, resistance and exiled governments) subsequently emerged, so they recognized control of local government as an essential component of their success.

Building a New Order (1939–42)

Convergence and Order

In the aftermath of their military successes in the years 1939–41, the German authorities were obliged to confront the challenge of working with and reworking local government. German plans varied strongly in specific occupied countries. The archenemy France first and foremost had to be permanently weakened, while the 'Aryan' Dutch and Norwegian populations had to be nazified and prepared for entry into the Greater-Germanic Reich. In general, however, in most countries – exceptions such as Denmark aside – the German occupying power wanted to create a 'New Order' that would gain legitimacy. This was also necessary to pursue the two main though contradictory goals of wartime Nazi rule: the short-term goal of economic exploitation and the long-term political goal of nazification. To achieve both these goals, the local level was clearly of crucial importance. Indeed, one might argue that everything converged on the local level of government. Unwilling to establish strong indigenous central regimes, the German authorities looked instead to local governments to carry out a wide range of both 'ordinary' administrative tasks as well as the 'exceptional' responsibilities inherent to wartime. At the same time local government became the principal arena in the Nazi ambition of building a New Order from the bottom up. A new and viable structure of local government was therefore central to 'the war for legitimacy' but also perhaps to the outcome of the entire war.

Unlike in many east and central European countries, German occupation did not lead to an immediate, radical rupture of local government and everyday life in north-western European countries. Different strategics aside, a return to administrative and economic normalcy and an efficient provision of basic needs (food, work and security) after the severe disruption of war and occupation, was the first priority for the different occupying regimes in north-western Europe in 1940. In this way, German plans met the initial expectations of local populations. War, occupation and the instalment of new regimes were profoundly disturbing experiences for local populations who were confronted with invading armies, material destruction and great personal uncertainty. After the profound shock and anxiety of war (however short it might have been), people understandably wished for a return to safety and normality.

In many countries – occupied Denmark being an exception – national authority fled (Belgium, the Netherlands and Norway) or was replaced (France). In this context, national civil servants and more especially local leaders and administrations were often highly visible islands of stability. Life immediately became more localized after the German invasion and subsequent occupation, as state authority disappeared at least temporarily and municipal administrations and local elites often became the most important or only source of authority.

It is important to note that the German authorities recognized the crucial importance of local administrative continuity. Political collaborators and sympathizers with the Nazi cause initially had few opportunities. In the Flemish areas of Belgium, some ambitious local members of the *Vlaams Nationaal Verbond* (VNV) could provoke support from the Germans in May and June 1940 to replace local municipal leaders, but these situations were quickly rectified. The Germans themselves wanted administrative stability and thus initial continuity. In Norway and Denmark (April 1940), Belgium and the Netherlands (May 1940) and subsequently France (July 1940), the Germans initially sought cooperation with the traditional elites and not with native fascist or national-socialist parties. Initiating a revolution by replacing pre-war, experienced administrators with inexperienced members of collaborationist parties on the basis of reasons of political kinship was highly illogical. The understaffed Germans needed both the legitimacy as well as the administrative experience of pre-war native administrators. These local administrative necessities loomed largest at the local level, where efficiently resolving the many practical problems created by war and invasion was an absolute priority.

During the first months, events at the local level were determined by a convergence of the material, practical interests of the Germans and those of the occupied country.[7] For a short and unique moment in the summer of 1940, German ambitions for their aggressive occupation policy seemed to have some sort of credible starting point in north-western Europe. This legitimating project was predominantly determined by the practical yet highly political and very vague notions of 'order', 'efficiency', 'stability' or even 'justice'.

Above all, this concerned issues of employment. In much of Europe, German occupation followed ten years of high unemployment; and in 1940 the Germans could appear as a solution to this long-term crisis. The Germans played on these hopes, juxtaposing these goals against a past period of democratic chaos, high unemployment, administrative corruption and political clientelism. The Germans propagated these vague concepts explicitly in their dealings with local populations and municipal administrations, who would be the first to have to bring these ideas into practice. Many municipal and regional administrations seem to have supported this German strategy. In many countries, local administrations were also obligated by pre-war democratic legislation to remain in office. This was the case in Belgium and the Netherlands. Foreseeing a repetition of the German invasion of 1914, pre-war Belgian law obliged mayors, policemen and other key officials to 'loyally support'

Figure 4.1 A German soldier in Denmark sticks up a poster ordering the local population to respect German commands. Courtesy of Netherlands Institute for War Documentation, Amsterdam.

German policy in the 'interest of the population'. Indeed, the population demanded this 'loyal support' from their local leaders during the first months. Local populations did not expect their local leaders to be patriotic resisters against the Germans. On the contrary, 'heroism' during these first months was more associated with remaining in place and working with the Germans. Order, stability, efficiency and thus also obedience were primary wishes for most populations during the summer of 1940. Local people wanted food and jobs, they wanted to see their homes and streets repaired, their neighbourhood safe from looters and their loved ones (who had fled or who had been taken as prisoners of war) returned as soon as possible . A large majority of local populations could probably strongly relate to German public demands denouncing any form of resistance, to collect all privately owned weapons or demands to the local police to conduct a strict maintenance of public order. And this could only be done by collaborating loyally and closely with the Germans. At a time when military operations were continuing but also appeared to be reaching a successful outcome, the Germans basically wanted the same things. The political goals of nazification remained as medium and long-term objectives, but did not appear to be a matter of urgency. Their hour would come, but in the meantime, there were more pressing priorities. Thus, political differences in national (occupied) regimes initially were not dominant factors at the local level.

This practical convergence of material interests was also closely tied to the essential characteristics of local and especially municipal government. Municipal government was accustomed to maintaining its own domestic sphere of government autonomously from central government.[8] Municipal government by character was able to return to a situation of 'business as usual' relatively quickly, almost regardless of the national changes of regimes. This was especially clear in the Netherlands, where the war was over in just four days in May 1940. It is however also remarkable to notice the real willingness of many mayors in the Netherlands, Belgium and France during the summer of 1940 to cooperate with the Germans out of an explicit need to demonstrate their administrative capabilities to the occupying authorities. This was especially clear in Belgium, where the Germans explicitly looked down upon the poor quality of local administrations. In most countries, providing efficient local government was also a way of shielding the population from German interventions. This was especially clear in France and Denmark. This dynamic of local convergence of interests was very strong during the first months of occupation. The fact the Germans set the priority by rebuilding roads and local economies and chose to collaborate with local leaders instead of systematically shooting or arresting them, gave the Germans a very real, significant platform for legitimation.

That some reforms were in order however, and that local democracy and autonomy would be severely limited, seemed inevitable, from the outset. The Germans did possess a general outline of reforms for most occupied countries. Some basic and general principles were centralization, de-politicization of local government, the implementation of the *Führerprinzip,* unification and centralization of municipal police and the neutralization of local autonomy and self-government, initially all in the name of administrative efficiency and the practical resolution of the many pressing problems.

However, the German regimes in most occupied countries lacked a clear programme of how to do this or how to obtain legitimacy for these future reforms and regimes. The general plan seemed to be one of absolute utopian centralization, whereby the municipal level would perfectly execute central orders, at the same time also making sure that local populations cooperated perfectly. Yet, the German enthusiasm for reconstruction was offset by a reluctance to interfere too directly in the professional responsibilities of officials. The Germans were, however, initially helped and stimulated in their reformist goal by the political-administrative elites in many occupied countries. For these countries the military defeat and subsequent occupation had not only been a military, but also a profound political and more especially administrative shock. Defeat had been above all a product of a failure of structures of organization. During the summer of 1940, there was a widespread feeling in many occupied countries of northern and western Europe that the implementation of some form of authoritarian 'New Order' was a necessary or even desirable road. That was not the same as an uncritical acceptance of Nazi models. Indeed, the willingness to consider authoritarian models of rule in 1940 in no way coincided with 'philo-Nazism'. The aspiration for a New Order was in that sense distinct from support for Germany, though this was a distinction that the Germans were perhaps understandably slow to recognize in the euphoric aftermath of victory.

Legitimation and Local Reform

Generally speaking, the 'success' of the German legitimation process during the summer of 1940 was short-lived. It appeared to have been exclusively bound to the period of sudden transition. It came from a combination of the initial vagueness of the German plans, the conviction of local elites that indigenous interests could be shielded and served by a policy of accommodation, a sense of general relief within the population after the invasion, a feeling of great uncertainty for the future and more especially a local convergence of German and native populations' immediate material interests. This convergence came to an end in most areas of occupied Europe over the winter of 1940–1 at the same time as it became clear that Great Britain would continue the war.

Paradoxically, however, it was only after the period of convergence had ended that several programmes for municipal reforms were carried out. Despite the national differences, October 1940 – October 1941 was a period of profound municipal reforms in most countries. Three examples will stand as representative of the different forms of reform that were enacted. France can serve as an example of a primarily indigenous course of reform. The 'phoney war' and the republican crisis had already led to the first drastic municipal reforms. After the Armistice (22 June 1940), the municipal situation in divided France was for the first two years mostly determined by the French themselves, even in the German-occupied zones. The Vichy regime wanted to eradicate the entire fabric of pre-war republican democracy. But unlike many other levels or structures, the municipal level was initially not radically reformed. Vichy could build on the Daladier reforms, so initial continuity in municipal administrative legality was strong.

Thus, in contrast to the abrupt suspension of the Third Republic at the national level in July 1940, there was a gradual, controlled process of municipal changes. In 1940, both Vichy and the German occupying forces implemented instructions to transform French municipal administrations into de-politicized, purely administrative and executive administrations. Efficient everyday administration ('good government') seemed to be the role municipalities had to play in the struggle for legitimacy for the new French regime and state.[9] This often meant that radical purges of municipal personnel were out of the question.[10] The 'new' local elite was initially still very strongly linked to the pre-war, republican elite. The ties with the (regional and local) republican elite were never broken and it was even strengthened after April 1942, with the return to power of the head of government Pierre Laval. His policy of reconnecting with the republican (regional and local) political-administrative elite, was primarily an attempt to use pre-war local-regional republican legitimacy to bolster the new state.

Theoretically, the local level had great importance for the struggle for legitimacy. Legitimation for the French New Order was a native and non-German project, in which great political importance was given to local communities. The ideological conception of state and society was essentially built on the idea of organically composed local communities. These mystical largely rural and Catholic local communities were crucial for merging both 'fatherland' (national) and 'family' (local), two legitimizing keywords of the new French state. Interior Minister Pierre Pucheu explicitly stated in December 1941 that the work of the government had to be connected with local representatives of 'le pays réel'. However, the Vichy regime seemed unable or unwilling to put these ideas about local government into practice. The new French regime would never resolve the classic choice between a highly centralized or a decentralized state organization. Once the regime encountered socio-economic, military and political problems by the end of 1940, it would also never resolve the contradiction (present in all New Order regimes) of how to build an 'organic', natural state that obviously was quickly losing public support and legitimacy.

France offers a prime example of this contradiction. The French regime lacked a vision as to how to integrate the municipal level in the new state. The regime considered an authoritarian prefect to be crucial and enlarged his powers from 1940 onwards. Other services and institutions were created, while the police and security forces were also radically reformed in 1940–1. This had a large impact on regional and local institutions and civil society. A chaotic conglomerate of new institutions emerged. In this wave of reforms, the mayor and the municipal administrations were more or less ousted. The new municipal law (16 November 1940) dealt solely with the appointment of mayors and *adjoints* for larger municipalities. The powers of the mayor and his administration were quickly hollowed out and eroded, especially in those two matters of crucial importance: the distribution of food and the maintenance of order. This meant that within the Vichy state model, a strong internal contradiction arose on the use of the local level in the struggle for legitimacy. Local administrations theoretically held key roles in the legitimation process but the ideological distrust of the regime towards these local administrations held the regime back from providing local administrations with the instruments actually to carry out this task. This discrepancy was a crucial failure in the local struggle for legitimacy.

Norway can serve as an example of a second type, in which German national-socialist ideology played a more dominant role. After two failed attempts at a coup by the Norwegian pro-Nazi leader of the *Nasjonal Samling* (NS) Vidkun Quisling, the German *Reichskommissar* Josef Terboven appointed a new provisional cabinet, with trusted professionals and Norwegian Nazis as directors of each ministry and Quisling as political head of the cabinet. A.V. Hagelin, deputy-president of the NS,

Figure 4.2 The Police were a central institution of the Vichy Regime's National Revolution in France. Courtesy of Archives Nationales, Paris.

headed the Ministry of the Interior. He wanted to install a Norwegian Nazi regime and for him, Norwegian municipal reform, which started after November 1940, was an obvious priority. On 21 December 1940 the *Führerprinzip* was introduced. District and municipal councils were abolished. In the municipalities a mayor and a deputy was appointed by the Ministry of the Interior and the head of the district appointed a number of advisory 'chairmen' (*formenn*) to the mayor, who had only advisory powers. This radical reform was instigated on Norwegian initiative, as Quisling and the NS emphasized themselves.[11] Indeed, although some reforms resembled the *Deutsche Gemeindeordnung* (1935), the distinctive Norwegian characteristics were stronger. Contrary to the German model for instance, the Norwegian municipal model explicitly upheld the separation of the party (NS) and the state and between the political and the administrative leadership. This model of imposed and ideologically inspired change was also largely enacted in Slovakia, where the creation of the new state led by Hlinka's Slovak People's Party led to the imposition of an authoritarian model of government.[12]

The Netherlands and, despite its politically 'neutral' military occupation government, Belgium also belong to this ideological course of reform. In this ideological model, often carried forward by the indigenous national-socialist collaborationist parties, the rupture with pre-war (municipal) legality was stronger and the German influence more obvious. The result was that the purely administrative arguments of 'good government' were used much more explicitly as a legitimating argument by the collaborationist parties and the Germans. They also drew explicit connections with discussions about local government that had taken place in those countries before the war, in order to present the New Order reform of local government as a logical internal evolution that had nothing to do *per se* with the German occupation. This was clear in the Netherlands where the radical police reform initiated by Rauter, the German police chief in Holland from 1940–1 onwards, was legitimated by connecting it to the pre-war discussions about the Dutch police.[13] The best example of such a course of change, however, was Belgium. Pre-existing convictions about the deficiency of Belgian institutions and administrations found fertile ground in 1940 after thousands of officials had fled to France in the face of the German attack rather than remaining at their posts.[14] The pro-German groupings, the VNV in Flanders and Rex in francophone Belgium recognized this weakness of municipal structures as the most useful tool to instigate their political changes. Both parties used a systematic campaign of 'objective', neutral information to attack existing Belgian local administrations. The success of this campaign and the relative strength of the VNV in Flanders, led to a series of radical reforms being enacted in 1941. Because these changes eroded Belgian administrative legality, the New Order mayors who were then appointed, were considered by many to hold their positions illegally. Since these mayors could not rely on legal arguments to legitimize their position, the provision of everyday 'good governance' became even more crucial in the process of gaining legitimacy.

The protectorate of Bohemia and Moravia serves as an example of a third 'model' to illustrate the diversity of local reform. The protectorate was created in March 1939 as an integral part of the German Reich.[15] The term 'protectorate' implied a colonial status.[16] Although theoretically the protectorate was merely a 'supervisory' regime,[17] the Czechoslovak local administrative level was quickly but fundamentally reformed into a highly centralized form of government. The *Wehrmacht* established twenty so-called *Oberlandräte* (April 1939), controlling the district and municipal level. These *Oberlandräte* had extensive supervisory powers, making the powers of the Hácha government purely formal. Policing and economic exploitation were governed through the district administration or directly by the *Oberlandräte*, which left the municipalities with less important tasks. In cities and towns with a German population, the municipal assemblies were replaced by a leading local German who was appointed as 'mayoral commissioner', subordinated only to the *Oberlandräte*. This was a common procedure, since most significant Czech towns had a German community. The original administrative framework continued formally to exist but in reality it was replaced by a parallel Nazi framework.[18] This dual administrative system was echoed by the sharp dual ethnic categorization obviously diminishing the legitimacy of many (German) town administrations.[19] The politicization in this 'imperial' or 'colonial' model was first and foremost carried forward on an ethnic basis, which demanded coercion and repression from the very outset and very little reliance on local forms of legitimation.

Legitimacy and 'Good Governance'

However these reforms of local government were implemented, it was essential for their legitimacy that they were perceived by their populations to fulfil the expectations of 'good governance' in the form of the impartial and efficient provision of services to meet the most urgent needs of the local community. In such cases, they could come close to being seen as 'their own' authorities. As we have seen, war and occupation had brought a set of severe problems, including refugees, administrative and financial disintegration and socio-economic problems such as high unemployment. The presence of the occupying forces also generated many practical problems (such as their high material demands), the security measures and the harsh penalties for small violations of the German regulations. In the larger cities of Belgium and France, a shortage of food and deteriorating social and labour conditions were rampant. Especially in the short term, all of these problems had to be dealt with primarily by local administrations.

In Belgium, the German authorities had supported municipal reform because they believed that the New Order mayors would improve administration, initially especially from the standpoint of food distribution, but later also public order and repression. The VNV and Rex had strongly emphasized and propagated this perception. Both parties however, failed to transform political rhetoric into administrative reality. They did not possess a practical programme to deal with unemployment, food shortages and deteriorating labour conditions, let alone the delicate matter of public order. The only practical instrument of policy of these collaborationist mayors was the increase of control and repression. This was a universal characteristic of 'New Order' local governments in occupied Europe. Disobedience was often unambiguously interpreted as the result of conscious political opposition. Their attitude clashed with the pre-war traditions of local democracy. Before the occupation, there had been many forms and ways by which local populations could protest against and directly influence the actions of local and regional administrations. Although all of these 'normal' forms of social protest had now 'officially' fallen away, local populations who were born and bred in this culture of local democracy, continued to use them. The consequence was a huge clash between the new collaborationist local elites and their populations. Although a majority of New Order mayors probably had a sincere wish to improve the lives of the local people, their only instrument of policy was top-down control, which quickly resulted in politically motivated persecution (with help from the German security services). Therefore, not only had these pro-German appointees no real administrative solutions, they were also blinded by their ideological mindsets and frameworks. In addition, the New Order in Belgium was poorly organized, often leading to confusion, internal competition and general chaos on the local level.[20] New Order measures led to conflicts with existing, traditional services and institutions, such as between the traditional police forces and nazified units.

Belgium was a prime example of the fact that German occupation in general presented a nearly impossible context for new local administrators to gain legitimacy through everyday administration. The gap between local sensibilities, expectations and local ways of expressing discontent and the way in which the new collaborationist local elite handled local government quickly proved impossible to overcome. Already in 1941, it was clear that hundreds of new VNV mayors in Flanders were not convincing local populations of the benefits of the superior National-Socialist administration. Rex in Wallonia faced even more severe problems in 1940–1. The party was plagued by disorganization, a lack of skilled party members and a lack of socio-economic or administrative plans. Despite the increasing attention of the party towards issues of social policy in the larger cities and Walloon industrial areas, its concrete initiatives remained either vague or nonexistent, which was also the case for their plans as to how to finance these potential social schemes.

The only true administrative advantage pro-German mayors in different countries initially had was their privileged position with the occupying authorities, giving them potentially a greater lever to obtain certain practical concessions. Many collaborationist mayors could gain results which other mayors could not in terms of alleviating collective German punishments. National-Socialist mayors did have an important potential legitimating tool here. But in France, the Netherlands and Belgium, many of these mayors did not use this tool in 1940–2. On the contrary, they were in a triumphant mood when appointed and excelled in political clientelism and providing favours for their own political membership. This was also connected to a feeling of *revanchisme*, compensating for pre-war frustrations when these parties had been ostracized by the political elite. Revenge, however, was not a means upon which to build legitimacy.

Even in countries where socio-economic conditions were relatively favourable during the first years of occupation, the New Order parties and the Germans experienced difficulties in turning 'good governance' into legitimacy. Not only political and ideological resentment, but also a general perception of administrative incompetence of party members, were obstacles to the New Order parties gaining any credibility. Thus, for example, in the Netherlands, the public for the time being supported the municipal apparatus led by its professionally trained civil-servant mayors.[21] As with the VNV and Rex, the Dutch national socialists of the *Nationaal Socialistische Beweging* (NSB) lacked an administrative programme. They used the same theoretical rhetoric of providing a more efficient and impartial administration to build the ideological bridge towards the Dutch population. Good local government became the main political task of NSB mayors. Pre-war Dutch mayors proved to be able to preserve their strong legitimacy. As the queen and her government had fled the country in 1940, mayors were often the most important and visible symbols of the traditional Dutch society, nation and state. Far more than Belgian mayors, for instance, some (state-appointed) Dutch mayors also played a role in giving a more civic, moral interpretation to the notion of 'reconstruction' and 'regeneration' after May 1940. Also, the mere fact that the presence of these pre-war functionaries was preventing an NSB member from taking over was often sufficient to enhance their legitimacy even when compromises with German demands were necessary. These socio-economic and political reasons were all necessary conditions for the legitimacy of Dutch mayors and other local leaders. Norway provided a similar example. As in the Netherlands, there was an initially relatively prosperous socio-economic situation. As with the NSB and Rex, the NS in Norway immediately faced the problem that they had nowhere near the number of competent members to fill the different seats in Norway's 20 districts and more than 700 municipalities. The NS did gradually manage to fill many mayoralties either with old NS veterans or more often with defectors from the pre-war parties. Again, these NS mayors faced the same problems as did the NSB in the Netherlands. The Norwegian population attributed any results of actual 'good government' to the remaining non-NS civil servants in the municipality, but the shortcomings to the NS mayor.

In the more 'imperial' model of Bohemia-Moravia, the Germans could implement a 'good governance' scheme more directly. In the Protectorate, because of the importance of its armaments industry, they decided to use social policies and labour market conditions as legitimizing tools towards the working population (a substantial part of whom worked in the armaments industry), with the initial elimination of unemployment and provisions of generous wages for certain industrial labourers.[22] The former unions were reorganized, depoliticizing the entire labour market while guiding the attention of the workers towards their material advantages. On paper, the German imperial model was more successful than indigenous collaborationist regimes and administrations in implementing these social strategies. In reality this 'success' was very relative and limited in time. Already in early 1941, this labour-market strategy was hard to maintain and unrest began to develop among workers. The classic German response in this imperial model was to harden repression while further centralizing local government. SS-General Reinhard Heydrich (who replaced

Reichsprotektor von Neurath in 1941) stripped the *Oberlandräte* of most of their administrative tasks, transferring direct power to the lower levels including the municipalities, which by then were mostly led by Nazi ethnic Germans.[23] This was accomplished by the autumn of 1942, but by then the aftermath of Heydrich's assassination (May 1942) had led the Czech nation to a situation of total reprisal terror.

The conclusion for all three models of reform was therefore similar. The initial strong convergence of practical interests that had propelled local 'good governance' to the centre of German New Order legitimation, quickly evaporated and could not be turned into local reality. The 'new' local administrations were unable to put good governance into practice and they generally responded extremely negatively towards protests from a population that was still steeped in a pre-war culture of local democratic participation.

Politicization

Alongside the evident lack of administrative quality of the New Order administration, the second factor undermining its legitimacy in 1941–2 was the counterproductive effect of the explicit politicization of the administrative apparatus in general and local administration in particular. The specific political-administrative status of each national occupation regime notwithstanding, politics and ideology were an inextricable part of the New Order and of everyday life. Indeed, the structural municipal reforms and the gradual replacement of the 'old' municipal political elite with a new one, was one of the main ways by which the populations of occupied Europe were confronted with the more political aspects of the New Order, National Socialism and the German occupation. Particularly where pro-German parties took over city halls, municipal life became highly politicized. In countries such as Belgium, the Netherlands and Norway, collaborationist mayors did not attempt to mitigate the political aspect of their rule. On the contrary, the large majority of these mayors not only remained politically active after their appointment to office, they often used their administrative position to express very explicitly their political commitment and propagate New Order and national-socialist ideas.

This politicization took many forms. Many New Order mayors integrated political symbols in town halls, such as replacing the picture of the royal family with pictures of Hitler or native party leaders, replacing national flags, hanging up German posters, wearing party symbols (or even uniforms) during office hours or changing the names of streets and squares. More serious acts were granting New Order militias the use of municipal buildings such as schools, using town halls for party meetings or rallies and giving an official municipal aura to public propaganda meetings. The equivalent in the state model such as Vichy France was a mayor or other local dignitary who simultaneously filled the position of local 'representative of information and propaganda' (*Délégués à l'information et à la propagande*), the local representative of the regime responsible for political activities. In fact, in the occupied zones, only a small minority of mayors seem to have filled this position. Otherwise, ideology as explicit political expressions or political behaviour in support of the regime was relatively absent from French town halls. The impressive Vichy propaganda machine obviously wanted representations or references to Pétain to be omnipresent in official or public buildings such as town halls, but the presence of these material representations of the regime in municipal buildings or town halls soon became a formality, not necessarily affecting a mayor's position to the same degree as was the case with collaborationist mayors in some other countries.

A good example of such politicization was the inaugural appointment celebrations of New Order mayors, occasions that in Flanders and the Netherlands were often used for explicit political demonstrations. In Flanders the appointment celebrations of VNV mayors, often with speeches and marches from New Order militias, were mostly for internal use to encourage party members. In the Netherlands, these inaugural celebrations carried a much greater formal importance, because in normal times they were symbols of the patriotic Dutch civil society. NSB mayors made a point of using these celebrations as an explicit political statement directed at the municipal personnel and local elite. A majority of NSB mayors used their speeches to promote national socialism and to demand strict obedience. Because of its high symbolic value in Dutch municipal culture (with the symbolic hanging of the ceremonial chain around the mayor's neck) the inevitable feeling was that Dutch town halls had been 'hijacked'.[24] Rexist mayors in francophone Belgium seem to have been much more careful in their explicit political demonstrations, probably because they had a realistic assessment of the general hostility towards them and their own isolation. In Wallonia, Rexists were confronted early on with more violent opposition and Rexist administrators generally seemed more careful in their openly political behaviour.[25] In Norway the explicit political actions of the appointees also provoked tensions, but notably less so than in Belgium or the Netherlands. A large majority of collaborationist Norwegian mayors adopted a more moderate political attitude than their Belgian and Dutch counterparts. The Germans supported these mayors in their ideological 'passivity'. In this respect, it was also essential that many pre-war mayors became NS members. They transferred their legitimacy and administrative experience to the NS. This transfer of legitimacy by traditional mayors to the New Order can only be compared to the French situation, where there was no clear transfer from one political class to another at the local level. Though the Vichy regime used its exceptional powers to purge those mayors (such as Communists or prominent freemasons) who were at odds with the National Revolution, they sought more often to incorporate the local municipal elite in the achievement of their goals. This incorporation could range, depending on local circumstances, from the merely symbolic to the highly tangible, with local officials effectively deciding how far they would choose to invest in the National Revolution. This was however rarely an entirely free choice. The supervision imposed by the superior Vichy authorities, by the German occupation authorities and the members of the pro-German parties and Vichy's propaganda organizations obliged many mayors to chart an often difficult course between national orders and local realities.[26]

Wherever it occurred, explicit politicization of local government was always irrational, clumsy and counterproductive. Not surprisingly, stressing and expressing your adherence to a foreign ideology in a context of occupation and quickly deteriorating socio-economic conditions proved to be a recipe for political and administrative disaster. In this respect, the arrogant behaviour of New Order officials was rather akin to previous instances of ineffective partisan government. The mayors of the NSB or the VNV were in this respect the modern equivalents of the *représentants en mission* of the Terror in France in 1793–4, provocatively installing trees of liberty (and guillotines) in recalcitrant French villages, or conversely the actions of local agents of the Bourbon Restoration in France who imposed an ostentatious royalist and Catholic ritual after 1815.[27]

There were other ways for ideology to undermine everyday legitimacy. In an increasingly difficult socio-economic situation, local populations encountered political favouritism on a daily basis. Collaborationist mayors, policemen and others favoured Party members, for example in terms of helping them to get jobs and other material benefits such as food products, or getting them exemptions for certain German or other unpopular measures. A collaborationist mayor always stood at the centre of these (alleged) arrangements. When the municipality had to organize the mandatory requisitioning of radios and bicycles New Order mayors could exempt their supporters. When a collaborationist mayor had to organize mandatory civil-guard duties he was often (rightly or not) accused of requisitioning local patriots or political opponents. In many cases, this was connected with strong sentiments of *revanchisme* compensating for their pre-war civil and political isolation. Another obvious aspect was that often illogical appointments were carried out. In many cases, it was clear that logical, capable candidates were blocked by external political candidates.

In some political cultures members of the 'new' elite of the New Order simply built on already existing foundations of pre-war clientelism. A rather extreme example of this was the Marseille local politician Simon Sabiani of the fascist *Parti Populaire Français* (PPF).[28] For many years prior to the war his political platform had been built on clientelism and favouritism, which had a long tradition in the ethnic melting pot of Marseille. In the 1930s he had bought political loyalty by providing his followers with public employment. After the German occupation of the Free Zone in November 1942 he collaborated enthusiastically with the *Sicherheitsdienst* and other German agencies and was thereby able to help his clientele avoid military service or labour conscription. Others were provided with jobs in the naval bases of the *Kriegsmarine* in the city.[29] Another negative political element was the role of paramilitary New Order militias. Many of these militias quickly gained an 'untouchable' position, being subjugated only to German law. This obviously led to (often violent) abuses of power. This disruptive behaviour contradicted the administrative, 'responsible' tasks of their party members within state administration. This was especially clear in Flanders for instance, where many VNV collaborators in certain administrative positions were highly critical of the actions of their own militias.

This politicization had very real and negative effects on administration. It not only damaged the relationship between a New Order mayor and his population, it also damaged the relationship with his own municipal personnel. In most occupied countries, New Order parties could only fill the top positions in local and regional administrations, simply due to a lack of sufficient competent party members. The body of the administrative personnel was often left intact. New Order mayors also depended on these experienced public servants to provide efficient administration. Alienating their own municipal personnel, therefore, did not help with administration. This was very clear in the Netherlands. Municipal personnel often rejected NSB administrative leadership, leading to open conflict and a refusal to follow orders. Many New Order mayors (especially in the Netherlands and Belgium) also withdrew themselves from higher administrative control believing it to be insufficiently radical in inspiration. Many pro-German mayors considered that pre-war administrative rules were no longer valid and preferred party instructions over administrative legality. They were stimulated in this 'revolutionary' attitude by their party leadership. Officially, party hierarchy had to prevail over administrative hierarchy. Collaborationist mayors had to be party members first and mayors second. Too much attention to administrative or legal details was considered to be 'un-National-Socialist' and even sabotage. The Netherlands is a prime example, where the NSB official and mayor of Rotterdam, Müller, presented himself as a 'shadow-minister' of the Interior who sometimes sent opposite instructions to NSB mayors when secretary-general Frederiks of the Ministry of the Interior had sent official orders to all Dutch mayors.

Remarkably, many collaborationist mayors provoked or sought out conflicts where these could easily be avoided. Administration in times of scarcity always provokes tensions and a diplomatic, tactical attitude on the part of local leaders seems crucial in finding solutions and bringing different local players to a consensus. Many New Order mayors seemed intent on adopting exactly the opposite attitude, creating problems where there were none before. Small acts of criticism could easily escalate. By adopting such an approach, New Order mayors generally showed a strong consciousness of their own illegitimate position and a profound insecurity about their authority. They often sought conflicts with strong pre-war leaders whom they considered to be competitors. In response, the mayors often fell back on the support of the German forces, apparently seeing no other means of maintaining their authority.

Their explicit politicization of local government entirely undermined their self-legitimation of providing 'objective' and 'superior' efficient administration.

Rather than 'order' and 'efficiency', public unrest and chaos increased where New Order mayors were nominated. Although the feelings of populations towards local government remain difficult to determine, it was quite obvious that in Norway, Belgium and the Netherlands, rejection of New Order mayors was already very strong by 1941. Large mass protests quickly became less frequent for obvious reasons, but small incidents between members of the local population and New Order mayors grew from 1941 onwards. This was especially clear in the more industrialized areas of Belgium and France. But also in the more rural areas of Flanders, the many incidents between the population and VNV mayors points to a general atmosphere of hostility and rejection. Protests often took on a social form: 'bread-protests' of women for better food provision and strikes and other forms of industrial action in factories by workers.[30] The local populations had good reasons to dislike and indeed to fear the decisions made by their local rulers. What was presented as protection could easily be turned against them. Regulating life, distributing scarce commodities, policing public order, all of these were techniques of control that had profound influences on everybody's life (or death). Town halls issued rationing cards (which could also be used for identification) and identity documents, decided who had to be sent to labour service in Germany, had to work on German-inspired defence projects, was to report for deportation as Jews, or would lose their jobs in education or other branches of administration. Thus, local government became a driving wheel in the implementation of the fundamental policies of the occupation and had to be mistrusted until proven otherwise.

Given its centrality to occupation policies, the evident lack of legitimacy on the local level was a major problem for the New Order parties as well as the Germans. It became acute when socio-economic conditions worsened. At such a time, the importance of shared basic goals or beliefs between local populations and their leaders became essential. Only administrators with strong legitimacy could have implemented the many unpopular measures required. Some New Order administrators did try to gain legitimacy by referring to some vague set of shared basic beliefs or common goals with their population. This had no success whatsoever. The attempts of Rex to present itself as the only 'true socialist' party in the larger Walloon cities of southern Belgium or to gain administrative credibility with the traditional Right-wing francophone elite failed completely. So did the attempts of the VNV to use the rich symbolism and history of the Flemish movement to reach out for broader support. The attempts of the NSB to link National Socialism to some form of 'Dutch nationalism' was doomed from the beginning. Their explicit politicization was a fatal mistake from the viewpoint of legitimacy and subsequently for the provision of good governance. In Norway, the NS explicitly used references to Norwegian historical mythology to legitimize their infiltration of local civil society. This stimulated a large movement of Norwegian local 'resistance', which first and foremost was a movement of local political-cultural rejection of Norwegian national socialism rather than resistance through the use of force.[31]

In a country such as Belgium, where public order was the main concrete goal of the Germans, it would at first sight appear strange that the German occupation authorities never even attempted to mitigate the explicit politicization of municipal administrations. That they did not do so does, however, demonstrate the degree of politicization that characterized German administrative structures across occupied Europe. It was not only in the 'frontier' zones of eastern Europe or the Balkans that 'ordinary' German officials operated according to highly politicized (and often racial) norms. In the more 'settled' administrations of western and northern Europe, the German administrative structures contained explicit agents of nazification such as the plethora of SS racial and ideological experts as well as a substantial cadre of experienced civilian and military officials who had nevertheless internalized the ideological assumptions of the Third Reich. In such circumstances, German concepts of 'order' were never as ideologically neutral as they initially appeared.[32]

In France, although the head of state Pétain could maintain some legitimacy during the first years of 1940–2, it had already became clear on the local level by the end of 1940 that the Vichy government itself had severe problems of legitimacy. The regime faced too many problems at the local level, through a combination of their failure to deliver good government and their obvious subjugation to the German authorities. The impact of the potentially extremely rich arsenal of shared French beliefs within the National Revolution foundered quickly at the local level.[33] A good example is the *Relève* in 1942, by which the regime tried to trade voluntary French labourers for French POWs in German captivity. The political scheme was that this barter would enhance national solidarity and strengthen the French nation and state. But it was a failure. The regime could not convince local populations that this *Relève* was anything other than deportation of French workers to Germany in the service of the German war effort. New Order regimes had proven totally incapable of motivating their populations in providing support, because these regimes were seen as the major causes of the problems.[34]

In 1941, it was clear the German New Order had failed to establish its legitimacy. Consequently, during 1941–2 in France, Belgium and Norway, legitimate government at the local level became 'up for grabs'. There was uncertainty and a lack of clarity among local populations and administrations about where and with whom national legitimate power rested: De Gaulle or Pétain, King Leopold III, Quisling, the governments in exile, Moscow or London. This uncertainty had immediate demonstrable consequences at the local level. Collaborationists with local administrative mandates not only succeeded in de-legitimizing the New Order, but gradually on a more general level also the very nature of public authority itself. The New Order identified itself completely with legitimate 'order' and 'authority', denouncing every form of disobedience or dissidence as 'resistance'. However, in countries such as Belgium and France, it was exactly this disobedience to public authority that was quickly becoming the more legitimate form of behaviour. Most people found relying on the black market for survival to be a more legitimate form of behaviour than obeying orders from collaborationist mayors or other German-supported administrators.

The localization of public authority and the context of everyday crisis caused a fragmentation of legitimacy. Legitimacy did not disappear or evaporate. It spread out over many different individuals and entities. The difference with a normally functioning civil society was the absence of any deeper or longer-term legitimacy. Powerful local leaders (sometimes pre-war mayors) and useful organizations or institutions could quickly gain and maintain local legitimacy. This was notably strong in rural areas, where interpersonal relationships between local authorities and the population remained more direct.[35] There gradually emerged a situation of 'localized' or 'compartmentalized' legitimacy in which individual leaders could win short-term personal legitimacy based on their leadership abilities in the face of direct, practical problems. The New Order's obvious failure to establish legitimacy by 1942 did not therefore lead to a vacuum of legitimacy at the local level. As far as long-term more deeply rooted legitimacy was concerned, however, the situation in 1941–2 resembled more a 'preparatory' situation. Strong local leaders were simply maintaining their positions often clandestinely, while waiting for new central legitimate institutions to be installed.

A Central Perspective Returns (1943–5)

The winter of 1942–43, was an international moment of political rupture. It became clear for many local populations living under German rule that occupation regimes and the New Order in general were no longer struggling for long-term legitimacy but short-term survival. German military might dwindled and socio-economic conditions worsened in most occupied countries. Legitimizing arguments such as 'efficiency', 'order' and 'just rule' were quickly replaced with the reality of total war. In terms of local government, this meant that Nazi Germany began imposing its own specific set of immediate short-term goals in occupied countries. Local administrations were increasingly ordered simply to carry out central orders, regarding forced labour, racial policies and the fight against the resistance. The Germans gradually abandoned their system of 'indirect rule' through local indigenous administrations and simply fell back on taking what they needed by force.

The general reaction in many occupied countries was further 'localization' of life. One of the key characteristics of this period was that central regimes found it increasingly difficult to control local administrations. In this way, the central level's lack of legitimacy became a very real, practical problem because central regimes were obliged to recognize that they were increasingly powerless to make local structures implement their orders. Central legitimation also became more openly political. Rather than using obsolete arguments of efficient and 'just' rule, the Germans and especially collaborationist regimes tried to maintain public support and legitimacy by referring to the fight of the Germanic West against the Bolshevik East. Local indigenous collaborators used the same strategy, warning the population about the dangers of 'Communist terrorism'. The danger of the Communist threat, however, had lost much of its immediate impact in the context of National Socialist rule. The local struggle for legitimacy strengthened, but its character had changed fundamentally. In 1941–2, local leading groups and individuals were simply maintaining local administration in a context where clear future goals and national legitimacy itself remained highly uncertain. The main goal was to keep the population happy while not attracting the attention of the higher administrative hierarchy or the Germans. In France mayors and local institutions formally supported the 'National Revolution' and the Vichy government, which in reality meant that they tried to stay out of politics and mediate on behalf of their population. Local notables – by now increasingly outside of the 'official' municipal structures – hid small 'pockets' of local legitimacy, waiting to be opened and used at a later date.

In 1943–4, however, the future perspectives became clearer. This changed the nature of the local struggle for legitimacy. The local struggle gradually regained its longer term 'national' goals in the preparation for the transition and the post-war order. It still remained unclear to local administrators which exactly was the legitimate central power to follow. As public authority gradually began to disintegrate, many mayors were left to their own devices, without administrative leadership. Governments in exile began to denounce the politics of administrative accommodation with the German authorities more strongly, while populations now became highly critical of the actions of their representatives. Indeed, the deteriorating material situation, increasing German repression, and the hope of some future liberation that had previously primarily affected the legitimacy of local representatives of the New Order, now began affecting representatives of the pre-war order as well. Pre-war mayors and other prominent local administrators who were still in office by the beginning of 1943 were obliged to recognize that the situation had changed dramatically in the course of one year.

A good example was the Netherlands, where the dilemma of staying in office or resigning had already been touched upon in a clandestine letter written in 1942 by the mayor of the rural town of Wisch in which he stated tersely that 'resigning without a conflict is desertion'.[36] What he did not say was which matters were worth resigning over. After the winter of 1942–3 (and especially after the national strikes which occurred in municipal administrations in May 1943) many pre-war Dutch mayors began to notice that their former legitimacy was quickly eroding. The ability of local administrations to protect their citizens, to deliver good administration and to mediate effectively with German authorities diminished quickly.[37] Citizens began to question mayors' decisions to stay in place and cooperate with the Germans. When the instruments to provide good governance diminished, mayors were only left with their role as instruments of nazification. As more and more mayors were replaced by National Socialists, an increasing shadow of suspicion was thrown on those mayors who were allowed to stay in office. While in 1940 staying in office, continuing to govern and cooperating with the Germans had seemed to be an act of patriotism, responsibility and bravery, exactly the same behaviour was increasingly looked upon as almost treacherous in itself. In the Netherlands, this even led to new official 'Instructions' in 1943 which were prepared clandestinely but officially recognized by the government in exile, that stressed the illegality of German rule in the Netherlands and denounced the strategy of staying in office as a way of lending legitimacy to the New Order. Especially after the May strikes of 1943, many (often younger) members of the Dutch municipal personnel began pushing for a more 'resistant' attitude, which often provoked conflict with more traditional-minded Dutch mayors who were conditioned by a lifetime of public service and obedience to central authority, and who found it difficult suddenly to adopt an attitude of systematic resistance.

All over occupied north-western Europe, local administrators were now directly confronted with the fact that continuing in their administrative office inevitably meant executing Nazi policy. Local Jewish families were deported, local men were arrested and deported as labourers, and the German security services began an all-out war against the underground resistance. In executing these and many other tasks, the Germans needed municipal administrations and local police forces. This near total nazification of local government placed most local administrators, even many members of collaborationist parties, in impossible positions.

In France, 'traditional' municipal government had been somewhat left out of the new organization of the state in 1940–1. This now became an advantage for many French mayors in 1943. They tried to concentrate on purely local interests, offering practical mediation where possible. As Gildea argues in his regional study of the Loire valley, the concrete interests of family, village, town, church and trade union became more important than making explicit choices for Vichy, London or Moscow.[38] Many French mayors were no longer supporting the central regime's legitimacy, but their own personal legitimacy and that of the political groups they represented. Many Socialist mayors for instance, found themselves in direct competition with the underground Communist (or the rapidly growing Socialist) resistance. While the French Communists felt that armed resistance was the best way of gaining post-war legitimacy, many republican mayors under Vichy felt that upholding local administration was the best means of reaching exactly the same goal. This was also the case in Denmark, where after the resignation of the government in August 1943 many Social Democratic mayors in larger cities saw their administrative allegiance to the state as a matter of safeguarding Social Democratic interests for the longer term in the face of Communist attempts to strengthen their future position in Denmark.[39]

As has already been said, even some collaborationist local functionaries had the same reaction. When the Norwegian Quisling government increased its general repression, many local NS mayors recognized the advantages of focusing on their day-to-day business and the provision of services for the community, while at the same time consciously scaling down the ideological aspects of their everyday administration. Obviously, this remained a delicate balancing exercise. Only a few municipalities managed successfully to withdraw fully. External conditions could often force collaborationist mayors to compromise themselves in acts of violent repression.

'Official' local governments were now caught in a local competition for legitimacy with a complex and heterogeneous patchwork of local networks that came to the fore. Diverse structures and individuals outside of the 'official' municipal governments began to act more explicitly and openly in a context in which some form of future transition became more certain by the month. These structures and individuals incorporated a wide variety of local and regional players in the economic, social, political, religious and cultural spheres, the exact composition of which differed depending on both national and local contexts.[40] Essentially however, the transition to the post-war period now became the main point of focus in the struggle for legitimacy. Notables and groups began to position themselves in order to be able successfully to make the transition.

Gildea's research on the occupation history of the small French village of Chinon shows a surprisingly active local associational life, even under the restrictions of Vichy and the Germans.[41] Vichy had never come close to eradicating the strong local positions of notables and mayors, partly also because the regime had quickly realized the potential value of these local pre-war leaders and structures for the consolidation of the regime.[42] Many pre-war structures and associations continued to evolve during the occupation, in an 'official' or clandestine form. These 'clandestine' associations and networks took away legitimacy from the official state organizations and associations (such as the *Légion Française des Combattants*). But the war and occupation also created new local structures and associations. In France, for example, the absence of many thousands of POWs gave rise to organized local solidarity actions.[43] Gradually in 1943–4 many of these local structures and individuals connected or merged with the underground resistance. Local resistance groups obviously were the most important among the newly established structures that played a crucial role in this struggle for local legitimacy. These resistance groups were often a combination of old and new, initially being based on pre-war (often non-political) local associations and structures but during the occupation gradually evolving into something entirely new. They used their struggle against the Germans and for national independence as well as their boldness and personal sacrifices as tools for constructing post-war legitimacy.[44]

In the more industrial, urbanized regions Socialist and Communist activists organized social protests into clandestine unions. In the more Catholic parts of rural Western Europe, religious leaders and associations played a crucial role. In 1943–4 the 'moral leadership' of the local clergy was endowed with an explicitly political character. Not only did the local clergy have a strong political or moral prestige, they also possessed the structures and institutions to provide a powerful counterweight to 'official' local governments.[45] During the German requisitioning of church bells in Belgium, the local clergy strongly protested, placing collaborationist mayors – many of whom were Catholic in origin themselves – in a difficult position.[46] In some (rural) parts of France and Belgium, the Catholic clergy and their local institutions played a crucial role in hiding Jews and other people in hiding. In Belgium, Catholic youth associations actively stimulated young people to evade labour conscription. The same situation arose in Vichy France, where many of the local clergy turned away from the regime and often their own pro-Vichy hierarchy. Vesna Drapac's study of parish life in Paris shows how the local church guided and organized its local communities to shield it from excessive collaboration and politicization. She argues that during the occupation 'Catholicism ... remained the single most cohesive force in French society'.[47] In Protestant Denmark and Norway the churches played a similar part. Certainly in Norway the church was a central institution in the protest against attempts to nazify civil society.[48]

Local clergy often played this role all over occupied Europe. Even in the mostly German-speaking province of South Tyrol/Alto Adige in Northern Italy (formerly a part of the Habsburg Empire), the local Church played a vital role in delegitimizing Nazism. Many German-speaking South Tyrolers welcomed the German occupation of Northern Italy in the late summer of 1943, but immediately rejected its blatant anti-Catholic policy. Since the First World War, the Church had been a key factor in German identity in South Tyrol. In 1943, the local (German-speaking) clergy became a main rallying point of opposition against the Nazis.[49] Local political leaders who had been cast aside during the New Order also played an important role in many localities. They often kept in contact with municipal personnel and the police, and could openly or secretly influence these people to obstruct certain orders issued by New Order appointees. In this localized struggle for legitimacy, old legitimacies were re-established and strengthened, while completely new ones emerged and took root.

The local struggle for legitimacy thus regained focus and purpose after 1943. But to exactly what purpose? It is far too simple to reduce this complex local struggle to a straightforward process by which the pre-war order was preparing a purge of the collaborators and their own restoration to power. It is also far too simple to reduce it to a struggle of local democracy against oppressive state-fascism. This restoration was still highly uncertain, as was the nature of the future transition or post-war order. The local struggle for legitimacy that was rekindled after the winter of 1942–3, involved local administrators searching for ways to survive the occupation and the transition with their personal legitimacy and that of their political entourage intact. So, despite the renewed focus on the post-war era, the struggle for legitimacy remained highly localized, with powerful local individuals and clandestine networks using their own means to secure their positions.

In this insecure context of forthcoming transition, collaborationist local leaders could maintain – or even for the first time gain – some form of short-term legitimacy. This legitimacy was pragmatic and temporary, based on good governance. Many pro-German administrators left political radicalism behind once they realized that the New Order was coming to an end. They began using their powers as mayors and policemen to help certain members of the local population.[50] The most obvious example was forced labour. More than any other German measure, this provoked broad public hostility and opposition from 1943 onwards in all areas of Europe where it was implemented. In response, New Order local officials began to protect certain citizens. This change in attitude was also tied to the growing frustration within collaborationist movements towards the Germans, who could or would not protect the physical safety of collaborators, were clearly only interested in their own war effort and (most importantly) were losing the war.

Thus, some New Order mayors could gain some form of very personal and very temporary legitimacy in 1943–4. A prime example was Flanders, where many VNV mayors consciously tried to re-establish their close pre-war links with the Flemish Catholic institutions. There were some clear examples of VNV mayors offering explicit protection to members of the local Catholic elite in 1944, in return for their support after the liberation. This was mostly successful in smaller villages where pre-war local and personal ties between the Flemish Nationalists and the Catholic Party had been strong. Allowing their municipal personnel to help people evading compulsory labour, or giving certain local key-figures personal protection were the main strategies used by these New Order mayors. Romijn also argues for the Netherlands that in smaller villages where a traditional, patriarchical mayoralty had always been dominant, New Order mayors could try to fill this role and thus gain some connection with the population.[51] Indeed, some NSB mayors left their blind ideological logic behind and opted for a more pragmatic relationship with their local surroundings. This often meant connecting with the local elite, and sometimes even the local resistance. During the often complete disintegration of public administration which occurred during the so-called hunger-winter of 1944–5, informal local leaders formed ad hoc committees and associations to take over the basic tasks of public power: food provisioning, medical care and the transportation of city children to the countryside.[52] These improvised local committees – that formed an important tool for a stable local transition in the period immediately after the liberation – were sometimes supported by pragmatic NSB mayors.

The same phenomenon happened in Norway, where the local resistance during the last phase negotiated with the mayoralty for the post-war transition. Also some collaborationist mayors who tried to soften measures from Oslo (and especially Hagelin's excessive policies) could gain some form of local legitimacy in the eyes of their population.[53] A good example was the large south-east Norwegian town of Fredrikstad, where several local protagonists declined the Ministry of the Interior's request to accept the post of mayor. Finally, the Ministry appointed a senior master at the local seafarers school who had recently joined the NS. This man was well respected; although considered to be politically naïve. After the liberation most people in the municipal administration and the general public agreed that he had provided fairly good administration and had mediated for the local community with the Ministry of the Interior.[54]

But the struggle for local legitimacy was about more than just 'good governance' and short-term personal benefits for groups. Ideology and long-term expectations about the outcome of the war also played an essential part. Fear of Communist 'terrorism' and of a possible future Communist takeover for instance, probably influenced some people's feelings and attitude towards collaborating mayors. This was especially the case in some areas in France.[55] Many Flemish VNV mayors could probably also count on some form of general support for their attempts at maintaining local administration against violent attacks, be it politically motivated or not. This was a legitimacy based on people's fears for their immediate safety and a – perhaps natural – tendency to identify with the authority of the mayor and his administration and not the anonymous resistance fighter. By the spring of 1944, fears – if not quite the reality – of civil war were widespread in German-occupied Europe.[56] This complicated preparations for a local transfer of power. The hopes of notables that they could direct a relatively ordered local transition were undermined by the 'terrorist' actions of collaborationist groups – such as Darnand's *Milice* in France – and of local resistance groups which, whatever their nominal loyalty to Communist front organizations or indeed Allied-controlled networks engaged in their own 'spontaneous' actions. The fears of the moment caused some radical political realignments, in which local figures sought protection from whosoever appeared best able to provide it, be it the resistance fighters in the hills, the semi-clandestine representatives of the Allies or of the government-in-exile or the local German commander.[57]

This same logic of desperation had long been present in many areas of southern and eastern occupied Europe. In many of these countries, legitimacy could not play the same role because German rule had meant an almost immediate regression to blind exploitation and brutal repression. In the most extreme examples, civil society was destroyed (or at the least severely disrupted) down to its local foundations. Here, the level of administrative disintegration on the local level came years earlier than in northern and western Europe. In these conditions local legitimacy simply evaporated. In Belarus, for example, the German occupation after the summer of 1941 severely disrupted everyday life with heavy repression, exploitation and racial extermination. The Germans left local administrations (*rayons* or districts and municipalities) formally intact, but local administration quickly disintegrated.[58] The Germans engaged the help of village elders to keep the agriculturally based economy operating and also to recruit young men for local police services who became involved in brutal German racial policies or reprisal actions. In response, the underground partisans evidently quickly and violently contested the collaborationist attitudes of these local authorities. It is difficult to determine the level of legitimacy of these village elders. The consequence here, as in many other areas of the Soviet borderlands, was an almost total breakdown in notions of legitimacy.[59] Survival was the first priority and in the face of an extreme and sudden descent into civil war, the situation of extreme violence, terror and permanent fear prevented local populations from accepting any legitimate rulers.

Many local police and village elders were purged and severely punished after the war by NKVD courts while local partisans could often not transform their wartime record and possible legitimacy into post-war power. Thus, rather than an internal process, one form of external authority was replaced by another. A similar situation was provided by Yugoslavia, that after German and Italian occupation quickly degenerated into an ethnically inspired civil war. Here also, legitimacy evaporated in the face of German reprisal terror, and rivalry between Communist partisans and the Rightist Chetnik-resistance movement. Here, the disruption of the Yugoslav state and its local government framework clearly facilitated the Communist takeover of the country in 1944–5.[60]

In some other countries, however, this disintegration of authority was a stimulating factor for local organization. Greece for instance, had since its occupation in April 1941 largely ceased to have any effective central authority.[61] The country was divided into different occupation zones, and the German zone was governed in what is sometimes called an 'authoritarian anarchy', with different German authorities competing with each other and three consecutive Greek collaborationist governments lacking any real power or control.[62] From the outset, legitimacy had not been a real issue for the Germans who even in 1941 implemented economic plunder and brutal repression. The Greek pro-German government tried to control the rising social protest and underground resistance in the larger Greek cities but could never extend significant control over large areas of the countryside. In the Greek mountains, a tradition of local self-government had developed for more than four centuries. The Ottomans had allowed these villages self-government in return for tax collections. During the occupation, the rural countryside fell back on this tradition and enhanced it, since self-government now became a tool to react against an increasingly brutal occupation. The Greek countryside effectively became a laboratory for developing new forms of local government. As early as 1941 local committees had sprung up that explicitly sought to promote total self-government replacing all state authority. By 1942, however, the underground resistance gradually took over these local structures, giving them a national 'goal' and making them an integral part of the struggle for Greek liberation. As the resistance expanded its influence over the countryside, they organized the areas that they more or less controlled with new systems of local government. The National Liberation Front even published the basis for a new municipal law in December 1942, completely re-organizing the entire fabric of local government. After some experimentation, this was followed by several new texts in 1943 and in August 1944 which gradually spread its geographical influence and implementation over central Greece during the final years of the German occupation.[63]

Even in north-western Europe, it is difficult to measure how far this localization – the gradual 'withdrawal' from the state and the local, personalized struggle for legitimacy – by many municipal administrations and the emergence of other local leaders or groups translated itself into new notions of local democracy. Many different groups defended many different and often contradictory ideas and goals. Most local players were concerned primarily with resolving specific local problems without explicit long-term goals. Nevertheless, many of these local networks and players were based on pre-war political parties, trade unions, religious networks or other associations. Their re-emergence in 1943–4 on the local terrain in many ways cleared the path for a post-war restoration of their positions of power and inevitably also their political ideas. On the other hand, the ideas of local self-government, local solidarity and resistance against higher state authority automatically involved ideas concerning 'local democracy' and the rights of local people. Thus, the clear local juxtaposition between freedom and civil rights on the one hand and occupation and oppression on the other, reinforced those democratic traditions that in many countries had been the norm for decades.

The most explicitly political local player obviously was the underground resistance and especially its press. Although for many local resistance groups, clear political ideological goals were subjugated to the goal of ousting the Germans and liberating their respective countries, most resistance groups had certain preferences about the political future. Obviously, the Communist resistance network had the most clearly articulated political goals. But the political programme of most local and regional resistance groups was often based on a vague programme of national 'renewal'. Thus, in 1944–5, 'renewal' and 'unification' became key legitimizing words, just as 'order', 'stability' and 'efficient, just rule' had been back in 1940. This shift in language did not influence greatly the consequent transition in power: the weight of Allied military power and the internal realities of local power structures counted for more than ideological rhetoric. But the language of renewal, though highly inchoate, did signify a shift in the nature of local legitimacy. The ambitions of 'good governance' so apparent in 1940 carried now a more democratic or participatory character. Legitimacy resided not only in the content of rule but in the fact that such rule was accomplished in accordance with the will of the people.

The Return of the Central State

In the last few months of the occupation, legitimacy had become localized and fragmented. The struggle for local legitimacy had become a process involving many players preparing for an uncertain post-war order. The liberation which for most countries in northern and western Europe came quickly (except in the Netherlands) and brought a sudden end to this fragmentalization and localization. For four or more years, local governments had been gradually forced to operate without legitimate central power and leadership. The liberation caused a sudden return of 'legal' state power. In most north-western European countries such as Belgium and France there was an immediate return to pre-war legality (and thus the pre-war administrative situation), which was also implemented at the local level. The return of the state meant that national (political) elements in the struggle for legitimacy came to the fore again and took over.

However, the local level continued to play an important role during the period of transition. The localized struggle for legitimacy was not simply integrated or absorbed into the national one, but rather had a fundamental influence on it. Moreover, the relationship and interaction between the local and national struggles for legitimacy was not without tensions and contradictions. The underlying tension lay in the fact that, while central regimes and governments preferred homogenous policies in order to strengthen national unity, local post-war sensibilities, needs and expectations were often highly diverse.[64] Communities that had to deal with strong German or collaborationist repression, severe hunger, or a highly politicized and polemical post-war transition had completely different expectations from neighbouring villages, which had escaped such experiences. In most countries, the central regime acted energetically to try to stabilize the local situation. In order to establish their legitimacy, central regimes had to do several main things: establish legal, democratic legitimacy (and reconnect with the pre-war order), implement the purges of local administrations and appoint reliable administrators and restore the quality of local government. But the attempts of new regimes and governments to establish their legitimacy, often did not converge with local wishes and expectations.

In most north-western European countries, a return of pre-war administrative legality theoretically meant the return of pre-war mayors and other local leaders. The reality was very different. Many of these men were not physically present at the time of liberation, and many of the men who were had to defend their position against local competitors. The local struggle for legitimacy was heightened after the liberation because now the different players could act openly. Many new local players presented themselves based on their wartime record and tried to transport their wartime legitimacy into the post-war order. Obviously, the most important group in this regard was the resistance. Immediately after the liberation, many local resistance groups used their moral prestige backed with their military might to attack local administrators. In many villages in France and Belgium, the Communist resistance briefly took over town halls temporarily pushing legal mayors and administrators aside. These 'illegal' situations were quickly rectified, but in many localities local resistance leaders and groups continued to dominate politics for many months. In many of these localities, resistance leaders were 'absorbed' by local political groups who sought to use their legitimacy in their political quest for power.[65] The local purges were an important factor in this political struggle, as well as one of the first post-war sources of frictions between the national and the local level. But another important factor in this struggle, remained the restoration of administrative efficiency and good government. In most countries in both eastern and western Europe, the last phase of the war and occupation had been characterized by a total disintegration of public authority, violence, food shortages and destruction. Quickly restoring 'order' and public life once the euphoria of liberation waned, was a serious challenge for all post-war governments and administrations.

A first condition was quickly to organize local purges. In countries where the politicization of local government had been high (such as the Netherlands, Belgium and Norway) administrative sanction procedures completely overlapped with judicial procedures, while in a country such as France the separation between the administrative and judicial element of the purges was more clearly defined. As Romijn points out for the Netherlands, although the purges and local restoration were legitimized in terms of restoring public confidence in local government, the real priority was restoring the central authorities' confidence in their local administration.[66] The central state only seemed to be able or willing to establish its own legitimacy, with a reliable local administration.

France and Belgium used two opposing strategies, but neither succeeded in neutralizing the contradictions between national logic and local expectations. The French provisional government chose the fast strategy with several early elections in 1945. Because of this hasty organization however, many French deportees who were still en route to their homes were denied the chance of participating in these crucial elections, giving rise to much local frustration.[67] The new provisional French government also took a firm grip on the transition process, with a rapid purge of departmental prefects, a tight organization of local resistance groups and the imposition of *Commissaires de la République* who were plenipotentiaries invested with vast administrative powers. Rapid and superficial administrative procedures judged local administrators and suspended or confirmed their position. New local players (notably from the resistance) had some influence on the local purges but in general the central state proved able to control matters fairly well. The first post-war municipal elections took place in May 1945, with Europe not even wholly liberated. This re-invested the municipal level with new democratic legitimacy, forcing new local contenders (such as the powerful French Communists) to integrate themselves in the democratic republican framework. On the surface, the French transition seemed quick and relatively successful. The local reality however, was different.

This is well illustrated in Koreman's detailed study of the transition in three small French towns.[68] She illustrates the three spheres in which local populations expected the new provisional republican government to provide 'just rule', notably (1) 'legal justice' through the purge of collaborators and restoration of the rule of law, (2) 'social justice' through good government (and especially an efficient and fair distribution of food) and (3) 'honorary justice' (the recognition of the local heroes and victims).

In contrast, the regime used a narrow definition of collaboration, dictated by the national logic to support the myth of the 'nation of resisters', to unite the country and to re-install quickly political stability. Only the most serious collaborators would be punished. This frustrated local populations, resisters and leaders who had expected a wider and more severe punishment of 'their' local collaborators. The national regime also often failed to meet the expectations of social justice, as they failed to organize food (and notably bread) distribution efficiently. The decision of the provisional government to introduce free-market principles in bread distribution in 1945 for instance, proved totally impossible to implement at the local level (and led to a bread crisis and the subsequent re-establishment of rationing). Moreover, De Gaulle's policy of using the resistance as the foundation of the myth of one homogenous French 'nation of resisters' left little room for individual recognition of local war heroes and victims, causing much local bitterness among the resistance and the many families of victims. The quick, French approach therefore covered up local tensions under a carpet of national unity; yet Koreman illustrates that the contradictions between central policies and local expectations in all three spheres forged tensions that would linger for many years.

But a deliberately slow strategy of political stabilization was no guarantee of success as Belgium well shows. This country opted for a long period of transition with municipal elections that were organized more than two years after the liberation in November 1946. The Belgian central and provincial authorities wanted first to stabilize local situations, before organizing elections. During this two-year period of transition, the national authorities needed strong, able and reliable local leaders (especially mayors). In order to do this, Belgian central and provincial authority was obliged to interfere more strongly than administrative legality normally allowed. The Belgian government wanted local leaders who were uncompromised by the occupation and who were good, efficient and dynamic administrators. Thus, many mayors and other local leaders who were considered undesirable solely for administrative reasons were purged together with political collaborators. Many local populations were often outraged to find their respected, patriotic (often elderly) mayor purged for administrative reasons together with New Order officials. This was especially the case with old mayors, for instance, who had a high moral prestige locally but were deemed undesirable by the national authorities because of their age and (alleged) lack of adaptability and administrative capabilities. The failure of the Belgian government to explain the administrative priorities of central policy to the wider public, would lay the foundations for many myths about a Belgian anti-Flemish repression that to a certain extent continues to exist in the Flemish movement today.[69]

A variant of this theme can be seen in the recreated Czechoslovak state, where the purges on the one hand had to serve the re-establishment of the new Czechoslovak National Front government yet also respond to strong local demands to purge the entire German population from the territory of the re-established republic.[70]

This was why Edvard Beneš (now again President of Czechoslovakia) and other members of the government directly encouraged local 'authorities' and citizens to embark on a wave of violence against the German minority and Czech collaborators after the liberation in May 1945. Beneš' decision to decentralize local government immediately after the liberation, also facilitated this violent retribution. Political tensions also complicated this process. While the democratic Czech political parties saw the purges as a tool for legitimizing the regime, the Communists (as in many other countries) regarded it much more as a political tool in the grander Communist strategy. Whatever their different reasons for doing so, the parties represented in the Czechoslovak government were less inclined than their Belgian, French or Dutch counterparts to control local demands for strong repressive purges. On the contrary, the Czechoslovak government approved local executions by 'People's Courts' before its legal foundations were even created. Only gradually did these local people's courts come under the control of the national regime and did they mitigate and render more objective their judicial proceedings. The so-called Small Decree on 'National Honour' (October 1945) gave local National Committees the authority to disenfranchise and deny persons 'certificates of national reliability'.[71] This devolution of control to the local level would in the end stimulate national political polarization, especially when after 1947 the punishment of economic collaboration became a burning issue. Here, Communists and their local allies clashed with their democratic partners in the National Front government. It became increasingly clear that the centre-Left parties opted for a legitimation of the republic with reference to the rule of law and democratic values, whereas the Communists openly began using the local dynamic of purges to legitimize an operation of cleansing society of its 'collaborationist bourgeoisie'.

From these case studies, it is clear that the first years of local transition (1944–6) did not proceed smoothly. Every country encountered local-national tensions, difficult political struggles between local strong men and problems with purges and good governance (concerning food distribution, for example). However, taking a more general and broader view of this transition period, one can only acknowledge its remarkable short-term success. Almost everywhere in north-western Europe, central state structures, governments and regimes were able to establish their democratic legitimacy remarkably quickly.

This was clear in terms of political continuity. In Denmark, Belgium, France and to a lesser extent the Netherlands there was a strong local political continuity, with the local political distribution of power in the post-war elections remaining more or less the same compared to the last pre-war elections. The initial Communist electoral gain to the disadvantage of the Socialists, would prove to be very temporary. There was a rupture of personnel however after the occupation in many countries. A younger generation of local administrators took over power, especially at the mayoral level. It is difficult to determine to what extent these new faces based their post-war career on a wartime legitimacy. Only very rarely could members of the resistance build a successful post-war local political career based on wartime legitimacy alone. Indeed, in general, the resistance could *not* capitalize upon their wartime legitimacy to achieve post-war political success at the local level. Just as they had pragmatically recognized the advantages of a moderate collaborationist mayor in 1943–4, local communities were in 1945–6 fairly quickly able to recognize the new priorities of the post-war era and the type of people who were now needed. After 1945, local communities did not need men with guns and explosives but people building houses and railways. Many new post-war mayors had already been strong figures during the 1930s. In many cases, a passive political attitude during the occupation even seemed a major asset, for instance in Belgium. Pre-war legitimacy was thus often transferred to the post-war period. This did not mean that the occupation had had no influence. Many new faces who were elected in post-war municipal elections had remained present in their localities during the occupation and had played some role, albeit not in the 'official' municipal administration nor in the resistance, but in the more clandestine and informal networks that had re-emerged after the winter of 1942–3. Generally speaking, one can therefore conclude that many post-war mayors and other local administrators had strengthened their legitimacy in 1943 and 1944, in effectively catering for local interests when local government had disintegrated.

An essential part of this successful national approach in north-western Europe to the restoration of democratic legitimacy, lay at the local level. The New Order had some small opportunities for legitimacy during the first weeks or months of occupation in some countries, but local reality evolved very quickly away from the occupying forces and their collaborators. Local structures proved very resilient. Often, pre-war leaders and structures could adapt very well and maintain their local centre of power, albeit in a non-direct and clandestine way. These local men and structures were little 'pockets of legitimacy', serving local expectations and interests and making legitimate German rule impossible. A wide variety of old and new local structures showed a strong continuity between the 1930s and the post-war era. They had evolved clandestinely during the occupation but had maintained their level of organization, their influence on the population and their legitimacy. One can also assume that this was about much more than local populations simply pragmatically picking the most convenient person. Local leaders who had been 'coming men' in the 1930s, who strengthened their position during the occupation and who could gain local or regional power after the liberation were people who first and foremost never seemed to have lost contact with the undercurrent of local expectations. When central power returned, it could build its structures on a foundation and framework of these local networks and individual leaders. In many ways, this continuity was entirely misleading: the reconstruction that took place followed years of discontinuity and upheaval. But the impression of continuity served to emphasize the failure of the preceding forms of experiment. Local legitimacy remained rooted within a recognizable, if much adapted, class of local notables who played a central role in the stabilization of the post-war political order.

Notes

1. E. Weber *Peasants into Frenchmen: The Modernization of Rural France* (London, 1977); U. Oestergaard *Peasants and Danes: The Danish National Identity and Political Culture. Comparative Studies of Society and History* 34 (Copenhagen, 1992), pp. 3–27; J. Stengers *Les racines de la Belgique* Vol. 1 (Brussels, 2000).
2. The powers and competences of modern local government were influenced by the tension between centralizing and localizing tendencies during the nineteenth century. See, for example, M.P. Brown 'The possibility of local autonomy' *Urban Geography* XIII (1993), 257–79; E. Page *Localism and Centralism in Europe: The Political and Legal Bases of Local Self-Government* (Oxford, 1991).
3. Regarding the importance of the modern local 'culture of democracy', see S. Weir and D. Beetham *Political Power and Democratic Control in Britain* (London, 1999); D. Beetham 'The idea of democratic audit in comparative perspective' *Parliamentary Affairs* LII (1999), 567–81.
4. Given that the nature of local government varied so greatly between different states, we have chosen to develop this chapter through examination of national case studies. These are predominantly drawn from northern and central Europe, though we will also use some southern examples (such as Greece). Attention will also be paid to other forms of occupation in wartime Europe, including the Italian occupation of areas of south-east Europe.
5. This was certainly the case after 1938 and even more after September 1939, when the Daladier government (1938–40) extended the powers of the central level over the local level: N. Wouters 'Localisation in the age of centralisation: local government in Belgium and Nord-Pas-de-Calais (1940–1944)', in B. De Wever, H. van Goethem and N. Wouters (eds) *Local Government in Occupied Europe (1939–1945)* (Gent, 2005), pp. 83–109.
6. K. Kjeldstadli *Et splittet samfunn 1905–1935. Norgeshistorie.* Vol. 10 (Oslo, 1994), pp. 206ff; J. Kanstrup and S. Ousager (eds) *Kommunal opgaveløsning 1842–1970* (Odense, 1990).
7. N. Wouters *Oorlogsburgemeesters 40/44. Lokaal bestuur en collaboratie in België* (Tielt, 2004), pp. 61–4.
8. P. Romijn *Burgemeesters in oorlogstijd. Besturen onder Duitse bezetting* (Amsterdam, 2006), pp. 94–127 and 161–8.
9. Although Peyrouton (6 January 1941) and Darlan (25 February 1941) both suggested they wanted to implement the system of a centrally appointed, technocratic mayor who could (politically or administratively) support the regime and its National Revolution, this was never accomplished.
10. There were strong regional differences in terms of purges of mayors and administrators. In the Nord-Pas-de-Calais the status quo was very high, while in

the free zone the Vichy regime stimulated a much more heavy purges of mayors. There was, however, no dominant French 'fascist' party and the conservative Vichy regime focused on the replacement of the local *Front Populaire* elite by a more traditional Right-wing elite.

11. S. Lorentzen 'Norsk lokalforvaltning under førerprincippet. Okkupasjonstidens kommunale nyordning 1940–1945', in S.U. Larsen (ed.) *Fra idé til dom. Noen trekk fra utviklingen av Nasjonal Samling* (1976), pp. 143ff.

12. Y. Jelinek *The Parish Republic. Hlinka's Slovak People's Party 1939–1945* (New York and London, 1976), p. 115.

13. G. Meershoek *Dienaren van het gezag: de Amsterdamse politie tijdens de bezetting* (Amsterdam, 1999).

14. In Belgium, propositions about municipal reform that had been popular during the 1930s resurfaced in 1940, the most important being the introduction of a centrally appointed civil servant-mayor and the merger of municipalities. This negative German perception was also strengthened by the German experience in Belgium during the First World War. For a general analysis of the importance of 1940 in Belgian society: J. Gérard-Libois and J. Gotovitch *L'an 40: la Belgique occupée* (Brussels, 1971).

15. V. Mastny *The Czechs under Nazi Rule: The Failure of National Resistance 1939–1942* (New York and London, 1971), p. 41; A. Teichova 'The Protectorate of Bohemia and Moravia (1939–1945): the economic dimension', in M. Teich (ed.) *Bohemia in History* (Cambridge, 1998), pp. 267–72.

16. Ethnic Germans were given the rights of German citizens, the Czechs were 'Protectorate subjects' and – from the summer of 1939 – Jews were defined using the criteria of the Nuremberg Laws: Mastny *op. cit.*, p. 14; Teichova *op. cit.*, p. 273. Von Neurath and Frank often disagreed on the political course for the Protectorate. Von Neurath would opt for a more moderate policy, whereas Frank would advocate a more ideological stance including forced Germanization of the Protectorate. As a long-term goal Hitler agreed with Frank's line but usually supported Von Neurath when he had to intervene between the two.

17. As in most north-western European countries, the Germans installed a controlling, supervising regime or *Aufsichtsverwaltung*. With the help of around 400,000 obedient Czech civil servants, Germany managed to administer the Protectorate with an administrative body of only 2,000 Germans. In addition, the German administration was assisted by the Sudeten Germans, many of whom were strongly Nazi, and knew Czech society and its language: A. Teichova *op. cit.*, p. 275; V. Mastny *op. cit.*, p. 201.

18. D. Brandes *Die Tschechen unter deutschem Protektorat. Part 1 Besatzungspolitik, Kollaboration und Widerstand im Protektorat Böhmen und Mähren bis Heydrichs Tod (1939–1942)* (Munich, 1969), pp. 32f; V. Mastny *op. cit.*, p. 93; A. Teichova *op. cit.*, pp. 274 and 296.

19. For the example of the town of Budweis/Budejovice, see: J. King *Budweisers into Czechs and Germans: A Local History of Bohemian Politics, 1848–1948* (Princeton, 2002), pp. 169–88.

20. For Belgium, see N. Wouters *De Führerstaat: Overheid en collaboratie in België (1940–1944)* (Tielt, 2006).

21. The party itself organized administrative courses with fully-fledged examinations for their candidate mayors, which were ridiculed by the population and only strengthened their image of administrative incompetence.

22. D. Brandes *op. cit.*, p. 154.

23. D. Brandes *op. cit.*, p. 222.

24. P. Romijn *Burgemeesters in oorlogstijd*, pp. 349–58.

25. A. Vrints 'Patronen van polarisatie. Homicide in België tijdens de Tweede Wereldoorlog', *Cahiers d'Histoire du Temps Présent – Bijdragen tot de Eigentijdse Geschiedenis* XV (2005), 177–204.

26. Y. Le Maner 'Town Councils of the Nord and Pas-de-Calais region: local power, French power, German power' in T. Kirk and A. McGelligott, (eds) *Opposing Fascism. Community, Authority and Resistance in Europe* (Cambridge, 1999), pp. 97–119.

27. C. Lucas *The Structure of the Terror: The Example of Javogues and the Loire* (Oxford, 1973); A. Spitzer 'The elections of 1824 and 1827 in the department of the Doubs', *French History* III (1989), 153–76; A. Lewis 'A Turbulent Priest? The Forbin-Janson Affair (1824–1839)', *French History* XIX (2005), 324–41.

28. P. Jankowski *Communism and Collaboration: Simon Sabiani and Politics in Marseille, 1919–1944* (New Haven and London, 1989).

29. P. Jankowski *op. cit.*, pp. 90–100.

30. L. Taylor *Between Resistance and Collaboration. Popular Protest in Northern France, 1940–45* (Basingstoke and New York, 2000), pp. 142–61.

31. A. Eriksen 'The Paper Clip War. The Mythology of the Norwegian resistance' in *La résistance et les européens du Nord* (Brussels, 1994), pp. 393–405.

32. For the ideological mentalities within the Third Reich administration, see, for example, G. Aly *'Final Solution'. Nazi Population Policy and the Murder of the European Jews* (London, 1999).

33. P. Laborie *L'opinion française sous Vichy* (Paris, 1990).

34. J. Jackson *France. The Dark Years 1940–1944* (Oxford, 2001), p. 220.

35. For local first-hand examples, see J. Teissier du Cros *Divided Loyalties: A Scotswoman in Occupied France* (republished Edinburgh, 1992); G. Millar *Maquis* (London, 1945).

36. P. Romijn *Burgemeesters in oorlogstijd*, p. 298.

37. P. Romijn *Burgemeesters in oorlogstijd*, pp. 503 ff.

38. R. Gildea 'Mediators or time-servers? Local officials and notables in the Loire Valley, 1940–1945', in B. De Wever, H. van Goethem and N. Wouters (eds) *op. cit.*, pp. 179–205.

39. H. Poulsen 'Denmark at War? The Occupation as History', in S. Ekman and N. Edling (eds) *War Experience, Self-Image and National Identity: The Second World War as Myth and History* (Södertälje, 1997), pp. 98–109.

40. For France, see notably J. Guillon 'La résistance au village' in J. Sainclivier and C. Bougeard (eds) *La Résistance et les Français. Enjeux stratégiques et environnement social* (Rennes, 1995), pp. 233–43; J. Sainclivier *La résistance en Ille-et-Vilaine, 1940–1944* (Rennes, 1993); Y. Durand and R. Vivier *Libération des pays de Loire. Blésois, Orléanais, Touraine* (Paris, 1974).

41. R. Gildea *Marianne in Chains. In Search of the German Occupation* (London, 2002), pp. 26 and 138.

42. Y. Durand 'Les notables' in J.-P. Azéma and F. Bédarida (eds) *Vichy et les Français* (Paris, 1992), pp. 371–81.

43. S. Fishman *We Will Wait. Wives of French Prisoners of War, 1940–1945* (New Haven and London, 1991), pp. 99–122.

44. F. Maerten 'Résistance et société en Hainaut belge. Histoire d'une brève rencontre', in R. Vandenbussche (ed.) *L'engagement dans la Résistance (France du Nord – Belgique)* (Villeneuve d'Ascq, 2003), pp. 77–98.

45. M. Conway 'The Age of Christian Democracy: The Frontiers of Success and Failure', in T. Kselman and J. Buttigieg (eds) *European Christian Democracy. Historical Legacies and Comparative Perspectives* (Notre Dame, 2003), pp. 43–67; J.-D. Durand 'L'épiscopat italien devant l'occupation allemande, 1943–1945', in J. Sainclivier and C. Bougeard (eds) *op. cit.*, pp. 95–108.

46. Regarding the mentality of local office-holders, see M. Conway *Collaboration in Belgium. Léon Degrelle and the Rexist Movement 1940–1944* (New Haven and London, 1993), pp. 206–8.

47. V. Drapac *War and Religion. Catholics in the Churches of Occupied Paris* (Washington DC, 1998), p. 28.

48. C.B. Christensen, J. Lund, N.W. Olesen and J. Sørensen *Danmark besat. Krig og hverdag 1940–5* (Copenhagen, 2005), p. 435.

49. K. Eisterer and R. Steininger (eds) *Die Option. Südtirol zwischen Faschismus und Nationalsozialismus* (Innsbruck, 1989); M. Lun *NS-Herrschaft in Südtirol. Die Operationszone Alpenvorland 1943–1945* (Innsbruck, 2004), pp. 243–9.

50. N. Wouters *Oorlogsburgemeesters*, pp. 542–9.

51. P. Romijn *Burgemeesters in oorlogstijd*, pp. 382–3.

52. P. Romijn *Burgemeesters in oorlogstijd*, pp. 590–601.

53. B. Nøkleby *Nyordning. Norge i Krig* Vol. 2 (Oslo, 1985), pp. 95ff; S.U. Larsen 'Kommunalforordningen', in H.F. Dahl et al. (eds) *Norsk Krigsleksikon* (Oslo 1995).

54. M. Dehli *Fredrikstad under krig og okkupasjon* (Fredrikstad, 1981), pp. 82–98.

55. H.R. Kedward 'The Vichy of the other Philippe' in G. Hirschfeld and P. Marsh (eds) *Collaboration in France: Politics and Culture during the Nazi Occupation 1940–1944* (Oxford, 1989), pp. 32–46.

56. C. Pavone *Una guerra civile: saggio storico sulla moralità nella resistenza* (Turin, 1991).
57. T. Todorov *A French Tragedy: Scenes of Civil War, Summer 1944* (Hanover, 1996).
58. B. Chiari 'Has there been a People's War? The History of the Second World War in Belarus, 60 years after the surrender of the Third Reich' in B. De Wever, H. van Goethem and N. Wouters (eds) *op. cit.*, pp. 221–41.
59. T. Snyder 'The Causes of Ukrainian-Polish Ethnic Cleansing 1943', *Past and Present* No. 179 (May 2003), 197–234.
60. J.R. Lampe *Yugoslavia as History. Twice there was a Country* (Cambridge, 1996), p. 196; J. Tomasevich *War and Revolution in Yugoslavia, 1941–1945. Occupation and Collaboration* (Stanford, 2001) and *The Chetniks* (Stanford, 1975).
61. M. Mazower *Inside Hitler's Greece. The Experience of Occupation, 1941–44* (New Haven and London, 1993); M. Mazower 'Structures of Authority in the Greek Resistance, 1941–1944', in T. Kirk and A. McGelligott (eds) *op. cit.*, pp. 120–32.
62. J. Hondros *Occupation and Resistance. The Greek Agony 1941–1944* (New York, 1983), pp. 60–1.
63. On wartime Greece, see notably M. Mazower, *Inside Hitler's Greece*; J. Hondros *op. cit.*; P. Carabott and T. Sfikas, (eds), *The Greek Civil War. Essays on a Conflict of Exceptionalism and Silences* (Aldershot and Burlington VT, 2004); S. Kalyvas *The Logic of Violence in Civil War* (Cambridge, 2006).
64. This is also shown by M. Koreman *The Expectation of Justice: France 1944–1946* (Durham NC, 2000).
65. For example, S. Farmer 'The Communist Resistance in the Haute Vienne', *French Historical Studies* XIV (1985), 89–116.
66. P. Romijn 'Ambitions and Dilemmas of Local Authorities in the German-occupied Netherlands, 1940–1945', in B. De Wever, H. van Goethem and N. Wouters (eds) *op. cit.*, pp. 33–67.
67. M. Koreman *op. cit.*, pp. 230–1.
68. M. Koreman *op. cit.*, pp. 5–7 and 258–63.
69. N. Wouters *Oorlogsburgemeesters*, pp. 609–20.
70. B. Frommer *National Cleansing. Retribution against Nazi Collaborators in Postwar Czechoslovakia* (Cambridge 2005), p. 29.
71. B. Frommer *op. cit.*, pp. 186 and 371.

–5–

Culture and Legitimacy*

'Everything that occurs here is ideological, but the ideology is fluid, undefined.'
(Kapuscinski on revolutionary Algeria, quoted in M. Mazower, 1993)

The sustained period of armed conflict and ideological flux that Europe experienced during the 'long Second World War' made politics a direct and often brutal part of the lived experience of every European. Even at the level of nation-states – the level most comprehensively covered by the political historiography – the struggles were not simply between different sets of rulers but between different conceptions of government and society. The convulsive history of the period between c.1936 and c.1949 problematized the very idea of the nation, on the one hand, collapsing it into a much more immediate sense of the local, particularly in the years after 1943; and, on the other, reproducing its rhetorical presence in a more grandiloquent and abstract way than had ever been the case before. Paradoxically, this was most emphatically so during the Second World War itself, a time of military engagement between nation-states, when established languages – such as patriotism – and identities – such as the loyal citizen – should have been most prominent. Instead, throughout Europe, individuals reappraised and renegotiated their relationship to authority and to community.

This was not, as this volume has made clear, a simple result of legitimizing strategies on the part of ideologically charged regimes, still less of political or state propaganda. Rather, the collapse of 'normality', of national structures and established modes of government meant a falling back on what was familiar – the local, the quotidian, the traditional – as political legitimacy was negotiated and contested within the everyday cultures that shaped and contextualized individual and group identities. If an authority is to be recognized as legitimate, its right to exercise power over others must be acknowledged, as early attempts to come to grips with the emergence, and the emerging popularity, of authoritarian regimes acknowledged.

The need to understand how fascist regimes were accepted rather than simply imposed has led to a historiographical impulse that can be traced back to Antonio Gramsci's writings on political consent. Gramsci's notion of 'consent' rested on his perception that the political domination of the Italian South originated in the cultural

---

* This chapter was written jointly by Mary Vincent and Erica Carter.

and social 'conditions of Southern ... existence.'[1] This understanding of consent was integral to Gramsci's notion of hegemony, which assumed that class domination, or 'rule', did not simply rely upon coercion and brute force. Instead, Gramsci's understanding of Fascist rule led him to emphasize that hegemony was, ultimately, generated not by the actions of the state but within what he termed 'civil society' and depended on complex processes of 'persuasion'.[2] This concept of hegemony has generated a substantial and often highly polemical historiography. In particular, it has often been assimilated, somewhat misleadingly, into Weberian models of legitimation, whereby in De Felice's formulation a 'consensus' emerged around the regime.[3]

Placing the focus on the cultural sphere can bring a distinctive approach to such debates, highlighting the limits of the ability of any regime to mould a society to its will through strategies of legitimation. More generally, however, culture demonstrates the complexities inherent in the apparently simple dialectic between regime and 'civil society'. Like his contemporaries elsewhere on the European Left, Gramsci identified the intermeshing of culture with politics as a distinctive feature of the drive for hegemony within European fascism. Mid-twentieth-century fascist regimes recognized modern mass culture as a powerful instrument for the creation of cohesive national communities, and for the mass orchestration of political consent. Concomitantly, late-twentieth-century scholars have emphasized spectacle, ritual and 'liturgy' in examining Fascism's visualization and virtualization of the political community.[4] Yet, as Gramsci's notion of hegemony suggests, there was always an indeterminacy inherent in the outcomes of Fascist mass cultural persuasion. In Mussolini's words, 'consent is as unstable as the sand formations on the edge of the sea'.[5]

Gramsci's culturalist redefinition of 'hegemony' proposed in particular a dynamic view of popular culture as generative of modes of cultural praxis that could in the right conditions give impetus to political opposition. Fascism's spectacular politics required 'the people', as both individuals and collectivity, to play a full part in public life, establishing their rapport with the regime through stance, word, and gesture. Hence the concern at the indifferent response of the workers when the *Duce* visited Fiat Mirafiori, a concern that Luisa Passerini sees as being reworked over time to represent a fundamental estrangement between people and regime. Despite the inherent ambiguity of silence, indifference came simply to mean dissent, even though it could be – and was – taken to signify the opposite, accommodation rather than opposition.[6] Indeed, as Victoria de Grazia argues, for industrial workers consent 'meant a silent industriousness', which in turn became one of the 'multiple specific meanings' that the idea of consent acquired in Mussolinian Italy.[7] The cultural instability of 'consent' was shown again by the Italian Communist Party leader Palmiro Togliatti's belief that the Fascist leisure organization, the *Dopolavoro*, offered real possibilities for Popular Frontism. The destruction of socialist subcultures – with their lending libraries, cycling clubs, and myriad other forms of social and cultural interaction – had left a flattened cultural landscape within which the Fascist organizations offered a rare possibility of mobilizing the working class and so, paradoxically, themselves became 'centres of resistance'. Decades later, Togliatti's heirs in Spain's Communist-led union, the *Comisiones Obreras*, came to the same conclusion as they organized within and through the official syndicates of the Franco regime.[8]

Such experiences show both how organizing was fundamental to attempts to foster consent through legitimating strategies but also more importantly how those strategies themselves depended on deeper, more nebulous and possibly less choate understandings of legitimacy. Similar examples of the complexity of popular consent were evident in wartime Europe. In the German-occupied territories, external offices of the *Reich* propaganda ministry served as conduits for a larger cultural project that aimed to establish legitimacy by restructuring everyday life around National Socialist conventions and norms. This could take the most banal of forms: efforts to inculcate German road-safety principles, or to promote ethnic German culture through children's play.[9] Sometimes such strategies worked to the benefit of the occupiers; at other points, the response was non-conformity, resistance, or what Boris Cyrulnic has termed 'resilience': the refusal by a social body of supervision and control.[10] In each case, the translation of ideas into collective acceptance involved a prior process of negotiation among competing symbolic systems and political ideologies, none of which existed autonomously. Rather, they overlapped with folk traditions, bourgeois etiquette, devotional practice, aesthetic arrangements of social and urban space and numerous other less stated cultural forms, all of which may lend legitimacy to authority, not simply by their appropriation, but through their contribution to a language of legitimacy, fashioned as the object of those identifications whereby individuals meld into collectivities, becoming part of the 'imagined communities' on which not only nations but also towns, regions, religions, and social classes all depend.[11]

Yet, as Gramsci had further discerned, that language also proved to be an idiom within which successful counter-claims to legitimacy could be articulated. Even in places where, it could be argued, a hegemonic culture existed – for example Hitler's Germany or Churchill's Britain – legitimacy could not be seen as universal. The way in which even authoritarian regimes seemed able to draw on remarkable reserves of loyalty within their populations illuminates how the mobilizing tools of those regimes could at times coincide with aspects of life regarded among the populace as commonplace, normal or right. But the experience of foreign occupation also demonstrated, often starkly, that legitimacy and even community had its limits. The short-lived, murderous regime imposed by the Croatian Ustaša early in the war attempted initially to forge a hegemonic legitimacy among Croatian men that rested upon racialized ideas of community, family, and masculinity, only to find its brutal vision of national community undermined by the very idea of a legitimate male violence that underlay it. For the Ustaša's 'nationalizing war strategy' unleashed what the *Wehrmacht* categorized as criminal 'butchery', 'slaughter', and 'terror': a frenzy of violence the dissolvent effects of which left no community available to imagine.[12] All that remained amid the turbulence and savagery of the eastern killing fields was the business of individual survival.

Clearly, then, cultural strategies of mass persuasion could not in themselves ensure hegemony. The unequivocal military victory achieved by General Franco, with the aid of his Axis allies, in 1939 was claimed as a victory for Christian civilization.[13] This, however, was little more than a *post-hoc* exercise in legitimation; to provide a basis for an enduring legitimacy, the 'crusade' had to coincide with aspects of life that more than the religiously committed regarded as right or normal. Efforts at legitimation, however determined and however sustained, did not in that sense bring about legitimacy; even those with the greatest firepower had to negotiate military victory into some kind of legitimacy. In Spain, the Francoist victory – brutally imposed through purging and the redemptive punishment of Republican prisoners – gave way during the 1940s to a regime of social 'peace' and effective government. Some kind of working social consensus emerged gradually around the regime in the isolated space afforded by non-belligerency during the Second World War. Military firepower was thus not sufficient to create legitimacy, but could serve as the starting point in a process towards legitimacy.[14]

The experience of defeat that was shared by Europeans from Spain to Norway in 1939–40 initiated what one might regard as a period of profound experimentation in the ways in which legitimacy is contested during changes of regime. The moment of occupation represented a caesura in political history, severing the regular political affiliations between national citizenship and sovereign national government. Crucially, however, that caesura neither erased agency on the part of those under occupation, nor did it efface cultural activity in public life. Rather, as they sought to reinvent purified national communities, the authoritarian regimes that dominated Europe in the war years made much of the mobilization of populations in public demonstrations of allegiance, from military parades, concert and theatre galas to charity collections for frontline troops. Where supposed affinities existed between the cultures of occupied peoples and the ruling regime, mass public events were used to flaunt them.[15] And, if what was at stake in those mass cultural spectacles was no longer consent, then it was in an enlarged sense of legitimacy, understood as a value around which the power of dictatorial, fascist or occupying regimes was established, negotiated and contested. For legitimacy is enacted through a myriad of evaluations, value judgements, critical choices and individual or collective acts. Culture, understood in its broadest sense as symbolic representation, cultural institution, and lived experience, was central to this process. It provides (and this all the more intensely in the absence of the possibility of political choice) an experiential terrain for the exercise both of judgement and of ethical choice: the choice to donate or withhold funds for *Winterhilfe* (Winter Aid) collections; to applaud (or not) visiting state dignitaries; to cough and sneeze throughout the German newsreels that were compulsory viewing for cinema audiences under Nazi occupation, or to maintain polite decorum, and tacitly acquiesce.[16]

Legitimacy seen in this way was during the war years a lived process involving decisions, choices and practical actions undertaken in space and time. This chapter examines how these choices were made in a broader cultural sphere. Capturing something of the mundaneness – the 'everydayness' of the cultural processes whereby individuals and collectivities situated themselves, under conditions of war and occupation, within struggles over the issue of legitimate rule – has led us to structure this chapter around categories (space, time, bodies) that delimit the field of embodied experience through which legitimacy is lived. These cultural fields are not separate from politics but nor are they encompassed by it. Rather, they define a domain of struggle that is both part of other struggles, and autonomous from them. The norms that defined the field of legitimacy during war and occupation had to be 'naturalized' in the sense suggested by Roland Barthes, cemented into a symbolic universe which allowed Europeans to conceive of themselves and their communities in terms of the everyday experience of legitimate rule. The overall goal of this chapter is therefore to investigate what Ian Clark has termed the 'rudimentary social agreements' that underpin legitimacy, based on a Gramsci-inspired notion of consent that comes primarily from within the norms of society rather than the legitimizing strategies of the state.[17]

Space

Among the bitterest of mid-twentieth-century cultural contestations were those fought around the spatial boundaries of European identities. War and occupation saw the disintegration of the pre-existing model of the nation-state, dissolving it simultaneously into both larger territories of conquest under Nazi and Fascist rule and smaller local spheres of lived experience. These multi-layered disjunctures between the geographical units in which people were placed and the communities to which they felt they belonged continued throughout the war years and beyond. 'Space' in that sense was about European populations working out the boundaries of their communities and responding to forms of identity imposed on them by rulers. Legitimate rule emerged when these internal and external concepts of the community overlapped sufficiently.

In Benedict Anderson's classic formulation, such rearticulations of 'imagined community' draw their impetus from a redrawing of imaginary cartographies, and from the delineation in particular of new boundaries for a cultural space, the integrity of which depends on it being perceived as 'inherently limited.'[18] Yet, in contrast to the territoriality that Anderson rightly perceives as intrinsic to understandings of the nation, the variants of hypernationalism which lay implicitly or explicitly within all European fascisms posited ideas of community that existed within and beyond the bounded nation-state. Such was the language of destiny, or the wider community of the *Volk*. According to the Spanish fascist leader José Antonio Primo de Rivera, Spain was 'a unity of destiny in the universal', a pithy phrase that conjured up visions of both the boundless (destiny) and the bounded (Spain). Such excesses of rhetorical hypernationalism depended upon a dual appeal, on the one hand to the community of 'nation' (an appeal that did not have to employ the biological racism of National Socialism, but always encompassed an ethnic and, at some level, exclusive understanding) and on the other hand, to the nation as limitless destiny.

Authoritarian and fascist nationalisms were thus both grounded in the nation space and simultaneously threatened its integrity; it was in part this contradiction that opened up a space for oppositional movements for a 'better nationalism' in which traditional liberties would be defended through appeals to popular community and national strength. Underpinning these alternative nationalisms were representations of occupation as a violation of national history, and assertions of oppositional identities forged in France for instance through Republican democratic lineage, or, in the Netherlands, through a heritage of political liberty and national independence.[19] Alongside these appeals to history and heritage, resistant nationalisms drew on the imagined geography of national landscapes to assert their oppositional visions of the nation. In wartime Britain, the recreation of the ordinary landscape, with allotments and air-raid shelters replacing lawns, parks, and gardens, confirmed nationalism as the defence of a national territory that was bounded and specific.[20] In occupied countries, the landscape – apolitical, natural, uncontestable – provided a refuge in a time of adversity. In the Netherlands, not only was the local and national landscape largely one and the same, but centuries of land reclamation had endowed the *polder* with moral virtue and national characteristics.[21] Pictures of sand dunes, articles on local cheese markets, and other features of traditional Dutch life thus punctuated newspapers and magazines, providing a resource for visions of an alternative national destiny that might supersede occupation and fascist rule.

The experience of occupation also created a new international order, within which 'Europe' became a redefined transnational community. The National Socialist vision of Germany as the economic, political, cultural and above all racial fulcrum of a revitalized 'Europe' comprising, essentially, the north-western Germanic lands, with some Latin outriders, was held in common by collaborationist leaders across the continent. Laval, Quisling, Mussert, Degrelle and others shared with the far Right in southern Europe a vision of a continental alliance under German hegemony, and of a transnational polity the subjects of which would share a 'sense of serving a community' of which they themselves were an 'intimate part.'[22] In cultural representation, Nazi Europeanism was legitimized through spatial tropes that situated Greater Germany as a symbolic territory that would restore to Europe a cultural integrity lost, in the transition from the Holy Roman Empire, to particularist nation-states.[23] This spatial extension of the German nation into Europe was also carried through in cultural production and practice as modern media forms created new possibilities for the cultural production of transnational identities. Goebbels' project after 1933, famously, was to generate a German film industry capable of displacing Hollywood as the dominant force in European film. Nazi cultural policy was intended to reverse the 1920s trend towards a liberal internationalization of European film and, under occupation, reorientate the cinema landscape towards German fare through bans on Allied imports and quota rulings in favour of German film. European broadcast and news media landscapes were similarly remapped, as Reuters was replaced with an international news agency under German control and bilingual and multilingual press organs promoted a Germanicized Europe throughout the world.[24]

Yet Nazi efforts to reshape Europe as a media and information space under fascist hegemony met with persistent challenges from popular audiences as well as organized resistance groups. In cinema, German newsreels were the object of especially vocal protest: Gestapo reports spoke of 'applause contests' in Dutch cinemas between pro- and anti-Nazi audience members; film reels were sabotaged in Czech movie houses, with pro-German sections secretly excised; clandestine propaganda campaigns aimed to undermine audience affiliations to the German light-entertainment films that dominated cinema screens after 1940.[25] The broadcast media, meanwhile, became the target of initiatives from beyond the borders of the occupied territories to establish a different Europe in the continental imagination. As governing elites, crowned heads, and other, less conspicuous refugees from the occupied countries joined exiles who had already fled National-Socialist Germany after 1933, so Europe's symbolic identity became increasingly ambivalent, multiform, and politically contested within a transcontinental space of exile that encompassed both the London exiles and those in North America. During the Second World War leaders in exile used the airwaves to reimagine the nation space – the territory of the 'free French' or the 'free Danes' – while Allied broadcasters and above all the BBC promulgated visions of a new transnational community rooted in core democratic values and forged through alliances between 'ordinary' citizens and the Allied cause. In this context, nations-in-exile could mount an assault upon their own territory, excoriating 'collaboration' as the work of traitors, depicting occupation regimes as violators and calling on ordinary citizens to assert democratic national visions.

Charles De Gaulle was perhaps the foremost instance of a leader in exile who used his key speeches from June 1940 onwards to call into being, in large part across the radio airwaves, a national community – Free France – envisaged as the sole legitimate embodiment of the French state and nation.[26] For De Gaulle, the centrepiece of his rhetoric was always the Republic, invoked not in terms of its pre-1940 reality but as the abstract collectivity of the French people. For other exile groups, such as the Norwegian and Dutch governments, it was the figure of the exiled monarch who served as the embodiment of the historic freedoms, national and constitutional, of their people. Common to all, however, was a sense of common purpose that transcended national boundaries. If the presence of the exiled

Figure 5.1 A poster produced in the Netherlands under German Occupation calls on the population to boycott the (German-controlled) cinemas. Courtesy of Netherlands Institute for War Documentation, Amsterdam

authorities in London did not quite generate a European Union, it did promote an oppositional transnational vision, an image of Europe as a continent of sovereign nations in alliance against fascist rule.[27]

A further site of struggles around legitimacy, especially in countries shaped by their own histories of colonial and imperial domination, was that of empire. Efforts were made by the Nazis and their allies to reshape global politics through an imperialist remapping of cultural space. In peacetime, the imaginary reconfiguration by European fascists of Europe as the space of an expansionist 'power bloc of fascist nations' (Oswald Mosley) went hand in hand with a strategic cultural imperialism realized in such showcase events as the Venice Biennale or the 1936 Berlin Olympics, and designed to cement in the international imagination an image of the superior cultural prowess of European fascism.[28] As the realization of Italy and Germany's imperial ambitions took the more violent form of military conquest, this renewal of 'eternal Empire' was legitimated by appeals to those two countries' 'vital needs' for expanded living space.[29] In Eastern Europe, German aggression was fuelled as much as was Italy's Mediterranean campaigns by fantasies of a restoration of the lost colonial space of a mythical medieval *Reich*. Hence Hitler's remark that

Figure 5.2 The radio of the Dutch government-in-exile broadcasting from London to the German-Occupied Netherlands. Courtesy of Netherlands Institute for War Documentation, Amsterdam

'[t]he Russian space is our India'.[30] In western Europe, Nazi occupation was often legitimated through appeals to a European common purpose in imperial domination. Those Dutch National Socialists who subscribed to 'Greater Dutch' conceptions of their nation stressed, for instance, the 'tribal kinship' between Holland and its Germanic neighbours and advocated ethnic solidarity between Dutch speakers in Europe, South African *Boeren*, and European settlers of Dutch extraction in the East and West Indies. As the war progressed, Dutch ethno-nationalism provided the ideological seedbed for Nazi propaganda, which seized on German victories as an opportunity to proselytize for a German-led restoration of the Dutch Empire within a world dominated by two fascist superpowers, Germany and Japan.[31]

Yet efforts to locate *Reich* or Empire as cultural ideals that legitimized occupation often proved ineffective, particularly as cultural and economic policies in the occupied territories collided. The requirement to fuel the hugely expanded war economy of the Third Reich demanded that other economies be stripped of all of the resources needed to stoke it.[32] The agents of Nazi and collaborationist propaganda strove to present service in the German armies on the Eastern Front or in the factories of the *Reich* as a 'European' cause in which national interest merged with the larger defence of European civilization against alien (Bolshevik, Slav, Jewish and American) attack. Yet the realities of migration and economic hardship rendered such discourses of imperial grandeur harder to sustain. As an ideological abstraction, 'empire' may have inspired many but, as colonial populations already knew, the lived experience of the colonized entailed the same collision that was now being experienced in occupied Europe. The French move from voluntary labour schemes to compulsory conscription in the form of the *Service du travail obligatoire* (STO) was but the most well known of numerous examples of the progressive hollowing out of the Nazi project of legitimation that occurred in the face of Germany's frontline defeats in 1942 and 1943. Rather than imperial grandeur, the coerced removal of sections of the population became for many the defining personal experience of the new *Reich*.

Lived experience thus undercut Nazi-led imperialist strategies of legitimation. And, as it became increasingly obvious that the grandiose ambitions of the New Order were impossible, so the opportunities for resistance increased. Bombing, conscription and hunger made simple survival a priority for millions of Europeans; the difficulties of daily life provoked a cultural shift from the national to the local and from the public to the private. In terms of everyday experience, the world narrowed, though localities were neither autonomous nor isolated. Radios broadcast news of battles in Africa and Asia (and incidentally stimulated a passion for maps); letters brought news of those far away; the passage of refugees, forced labourers and foreign troops brought the outside world into all but the most isolated communities. But the dominant current was towards localism. As occupation became more difficult and resistance grew, so the relationship between people and territory changed and the nation was re-imagined 'as a form of localness'.

The local territory was vital to resistance, above all to the partisans' struggle to be regarded as the legitimate representatives of the true, free, nation. From France to Yugoslavia, the pursuit of guerrilla war demanded an intimate knowledge of topography, enabling fighters to 'disappear' into the landscape, sheltered by the land itself. For the fluid, fragmented, underground and oppositional movement that became known as 'resistance', the rural hinterland was the source of the most militant challenges to the occupying authorities. The sudden and unexpected actions of mysterious (and mythologized) groups of fighters left traces of a submerged mass presence emerging from liminal spaces (mountains, woodland, cellars, attics, the underground) to lay claim to the land. Such acts, whether militarily effective or not, located the occupying forces – and their collaborators – as alien, incapable of possessing the heart of the people made nation.

The association between resisters and liminal rural space, particularly woodland, also conjured up older associations with outlaws and social bandits, those excluded by the law but not by the community.[33] After the war, such myths would be reworked into a firm assertion of the intrinsic relationship between resistance and nationality, but the actual resisters were far less bounded. Spaniards, Poles, and a wide variety of refugees, forced labourers and deserters fought in the French resistance, creating a mobilization of transnational identities that echoed the character of the International

Brigades during the Spanish Civil War. Exile and dislocation had created a Left-wing diaspora that had fought in Spain and now continued the struggle in occupied Europe. After Liberation, many would again cross the Pyrenees, to maintain the anti-fascist struggle in Franco's Spain.[34]

Relations between resistance fighters and local communities were invariably ambiguous, as had always been the case with 'social' bandits. In some rural areas, resistance groups were perceived as dangerous outsiders, living marginal and criminal lives, and bringing upon their host communities the unwelcome threat of German or collaborationist reprisals.[35] Yet the reconstituted relationship between locality and legitimacy remained; those struggling against occupation had asserted an umbilical relationship between resistance and the land. This helps to explain the importance of the resistance to the foundational myths of post-war regimes; legitimacy lay in the struggle against an alien occupation. The rural landscape had served as testimony to pre-war existence and so, by inference at least, to post-war survival. The survival of the countryside meant cultural continuity: in contrast to the ravaged towns, the rural landscape acted as a palimpsest, containing within itself the history and memory of all that had gone before.

Time

In an episode from her autobiographical account of resistance activities smuggling refugees across the border into Spain from Vichy France, Lisa Fittko remembers one formerly prominent art critic and polemicist against Nazi art policy, Paul Westheim:

> Westheim showed us a paper: a visa for Mexico... We celebrated with one of the last bottles of wine, and Westheim ... spoke of the future – perhaps his outpouring remains in my memory because in those days one sometimes forgot there was a future. He spoke of the cadres [who] must be preserved for the culture of the Germany of tomorrow.[36]

Fittko's book pays tribute to the many thousands of escapees of Westheim's ilk for whom occupied Europe became a network of clandestine spaces suspended in time: underground waiting rooms, whose occupants 'sat with a few other emigrants... and waited until time came to listen to the BBC broadcast in the back room.'[37] For Westheim, escape to Mexico was a chance to cross the threshold from the back room, and to re-enter history as one of the 'cadres' preserved for a post-fascist Germany; and his bid to seize the future illuminates the larger struggles that marked the relationship under conditions of occupation between culture, legitimacy and time.

For the émigré generation, escape from fascist Europe was an escape also from stasis into the time of a historical narrative that mastered the catastrophic present with the promise of a future beyond occupation, persecution, genocide and war. This quest to construct a coherent sense of time was confronted by millions of

Europeans during the war years. How should they locate their own existence within the divergent concepts of time expounded by the different political forces during the war years? As Westheim escaped across the mountains in 1941, stable linear concepts of time, familiar since the Enlightenment and rooted in liberal values, appeared to have evaporated. In their place had emerged competing rhetorics of millenarian and eschatological time, which sought to convey to Europeans that they were living through a decisive moment in European history. Millenarianism has been said to combine 'a representation of time that is both historical (impending dénouement) and mythic: cyclical and eternally repetitive time.'[38] This volatile combination of teleological and mythic narratives of historical time was evident across European fascisms, all of which embraced a paradoxical blend of modernist fervour with racial or religious myth. In Nazi Germany, fascist culture fused a *völkisch* adulation of the messianic figure of the *Führer* with an idealist vision of fascist modernity as the apotheosis of bourgeois cultural tradition. Hence Nazism's mythic constructions of bourgeois ideals of beauty and sublimity as qualities imbued with the spiritual capacity to 'liberate' social subjects from 'the conceptual world', and rekindle the deepest of 'affinities' with *Führer* and *Volk*.[39] Fascist movements that took their cue from Nazism rooted their claim to legitimacy in a similar amalgam of bourgeois cultural values and a racialized messianism. The Dutch *Nationaal Socialistische Beweging* (NSB) promoted a blend of cultural conformism and cultural activism that was encapsulated in 'de Nieuwe Gedachte' (the New Way of Thinking) of the movement, a loose set of mythological ideas closely linked to an expanded Nazi New Order in Europe. As late as 1944, Goebbels' Propaganda Ministry continued to invest energy in 'politically desirable' work with the NSB and other collaborationist groups, whom they saw as the bedrock of a pan-European elite wedded to Germanic cultural heritage, but willing also to carry the torch for Nazism's chiliastic vision of cultural modernization.[40]

The German imaginary had a particular resonance in northern Protestant countries, tied to the *Reich* by a common cultural and, in Nazi eyes, racial past. In other contexts, fascism's millennial understanding of the immanence of time was explicitly religious. Franco's Crusade was waged as much for Christ as against communism, as the millennial understanding of the immanence of time – also seen in the new fascist man and the Nazi new age – became eschatological. In Spain, a curiously literal belief in the 'social reign of Jesus Christ' brought with it a vision of the dead as 'living stones' in the monument the Heart of Jesus was building in Spain. The same reworking of time was seen in the claim that 'Christ and the Ustaša, Christ and the Croatians – all march together through history'.[41] National redemption would be achieved through blood-spilling, just as Jesus' sufferings wrought the salvation of the world. The deaths of these Christian warriors thus became martyrdom: their sacrificial and redemptive suffering echoed the passion of Christ himself. Yet, the language of martyrdom also had a wide range of secular meanings, particularly when commemorating fallen soldiers: resistance movements had their martyrs while war memorials everywhere spoke of sacrifice.[42] Such a generic style of commemoration, however, lacked the specific temporal meanings of Christian martyrdom. The campaigns to beatify the priests and members of religious orders killed in the anticlerical massacres of the Spanish Civil War made these men and women – who died without bearing arms, elected as victims simply because of their clerical office – into the central focus of a transcendental drama enacted throughout and outside historical time. In this story – the story of the redemption – the Spanish Civil War was simply a location for the eternal symbolic struggle between good and evil.[43]

The forcible sacralization of public space that marked the aftermath of victory in Franco's Spain thus collapsed historical time.[44] Verticalism, a hierarchical ordering of time and space, abandoned linear ideas of progress as time became simultaneously mythic and static. In the pharonic monument to the Francoist war dead that would also serve as the *Caudillo*'s mausoleum, 'the stones … rise up… to challenge time'.[45] Victory posters announced that 'Spain was, is and will be immortal' while a school textbook introduced the mission of the New State with the words, 'Our past waits for us to create the future'.[46] Whether embodied in the crusading 'empire leading towards God' [*imperio hacia Dios*] or in the immortal *Reich*, the ideal of each fascist regime was not only to embody all that was best in the nation's past, but to produce the nemesis of all that was not. The New Order would storm the gates of heaven and, at the apocalypse, time would stop. It is this perhaps that explains the continuing ability of apocalyptic visions to inspire fervour, encourage mobilization, and contribute to commitment even in the face of impending defeat. Why many members of the *Wehrmacht* fought to an increasingly bitter end, even after the war was clearly lost, not only needs explanation but also suggests that the Nazi vision was never during the war period entirely emptied of legitimacy, at least for a proportion of Germany's fighting men.

Among civilian populations, fascist millenarianism was harder to sustain. For fascist regimes at home as in the occupied territories, legitimacy depended on the embedding of larger historical narratives of fascist triumph within the temporal structures of everyday pragmatic action and embodied experience. Italian and German fascism had striven after just such a fusion of historical narrative with the everyday experience of time through an alignment of the calendrical year with recurrent fascist rituals. In Germany, the national celebration of a reinvented Mothers' Day remade this family and Christian ritual into a *völkisch* tribute to motherhood and national-biological renewal. In contrast, Fascist Italy celebrated Mothers' Day on Christmas Eve and Francoist Spain on the feast of the Immaculate Conception – appropriations of the Christian calendar that paradoxically emphasized virginity rather than reproduction.[47] All three regimes rewrote the calendar as a cultish re-enactment of fascist triumphs: in Italy, 28 October – the date of the March on Rome – became the start of the Fascist year; in Spain the years were renumbered from 1939 – *I año triunfal* – and the date of the Nationalist rising, 18 July (which fortuitously coincided with older festivities for the Virgin of Mount Carmel) was declared a national holiday.

But the hyperbole of these new calendars, so reminiscent of the French Revolution, never succeeded in taking hold of the imagination of Europeans. The disjuncture between these concepts of millenarian time and the mundanity of daily life undermined the legitimacy of the New Order regimes. Patterns of cultural consumption under occupying regimes offer one instance of a common determination to escape from grand history into the habitual temporality of well-worn modes of popular or middlebrow entertainment. Operetta, melodrama, comedy and vaudeville all flourished during the war years as accustomed patterns of leisure consumption proved a means of normalizing everyday life under new regimes. In France, the occupation saw a tripling in music-hall attendance; in Francoist Spain light-entertainment radio boomed.[48] Cinema attendance might have plummeted by a third in Oslo in the occupation's initial aftershock; but within two years it topped pre-war levels as audiences returned to watch 'harmless thrillers and comedies'.[49] Even in Poland, where Nazi racial policy restricted Poles to third-rung entertainment venues, audience figures appear to have risen equally sharply, despite the meagre diet of newsreels, propaganda titles and subtitled features on offer for Polish cinemagoers under German rule.[50]

The vehement resistance to cinema attendance from within the Polish underground – not only were cinemas sabotaged, but Polish cinemagoers themselves were subjected to anything from verbal abuse and public stigma to physical attack – shows how unequivocal was the equation by some at least among the civil resistance between cinema attendance, and popular endorsement of the legitimacy of the Nazi regime.[51] Yet a return to established leisure habits was also a return to the time of the everyday and it was from within that temporality that fascism's claim to modernity was often most effectively disputed. Millennial notions of time had challenged established secular ones but they did not always defeat them. There was a secular vision of mythic time, which collapsed time into an historic past in which national identity was defined through proximity to popular experience. Under the Second Spanish Republic, the *Institución Libre de Enseñanza* and its off-shoot, the *Misiones Pedagógicas*, had actively promulgated their belief that the essence of a nation, its 'internal history', was to be found in its literature, by taking Golden Age drama to the remotest pueblos of the peninsula.[52] As in France, this republican vision was reformist rather than mystic, looking to create informed and educated citizens, not a millennial future. As such, it undercut fascism's mythic visions with a civic understanding of time within which a sense of struggle encompassed setbacks and reversals, as well as victories and success.

Resistance movements, similarly, mobilized pre-existing ideas of a secular national time rooted in day-to-day collective effort. The nation was being renewed; its lifeblood, the young resisters, was rejuvenating the body politic.[53] Their vision was rooted in lived experience; the resistance was actively recreating the nation through an alternative civic modernity that would triumph not only as a result of those acts of personal bravery that found their symbolic place in the heroic time of the resistance myth, but also through technical expertise and pragmatic action in everyday time. While the methods of guerrilla war were long established, their success depended on technical expertise. Stealth and resolve were prized by the Maquis, but these qualities were exemplified by skill with explosives and telecommunications. Their fight depended upon the radio and the parachute, as well as the gun.

In the case of the resistance, this alternative modernity was enhanced by modern cultural modes, particularly those, such as photography and the cinema, which would do so much to fix its representation in the popular imagination after the war. Nor was it only in the resistance that understandings of modernity were established by praxis. The armed forces, particularly those branches such as air forces and tank divisions, depended upon technology and the ability to control it. Scientific understanding was long established as a prime constituent of modernity and such knowledge was widely distributed during the Second World War, among ambulance drivers, aeroplane mechanics, and hospital nurses.[54] Professional competence and bureaucratic efficiency thus provided other conduits of modernity, aspects of a techno-cratic identity and practice that was to become much more prevalent in the post-war decades, running through democratic, state-socialist, and authoritarian regimes.

Throughout war and occupation, the conduct of mundane business therefore existed within a discursive framework of modernity that at specific times had seemed the preserve of the fascists, particularly during the early phases of the war and German military success. No one could dispute the salience of modernity when confronted with its apparently unstoppable triumph. Defeat, by contrast, brought to the fore a collective experience of destruction and loss, and revived submerged traditions that framed everyday experiences of historical time within pragmatic strategies for the construction of a liveable present. Those strategies might include an engagement with history but this often took the form in everyday life of individual and collective grieving and in the public domain of an emphasis on the need for survival and reconstruction. In numerous contexts, the post-war years did eventually see a restructuring of popular memory around national myths of heroic resistance, or of popular dissent.[55] But in the immediate aftermath of world war, a broad-based pragmatism displaced both nationalist and fascist Utopias, replacing these as legitimizing ideologies with a low-key patriotism that prized negotiation and compromise over historic change, and promoted pastoral, not millenarian visions of 'a better, a more beautiful, and a happier Fatherland'.[56]

Bodies

In an essay from 1941, Pierre Drieu la Rochelle elaborated thus his vision of fascist social transformation: '[t]he Revolution which is taking place in Europe is total because it is the revolution of the body, the restoration of the values which have come forth from the body [and] the revolution of the soul which discovers and redefines its values through the values of the body.'[57] Drieu's claim is supported by the common recourse across European fascisms both to bodily metaphor as the organizing centre of fascist rhetoric, and to new forms of bodily discipline as the material practice through which the mid-century 'new order' was to be generated. Under Nazism, 'biology, not culture' became 'the defining factor in definitions of national identity'; both the Nuremberg laws, and the Italian race laws of 1938 consolidated long-held desires to purge the national 'body' of degenerate 'foreign' elements.[58] Indeed, the wartime radicalization of national conservative and fascist movements beyond the Axis countries invariably involved a shift towards socio-biological or emphatically racialized conceptions of the collective body of nation or *Reich*. The transition evident in 1940–1 among some Dutch National Socialists from the cultural nationalism of the pre-war era, to the socio-biological rhetoric of 'tribal kinship', was mirrored in the Austrian case by the radicalization after the *Anschluss* that provoked a wave of anti-semitic violence – public murders, confiscation of Jewish houses and property: the first salvos in an onslaught that promised to purge the Greater German social body of what Hitler's *Mein Kampf* had famously called the 'parasite in the body of other nations', the Jew.[59]

If, however, it was in part around representations of the body that fascism staked its early-twentieth-century claim for European hegemony, then the meanings of the body in political ideology were multiple and ambiguous. In its appeals to the body, fascism took to a new plane the wider discourse of organicism that in fact imbued all political languages in the inter-war period, from paternalist conservatism to the radical communitarian vision of libertarian communism. At one level, there was a struggle over the ownership of the body: its subordination as an agent of the collectivity for reproduction, fighting or other purposes. At another level, it was an object of mobilization: the massed crowd, choreographed and disciplined, was a fundamental element of the public display common to many regimes. Finally, the body was a metaphor in which individual bodies became merged in an abstract social collective, the body of the people. By the mid-1930s, certain of these uses were well established in both fascist and Communist culture. In political rituals of both the organized Left and Right, the social body was reconstructed around neo-classical principles of mass homogeneity, order, inner symmetry and internal coherence. In Italy, *Il Duce*'s conception of the popular masses as a 'herd' that must be 'conquered and domesticated' was mirrored and reinforced by a national culture of mass spectacle: military parades, public festivals, tourist outings, exhibitions, open-air film screenings and theatre spectacles, in pursuit of a 'new fascist art of secular celebration.'[60] In Nazi Germany, the myth of *Volksgemeinschaft* found material expression in a culture of the organized mass that spanned political rallies and popular parades; public pageants; organized tourism, evening classes, collective theatre outings, sports and gymnastics programmes designed to harness the 'tremendous spiritual and emotional energy' of the working classes to 'efficient' production in the service of the regime;[61] or remodelling of the built environment through architecture, design and public art that ran the stylistic gamut from a monumentalist post-Bauhaus modernism, to neo-Hellenic public buildings adorned with colossal statues in an ostentatious celebration of state and party as embodiments of the popular mass.[62]

None of these uses of the body was, however, exclusively fascist in character. The cultural policies adopted by a wide variety of regimes, including Italian Fascism and the French Popular Front, all looked to refashion the national body, inscribing all members of the body politic within a new cultural community. That these ideologically highly distinct regimes shared such a common rhetoric was significant. Fascist ideas about the body intersected not merely with those of other political forces but with concepts of the body rooted in established social and cultural traditions. Thus on the one hand, such cultural experiments as the French dramatist Copeau's 'theatre of communion', or the folk festivals and mass mystery plays of Austria's pre-*Anschluss* period mobilized bodies in mass formation as the metaphysical expression of a supranational authoritarian popular spirit or soul.[63] Yet, just such a theatrical discourse had characterized attempts in the 1930s by both Communists and Catholics to create an integrative, participative aesthetic performance. Under the French Popular Front, a concern to represent new communities – and to counter the cultural anxieties of modernity, change, and flux – led to liturgical and theatrical displays that involved a mass of embodied individuals used as actors rather than audience.[64] Parallels with Mussolini's Italy, where the *Duce* also saw himself as an artist sculpting the national body,[65] were not difficult to seek and cannot have been lost on contemporaries. Representing the people as a 'mystic community'[66] engaged in forging a world within which integration and unity would lead to reconciliation and a remaking of the national body was an enterprise of both Right and Left in the 1930s and this common endeavour left a common legacy.

Similarly prevalent in both Right and Left political discourse was the presentation of putatively 'natural' bodily distinctions as the basis of social institutions and hierarchies. French fascisms promoted, in Francine Muel-Dreyfus' formulation, 'a hierarchical social order ... legitimised by the ideology of the natural gift.' Muel-Dreyfus explores how 'symbolic representations of the male/female opposition' gained political effectiveness in occupied and Vichy France through interventions into socio-cultural policy and practice – in the workplace, education, the family and, via eugenics and medicine, into reproduction and public health – which in turn restructured the 'symbolic and practical organisation of social life.'[67] Collaborationism under Vichy sought further legitimacy through appeals by cultural conservatives for what Henry de Montherlant dubbed a 'masculine order' of 'courage, violence and death', set in opposition to 'a feminine world of sexual passion and sentimentality.'[68] Accompanying this symbolic realignment of relations of gender was a widespread recasting of practices of the body in everyday life. The 'Spartan severity' of the women's section of the Nazi *Reich* Labour Service, which promoted an ideal feminine type trained 'to do without cosmetics, to dress in the simplest manner, to display no individual vanity, to sleep on hard beds, and to forego all culinary delicacies', was just one example of a characteristic grooming and drilling that streamlined the physical body to the gendered social structures and *habitus* of the fascist populace or *Volk*.[69] That gendering of the social body intersected with fascist racial policy through institutional interventions – pro-natalist family policies, eugenics programmes and the like – which sought to restore gender and racial 'balance' by quashing what the 1931 Italian Penal Code, referring to contraception and abortion, termed 'crimes against the wholeness and health of the race.'

Fascist attempts to root their legitimacy in a culture of the body foundered, however, on the incoherences of fascist rhetoric. Many of Fascism's pro-natalist provisions for women – family allowances, health-care provision, protective legislation – echoed 'progressive demands elsewhere for benefits as the right of citizens and the duty of the state.'[70] This was more than coincidence. The embodied vision of paternalism – with its organic communities, hierarchical families, and male authority – intersected with all forms of pre-war politics. Paternal authority emanated out from the family in a 'natural' hierarchy that set the pattern for the wider ordering of society. Welfare schemes that encouraged a pro-natalist demographic policy but also protected marriage and reinforced masculine authority reworked the assumption that, as the man was the head of the household, the wife was its heart.[71] Paternalism was also essential to the corporatist vision, in both its Fascist and authoritarian guises. Alongside the verticalism of the syndical state, existed a nostalgic and often sentimental idea of small communities – localities, families, guilds – evolving organically into a wider 'state' and so marrying political organization with social harmony.[72]

The health of the social body depended, then, on understandings of natural order, hierarchy, and social peace that coincided with fascism but were not defined by it and would indeed remain intact after its fall. These lines of tension also undermined the ability of fascist and authoritarian regimes to bring about their ideal of a mobilized community. The mobilization of the people, both in their abstract totality and in their physical form, was an important means by which all authorities in wartime and liberation Europe sought to invest their rule with legitimacy. Only very rarely could mobilization assume the formal political guise of elections and referenda: the 1943 national and local elections in Denmark, for instance, were an exceptional example of elections being used as a powerful means of legitimation amidst the circumstances of occupation. More commonly, numerous informal modes existed through which 'the people' were to establish publicly their allegiance to occupation regimes. Levels of participation in the occupied territories in Winter Aid were closely scrutinized by Nazi authorities, who considered them both a barometer of public acquiescence in occupation, and an important symbolic mechanism in the formation of an imagined community of subject peoples. The extensive press, radio and newsreel coverage of the *Winterhilfe* in the Nazi-occupied territories testified to the strength of hopes that donations of charitable aid for the poor and likewise the active, embodied agency of those who served in canteens, packed parcels or knitted and sewed clothes for soldiers might function as a broad-based popular re-enactment of more explicitly political rituals of subservience: speeches by national leaders in praise of the occupying authorities, or government declarations calling on the polity 'universally to declare their loyalty to the idea of the *Reich*, and to the reordering of Europe by the *Führer*'.[73]

But in practice, popular mobilization around the notion of a collectivity united by a common purpose proved an elusive goal. Across Europe, authoritarian visions of a popular community failed to obliterate other allegiances, such as those to Catholicism or the working class, and often sat uneasily with entrenched popular attachments to the sovereign nation and to national culture. The problem lay in part in the causes being advocated, but also in the nature of human bodies, which were much less susceptible to discipline and mobilization than fascists (as well as many others) believed. As historians have long since demonstrated, the natalist policies of all regimes (Fascist and Nazi included) rarely succeeded in influencing personal decisions about family life.[74] The mobilization of European citizens in more public arenas was also often less than entirely successful, and well demonstrated how concepts of individual choice and taste cut across efforts at social mobilization. Personal testimony has revealed how cultural tastes in everyday life were often shaped by affiliations to modes of experience that implied at the very least a disaffection with, if not outright repudiation of, the body in its ordered and regulated authoritarian form.

Anne Frank's diary offers one suggestive instance. Throughout her period in the secret annexe, Frank was made 'happy every Monday' by her father's business partner bringing weekly copies of *Cinema and Theatre* magazine. Her film-star 'hobby' was denigrated by 'the less worldly members of our household' as 'a waste of money ... yet they never fail to be surprised at how accurately I can list the actors in any given film.'[75] Her bedroom in the Anne Frank House on Amsterdam's Prinsengracht is embellished with magazine images; alongside Dutch favourites (Lily Bouwmeester), Frank's favourites included Hollywood icons (Ginger Rogers, Deanna Durbin) and émigré European stars (Greta Garbo, Sonja Henie). A surprising addition is the German comedian Heinz Rühmann, Nazi cinema's 'archetypal' little man.[76] His inclusion in Anne Frank's film-star pantheon demonstrates the 'unstable' and 'invariably provisional' relation between Nazi politics, and discourses of the body in popular entertainment.[77] Third Reich film culture was certainly committed at the level of cultural policy and Nazi rhetoric to a dictatorial regimentation of practitioners and audiences across Germany and beyond. But film stars functioned also as focal points for social fantasies of cosmopolitanism, of sexual energy or of a hedonistic pursuit of physical thrills. Sonja Henie had been a Norwegian skating champion and three times Olympic gold medallist before launching into a career in film. Garbo, Durbin and Rogers evoked a raw physical and sexual energy that ruffled the ordered surface of authoritarian culture's organized mass – as did Heinz Rühmann, albeit differently, with his peculiar combination of physical awkwardness with charisma and romantic charm.

The international film culture that was so clearly a source of solace for Anne Frank was organized symbolically around a popular modernist aesthetic that pitched the mobile, sensuous, culturally hybrid and pleasure-seeking individual body against fascism's conception of regulated bodies in the organized mass. This merged with modern forms of individualism that had multiplied across Europe over the preceding generation: Hollywood dreams, fashionable clothes, jazz music and bobbed hair were all elements of a modern culture that worked against not merely fascist mobilization but any attempt to subordinate individuals to a disciplined collective.[78]

Figure 5.3 Image from Anne Frank House of Ginger Rogers. Courtesy of Anne Frank Stichting (AFS), Amsterdam.

Figure 5.4 Image from Anne Frank House of Greta Garbo. Courtesy of AFS, Amsterdam.

Figure 5.5 Image from Anne Frank House of Heinz Rühmann. Courtesy of AFS, Amsterdam.

Appropriation and control of the body thus proved to be an elusive means of legitimating political rule. The ideal of an acquiescent organized collectivity, composed of disciplined bodies, could be achieved in propaganda but rarely in reality. The 'democracy of the public square' – that political spectacle orchestrated by fascist and authoritarian regimes in order to demonstrate that they acted in accord with the will of the national body – performed legitimacy, and its performative aspect meant that those same embodied individuals could confer or deny it. This was not simply a matter of participation – which could easily be coerced – but of gesture, stance and appearance. Even amongst those taking part in the same political ritual, differences in self-presentation conveyed enthusiasm, indifference, acquiescence or even outright opposition. Thus, though all too occasional, there was resistance too to fascism's socio-biological vision of a racially purged transnational folk body. When Nazi authorities set out to implement *Gleichschaltung* in the occupied countries through the compulsory licensing of cultural practitioners, they also opened the way to forms of obduracy (refusals to register, foot-dragging over declarations of racial heritage) that signalled at the very least a refusal of identification with a racially and politically purged community of cultural producers under fascist rule.[79] Similar contestations were evident in the instances of yellow stars worn by Gentile populations under fascist occupation: a strategy that punctured fascism's fantasy of a popular body whose face mimetically reflected a racialized soul.[80]

Conclusion: Making Peace

In sum, then, the attempt of Nazis and others to legitimate their rule by manipulating concepts of space, time and the body can only appear as part of a failed experiment, albeit one that cost the lives of millions of Europeans and the happiness of many millions more. This failure was also, however, a sort of victory: it demonstrated the resilience of socially rooted concepts of legitimacy that lay in notions of the community, the family and the individual. These concepts were given material expression in the post-liberation years, which witnessed a renewed convergence of culture and consent that helps to explain the rootedness of the post-war order.

After 1945, millions of Europeans felt that they were returning home. That process of coming home took many, often difficult, forms. Many had no home to return to, or were obliged, as Displaced Persons, to return to places that had never truly been home. For others bereavement or family breakdown meant that home no longer existed in anything other than its geographic sense. The evident passion with which European sought to return home was, however, an indisputable fact. Moreover, once there, Europeans showed an obstinate determination to rebuild their homes and, with them, their lives. This may be seen as a reaction to trauma, what Richard Bessel and Dirk Schumann have aptly termed the collective phenomenon of 'life after death'.[81] But, as this chapter has sought to argue, there was a considerable continuity of value systems in European culture throughout the mid-century upheavals, which explains the almost obsessive post-war concern with 'normalcy'.

Gramscian notions of hegemony thus provide us with a means of appreciating the importance of forms of embodied cultural experience in the reception of political rule. Even during the displays of raw power that characterized invasion and occupation, twentieth-century rulers rarely if ever operated on a blank sheet. If they were to achieve legitimacy, their forms of rule had to be negotiated with the populations over whom they ruled. This cultural consent was the key to durable, acceptable government and, while largely lacking under conditions of wartime occupation, it proved to be much more attainable in postwar regimes.

Notes

1. M. Landy 'Culture and Politics in the Work of Antonio Gramsci', *boundary 2*, XIV *The Legacy of Antonio Gramsci* (1986), 50.
2. A. Gramsci *Selections from Prison Notebooks* (London, 1971), pp. 210–76; V. de Grazia *The Culture of Consent: Mass Organization of Leisure in Fascist Italy* (Cambridge, 1981), p. 22.
3. The debate centres on the Italian experience although the Franco regime has also been examined in very similar terms. For overviews see R.J.B. Bosworth *The Italian Dictatorship: Problems and Perspectives in the Interpretation of Mussolini and Fascism* (London, 1998), especially pp. 12–36 and 106–32 and I. Saz Campos *Fascismo y franquismo* (Valencia, 2004), pp. 171–96.
4. Among the clearest examples is S. Falasca-Zamponi *Fascist Spectacle: the Aesthetics of Power in Mussolini's Italy* (Berkeley, 1997). See also the enormously influential body of work by E. Gentile, most notably *The Sacralization of Politics in Fascist Italy* (Cambridge MA, 1996).
5. V. De Grazia *Culture of Consent*, p. 225.
6. L. Passerini *Fascism in Popular Memory: The Cultural Experience of the Turin Working Class* (Cambridge, 1987), pp. 183–98.
7. V. De Grazia *Culture of Consent*, pp. 4–5.
8. By the dictator's death, it was common for the same Left-wingers to hold office in both sets of unions: S. Balfour *Dictatorship, Workers, and the City: Labour in Greater Barcelona since 1936* (Oxford, 1989), pp. 210–18; V. De Grazia *Culture of Consent*, pp. 233–5.
9. Bundesarchiv (Henceforth BArch) R55 1337, 113: Memo to Goebbels from Reichsführer-SS and Chief of German Police re. Belgian traffic regulations, 27 February 1942. On children's cultural activities, see R55 1228, 52ff,

correspondence between Reichspropagandaamt Danzig-Westpreussen and RMVP Berlin, 19 April 1943.

10. B. Cyrulnic *Un merveilleux malheur* (Paris, 2002). The book is the first in a series of psychiatric studies in which Cyrulnic explores the concept of resilience as a response to psychic trauma. See also D. Peschanski 'Legitimacy/Legitimation/Delegitimation: France in the Dark Years, A Textbook Case' *Contemporary European History* XIII (2004), 416–17.

11. B. Anderson *Imagined Communities: Reflections on the Origin and Spread of Nationalism* (London, 1983).

12. M. Bokovoy 'Croatia' in K. Passmore (ed.) *Women, Gender and Fascism in Europe, 1919–45* (Manchester, 2003), pp. 115–23; J. Gumz '*Wehrmacht* Perceptions of Mass Violence in Croatia, 1941–2', *Historical Journal* XLIV (2001), 1015–38.

13. P. Preston *Franco: A Biography* (London, 1993), pp. 322–3 and 330; H. Raguer *La pólvora y el incienso: La Iglesia y la Guerra Civil española, 1936–1939* (Barcelona, 2001), pp. 392–9.

14. S. Kalyvas *The Logic of Violence in Civil War* (Cambridge, 2006), pp. 87–145, especially pp. 111–32.

15. In the German case, the significance afforded to mass cultural spectacle as the mode through which ideological links would be forged with subject peoples is illustrated by the detailed attention afforded by the Propaganda Ministry's external offices to the question of public space, and to its encoding as culturally Germanic. *Viz* for instance State Secretary K.H. Frank at the inauguration ceremony for Prague's Mozart memorial in December 1941, a monument he saw as celebrating 'the eternal right of *Heimat* that Wolfgang Amadeus Mozart enjoyed in this city': BArch R55 1337, 29. Further instances include the Ministry's detailed attention to the promotion of fashion as a cultural form that might stamp a 'quality' German imprint on the public culture (BArch R55 795); or its emphasis on the acquisition by the *Cautio Treuhand, Ufa* and *Tobis* of cinema chains in the occupied territories, film exhibition being seen as a key space of public spectacle, and thus as crucial to the overall project of steering film culture 'in the proper direction' (BArch R55 1319, 151).

16. Tytti Soila gives various examples of passive resistance by Danish and Norwegian audiences to German cinema fare: see T. Soila (ed.) *Nordic National Cinemas* (London and New York, 1998), pp. 14 and 120.

17. I. Clark *Legitimacy in International Society* (Oxford, 2005), p. 2.

18. B. Anderson *Imagined Communities*.

19. J. Romein and A. Romein-Verschoor *Erflaters van onze Beschaving* (Amsterdam, 1939); J.H. Huizinga *Nederlands geestesmerk* (Leiden, 1935), p. 18; J. Faber *Naar wijder horizon* (Utrecht, 1935); H.R. Kedward *Resistance in Vichy France* (Oxford, 1978), pp. 150–64.

20. D. Matless, *Landscape and Englishness* (London, 1998).

21. S. Schama *Landscape and Memory* (London, 1995).
22. M. Mazower *Inside Hitler's Greece: The Experience of Occupation 1941–44* (New Haven and London, 1993), pp. 79–82.
23. A prominent exponent of the Nazi conception of the German *Reich* as 'the buttress to Europe' was the pedagogue and philosopher Ernst Krieck. On the reception of his writings on Europe by the regime, see for example, memorandum to RMVP from Director of Student Cultural Exchanges in *Reich* Student Association: Bähr to Heinrichsdorff, 9 December 1941. BArch R55 626, 10.
24. See, for example, BArch R55 356: 30.3.1935: R55 409: 4.11.41, on Propaganda Ministry support for *Das neue Europa*, a magazine dedicated to restoring 'a feeling of commonality' among European peoples through its elaboration of a vision of 'the new Europe' as 'the great historical act of the *Reich*'. See also R55 826: 20.4.41, on visit by press chief Brauweiler to Europa-Press in Frankfurt.
25. K. Kreimeier, *Die Ufa-story. Geschichte eines Filmkonzerns* (Munich, 1992), p. 392. See also R. Vande Winkel and D. Welch (eds), *Cinema and the Swastika* (Houndmills, 2007).
26. We are indebted to Denis Peschanski for this insight.
27. M. Conway and J. Gotovitch (eds) *Europe in Exile. European Exile Communities in Britain 1940–45* (New York and Oxford, 2001).
28. O. Mosley 'The World Alternative' *Fascist Quarterly* II/III (1936), p. 395. James Hay refers to Cinecitta's 'intent to export Italian culture and to "conquer" foreign markets' in J. Hay, *Popular Film Culture in Fascist Italy: the Passing of the Rex* (Bloomington IN, 1987), p. 181. This was mirrored in Germany by *Ufa*'s commercial war with Hollywood: see for example M. Spiker, *Hollywood unterm Hakenkreuz. Der amerikanische Spielfilm im Dritten Reich* (Trier, 1999), especially Chapter 7; and by Nazi efforts throughout the 1930s to support German penetration of cultural markets abroad. The activities of the *Werberat der deutschen Wirtschaft*, active in fields as diverse as tourism and advertising, film and fashion, were especially significant here; see BArch R55 360 & R55 356.
29. 'Vital needs' was Benito Mussolini's formulation, cited in R. Griffin (ed.) *Fascism* (Oxford, 1995), pp. 74–5. Griffin also reproduces (pp. 75–6) a marching song from the Abyssinian campaign, referenced here in the appeal to 'eternal Empire'.
30. J. Zimmerer 'The birth of *Ostland* out of the spirit of colonialism: a postcolonial perspective on the Nazi policy of conquest and extermination' *Patterns of Prejudice*, XXXIX (2005), 197–219.
31. 'One even hears the hope expressed that Hitler might eventually intervene with Japan to achieve a restoration of the Dutch Indies': RMVP report, 19.1.42, BArch R55 1337 56ff; 14.12.42 to November 1942; RMVP reports on Dutch responses to war in the Far East, and on the RMVP's own use of Dutch losses

in the colonies to undermine the credibility of the government in exile, and to court Dutch support for a fascist-dominated resolution to the war.

32. J.A. Tooze *The Wages of Destruction: The Making and Breaking of the Nazi Economy* (London, 2006); M. Mazower *Dark Continent: Europe's Twentieth Century* (London, 1991), pp. 153–84.

33. E. Hobsbawm *Bandits* (London, 1969).

34. S. Serrano *Maquis: historia de la guerrilla antifranquista* (Madrid, 2001); J.A. Vidal Castaño *La memoria reprimida: historias orales del maquis* (Valencia, 2004).

35. R. Gildea *Marianne in Chains: In Search of the German Occupation, 1940–1945* (London, 2002), pp. 243–59; R. Gildea 'Resistance, Reprisals and Community in Occupied France' *Transactions of the Royal Historical Society* XIII (2003), 163–85; F. Moreno Gómez *Córdoba en la posguerra: la represión y la guerrilla, 1939–50* (Córdoba, 1987); Mazower *Inside Hitler's Greece*, pp. 265–91 and 322–39; S. Kalyvas, *Logic of Violence in Civil War*, pp. 246–329; B. Moore (ed.) *Resistance in Western Europe* (Oxford, 2000).

36. L. Fittko *Escape through the Pyrenees*, trans. D. Koblick (Evanston IL, 2000), p. 176.

37. *Ibid.*, p. 175.

38. F. Muel-Dreyfus *Vichy and the Eternal Feminine. A Contribution to a Political Sociology of Gender,* trans. K.A. Johnson (Durham NC and London, 2001), p. 4.

39. A. Hinderer 'Die Bedeutung Des Films', in Landesverband Berlin-Brandenburg-Grenzmark (ed.), *Filmtheaterführung. Die Vorträge des ersten Schulungsjahres 1934/35 der Fachschule der Filmtheaterbesitzer des Landesverbandes Berlin-Brandenburg-Grenzmark E.V.* (Berlin, 1935), p. 61. See also E. Carter *Dietrich's Ghosts. The Sublime and the Beautiful in Third Reich Film* (London, 2004), p. 86.

40. The RMVP, for example, enlisted the support of the external affairs department of the German lecturers' association (*Auslandsamt des Dozentenverbandes*), with a view to creating a pan-European body that would absorb colleagues from 'the eastern countries' from Poland to Czechoslovakia and beyond; 'the South-East'; France, Belgium, and the Netherlands. R55 1218, 8 December 1944 and *passim.*

41. A. Perez de Olaguer *'Piedras Vivas': biografía del Capellán Requeté José Mª Lamamié de Clairac y Alonso,* (San Sebastián, 1939); M.T. Camarero-Núñez *Mi nombre nuevo 'Magnificat': M^a del Pilar Lamamié de Clairac y Alonso* (Madrid, 1960); Croatian newspaper 1941 quoted in J. Gumz 'Wehrmacht Perceptions of Mass Violence', 1025.

42. J. Winter *Sites of Memory, Sites of Mourning: The Great War in European Cultural History* (Cambridge, 1995); J. Winter and E. Sivan (eds) *War and Remembrance in the Twentieth Century* (Cambridge, 1999); S. Farmer *Martyred*

Village: Commemorating the 1944 Massacre at Oradour-sur-Glane (Berkeley and London, 1999).

43. M. Vincent "'The Keys to the Kingdom": Religious Violence in the Spanish Civil War, July-August 1936' in C. Ealham and M. Richards (eds) *The Splintering of Spain: Cultural History and the Spanish Civil War* (Cambridge, 2004), pp. 68–92.

44. G. di Febo *Ritos de guerra y de victoria en la España franquista* (Bilbao, 2002); M. Richards *A Time of Silence. Civil War and the Culture of Repression in Franco's Spain, 1936–1945* (Cambridge, 1998), pp. 7–11 and 67–74.

45. Quoted M. Richards *Time of Silence*, p. 7; on verticalism, see 67ff.

46. C. Boyd *Historia Patria: Politics, History and National Identity in Spain, 1875–1975* (Princeton, 1997), p. 252.

47. V. de Grazia *How Fascism Ruled Women: Italy 1922–1945* (Berkeley, 1992), pp. 71–2; *Medina (Semanario de la Sección Femenina)* XXXIX (14 December 1941).

48. C. Lloyd 'Divided Loyalties: Singing in the Occupation' in H. Dauncey and S. Cannon (eds) *Popular Music in France from Chanson to Techno* (Aldershot, 2003), p. 169; L. Díaz, *La radio en España, 1923–97* (Madrid, 1997).

49. G. Iverson 'Norway', in T. Soila (ed.) *Nordic National Cinemas*, p. 120.

50. Ethnic Germans and Ukrainians had precedence in first and second-rung cinemas, with a total prohibition on Jewish attendance: see G. Stahr *Volksgemeinschaft vor der Leinwand? Der nationalsozialistische Film und sein Publikum* (Berlin, 2001).

51. *Ibid.*

52. S. Holguín *Creating Spaniards: Culture and National Identity in Republican Spain* (Madison, 2002); E. Otero Urtaza *Las misiones pedagógicas: una experiencia de educación popular* (Coruña, 1982).

53. H.R. Kedward *In Search of the Maquis: Rural Resistance in Southern France, 1942–1944* (Oxford, 1993) and *Resistance in Vichy France*; A. Prost (ed.) *La Résistance: une histoire sociale* (Paris, 1997).

54. R. Cooter, M. Harrison and S. Sturdy (eds) *War, Medicine and Modernity* (Stroud, 1998); H. Joas *War and Modernity* (Oxford, 2003).

55. P. Lagrou *The Legacy of Nazi Occupation: Patriotic Memory and National Recovery in Western Europe 1945–1965* (Cambridge, 2000).

56. *Het Belfort* 28 October 1944, cited in M. Conway 'Belgium's Mid-Twentieth Century Crisis: Crisis of a Nation-State?' *Revue belge d'histoire contemporaine* XXXV (2005), 577.

57. P. Drieu la Rochelle 'Renaissance de l'homme européen' in *Notes pour comprendre le siècle* (Paris, 1941), p. 162: translated in R. Griffin (ed.) *Fascism*, p. 203.

58. J. Herf *The Jewish Enemy. Nazi Ideology and Propaganda during World War II and the Holocaust* (Cambridge MA and London, 2006), pp. 17–49;

R. Ben-Ghiat 'Envisioning Modernity. Desire and Discipline in the Italian Fascist Film', *Critical Inquiry* XXIII (1996), 115. See also Z. Sternhell *La droite révolutionnaire 1885–1914. Les origines françaises du fascisme* (Paris, 2nd edn, 2000), pp. 161–88 and L. Joly 'Les débuts de l'Action Française (1899–1914) ou l'élaboration d'un nationalisme antisémite', *Revue historique* CCCVIII (2006), 695–717.

59. A. Hitler *Mein Kampf* ed. D.C. Watt (London, 1969), p. 277. On the Austrian case, see S. Friedländer, *Das dritte Reich und die Juden, Die Jahre der Verfolgung 1933–1939* (Munich, 1998), p. 263.

60. E. Gentile 'The Theatre of Politics in Fascist Italy' in G. Berghaus (ed.) *Fascism and Theatre: Comparative Studies on the Aesthetics and Politics of Performance in Europe, 1925–1945* (Providence and Oxford, 1996), p. 73. See also R. Ben-Ghiat 'Envisioning Modernity', 112.

61. Ingenieur Arnhold *Der Betriebsingenieur als Menschenführer* (Berlin, 1927) cited in R. Grunberger *A Social History of the Third Reich* (Harmondsworth, 1991), p. 254.

62. As Hitler declared at the NSDAP Congress in 1937: 'our buildings arise to strengthen [our] authority.' J. Hiden and J. Farquharson *Explaining Hitler's Germany* (London, 2nd edn, 1989), p. 51. See also R. Taylor *The Word in Stone. The Role of Architecture in the National Socialist Ideology* (Berkeley and London, 1974).

63. K. Müller 'Vaterländische und nazistische Fest- und Weihespiele in Österreich' in H. Haider-Pregler and B. Reiterer (eds) *Verspielte Zeit. Österreichisches Theater der dreissiger Jahre* (Vienna, 1997), pp. 150–69. On the 'theatre of communion' see S. Added 'Jacques Copeau and Popular Theatre in Vichy France', in G. Berghaus (ed.) *Fascism and Theatre*, p. 252 and *passim*.

64. J. Irons 'Staging Reconciliation: Popular Theatre and Political Utopia in France in 1937' *Contemporary European History* XIV (2005), 279–94.

65. S. Falasca-Zamponi *Fascist Spectacle*.

66. J. Irons 'Staging Reconciliation', 287.

67. F. Muel-Dreyfus *Vichy and the Eternal Feminine*, pp. 1–2, 209 and 252.

68. R.J. Golsan 'Henry de Montherlant. Itinerary of an Ambivalent Fascist' in R.J. Golsan (ed.) *Fascism, Aesthetics and Culture* (Hanover and London, 1992), p. 155. Golsan bases his comments on de Montherlant's 'ordre mâle' on two novels, *Le Songe* (1922) and *Les Bestiaires* (1926). Regarding De Montherlant see J. Jackson *France. The Dark Years 1940–1944* (Oxford, 2001), pp. 206–7. For a parallel Spanish example, see Mary Vincent on notions of a Françoist 'crusade' that culminated in the declaration of war on the Spanish Republic in 1936 and which was similarly underpinned by 'particular Catholic ideas of masculinity, which provided a sense of moral order, an image of heroism against the infidel, and a construction of martyrdom in which the whole idea of the crusade finds its ultimate expression.' M. Vincent 'The Martyrs and the

Saints: Masculinity and the Construction of the Francoist Crusade' *History Workshop Journal* XLVII (1999), 71.

69. R. Grunberger *Social History*, p. 335.

70. L. Caldwell, 'Reproducers of the Nation: Women and the Family in Fascist Policy' in D. Forgacs (ed.) *Rethinking Italian Fascism. Capitalism, Populism and Culture* (London, 1986), p. 135.

71. The clearest example is Francoist Spain but welfarism in Fascist Italy was also profoundly marked by Catholicism. See M.S. Quine *Italy's Social Revolution: Charity and Welfare from Liberalism to Fascism* (Basingstoke, 2002) and *Population Policies in Twentieth-Century Europe: Fascist Dictatorships and Liberal Democracies* (London, 1996).

72. See, for example, Victor Pradera *El Estado Nuevo* (1935) discussed in M. Blinkhorn *Carlism and Crisis in Spain, 1931–1939* (Cambridge, 1975), pp. 146–52. Corporatist ideas achieved great prominence in conservative circles throughout Europe during the 1930s, stimulated both by the examples of Italy and Portugal and Pius XI's *Quadragesimo Anno*.

73. BArch R55 1337, 22–3: weekly report from RMVP Prague to *Reich* Minister Goebbels, 12 and 14 January 1942. On the *Winterhulp Nederland*, see P. Romijn *Burgemeesters in oorlogstijd. Besturen onder Duitse bezetting* (Amsterdam, 2006), pp. 202–16.

74. M. Nash 'Pronatalism and Motherhood in Franco's Spain' in G. Bock and P. Thane (eds) *Maternity and Gender Policies: Women and the Rise of the European Welfare States, 1880s–1950s* (London, 1994), pp. 160–77; C. Koonz *Mothers in the Fatherland. Women, the Family and Nazi Politics* (London, 1986), pp. 185–98; P. Corner 'Women in Fascist Italy. Changing Family Roles in the Transition from an Agricultural to an Industrial Society', *European History Quarterly* XXIII (1993), 51–68; P. Willson 'Women in Fascist Italy' in R. Bessel (ed.) *Fascist Italy and Nazi Germany: Comparisons and Contrasts* (Cambridge, 1996), pp. 84–93.

75. A. Frank *The Diary of a Young Girl* (eds) O.H. Frank and M. Pressler (London, 2001), p. 176. See also p. 252.

76. S. Lowry 'Heinz Rühmann – The Archetypal German', in T. Bergfelder, E. Carter and D. Göktürk (eds) *The German Cinema Book* (London, 2002), p. 83.

77. S. Hake *Popular Cinema of the Third Reich* (Austin, 2001), p. ix.

78. M.L. Roberts *Civilization Without Sexes: Reconstructing Gender in Postwar France, 1917–1927* (Chicago, 1994); S. Reynolds *France Between the Wars: Gender and Politics* (London and New York, 1996), pp. 63–4: V. De Grazia *How Fascism Ruled Women*.

79. See e.g. BArch R55 1337, 46: Bergfeld to Schaeffer, 23 February 1942: appendix to weekly report from RMVP Netherlands, concerning refusal of Dutch theatre guild to comply with licensing regulations.

80. On 20 May 1942, the RMVP weekly report from Den Haag reported that 'a number of Aryans have adopted the Jewish star to demonstrate their sympathy. These were only isolated cases (though) rather more frequently, yellow flowers were worn instead of the yellow star, or seats in trams ostentatiously vacated to make way for Jews.' BArch R55 1337, 39.
81. R. Bessel and D. Schumann (eds) *Life after Death: Approaches to a Cultural and Social History of Europe during the 1940s and 1950s* (Cambridge, 2002).

–6–

Legitimacy and the Making of the
Post-War Order*

In November 1953 the governor of the eastern Austrian province of Burgenland, Lorenz Karall, attempted to explain the relative political stability in his province despite continuing economic insecurity and international tension caused by its position on the border with the Soviet bloc. Karall argued that this political stability was in part a product of the fact 'that the Austrian population has learned from the hard school of the past thirty-five years to be discriminating and seems thus to be immune to demagogic rhetoric.' Behind this lay a more profound shift in the nature of popular expectations of their political leaders in that 'Austrians today have more profound material than ideological needs.'[1] The deep seated materialization of popular expectations of politics occurred as part of a reproduction of continuity in the first decade following the end of the Second World War, which saw the reassertion of social democracy[2] and political Catholicism[3] as the two dominant political traditions in the new republic, as they had been prior to the disappearance of political pluralism in 1934. While political polarization had marked relations between these two political traditions between the wars, in the circumstances of occupied post-war Austria this was replaced with a durable politics of consensus. Karall, as the most prominent local beneficiary of this shift, was uniquely placed to observe the changes in popular attitudes that underpinned this transformation. Originally a political representative of Burgenland's Croatian minority Karall had risen to prominence in the late 1920s as a member of the Catholic Christian Socials. He served as a member of the last elected government in the province between 1930 and 1934, and was a prominent local advocate of the party's authoritarian turn thereafter, only to return after Nazi rule to serve as the provincial governor from 1946 managing a grand coalition of Catholics and Socialists.[4]

The dynamic of continuity and change visible in post-war Austria was discernible right across Europe. In the six years that followed the end of the Second World War many of the political traditions that had shaped political identities across the continent from the end of the nineteenth century reasserted themselves. They did so in a new context in which the experience of economic crisis, brief recovery and even war had reshaped popular expectations of both politics and of government.

---

*This chapter was written by Mark Pittaway, with Hans-Fredrik Dahl as co-author.

Populations demanded that politics and state action should focus on the immediate needs of local communities for physical and material security. Post-war publics were most comfortable with a protective state, which limited the space for overly ideological, transformative politics. This chapter argues that these complex and sometimes contradictory dynamics shaped a particular notion of legitimacy and thus the contours of a discernible political culture across Europe. While it was in north-western Europe, transformed politically by the dynamics of 'liberation' and the creation of limited liberal democracies during the early years of the Cold War that this shift was most visible, the reproduction of political cultures and the materialization of popular demands of the state could also be seen elsewhere. In traditionally Catholic and conservative western Hungary, for instance, political Catholicism not only mobilized majorities of voters behind centre-Right parties in elections in 1945 and 1947, just as it had ensured the loyalty of rural populations to the Horthy regime in the inter-war years, but participation in church processions during the early 1950s provided a focus for populations in conservative villages and small towns to express their opposition to the policies of the country's socialist dictatorship.[5] While renewed political cultures could provide a focus through which opposition was expressed, it was discontent about material circumstances in the face of the shortages of food, basic goods and heating during the era of socialist industrialization in the country that proved to be most corrosive for the legitimacy of the regime.[6]

The dynamics that lay behind these phenomena were difficult to discern as the post-war order was constructed across Europe during the late 1940s, for they lay in a semi-visible sphere somewhere between the realm of high politics and the everyday concerns of ordinary Europeans. They did, however, play a profound role, albeit with other factors, in defining the constraints under which political actors operated, creating hidden boundaries that forced political projects to move in directions unintended by their originators. The dynamics of legitimacy generated by the interaction between political projects and transformed popular expectations also created opportunities for political actors. Exploring these dynamics is essential to an understanding of the development of the various post-war settlements that arose across the continent. Hitherto the historiography of the development of Europe's post-war order has been dominated by writing on the origins of the early Cold War in the continent as if, after the mobilizations of the inter-war years and the Second World War, the shaping of political regimes was determined by the interaction between domestic political elites and the victorious great powers.[7] At the same time the history of the social realm in the immediate post-war years is still relatively under-researched, though historians have begun to focus on the social consequences of the violence of the war for the stability of the post-war era.[8] Yet there has been relatively little concentration on how the dynamics of changing political attitudes and expectations with their roots in the war years contributed to the development of post-war political settlements, expressed in a marked shift from relations between political traditions that was characterized by conflict to ones characterized by bargaining, despite the potential this approach has for understanding the distinctive character of the post-war order.[9]

From the perspective of international history the immediate post-war years seem to constitute a transition from the military outcome of war to the creation of the bi-polar order across Europe. When the immediate post-war years are examined from the standpoint of the struggle for legitimacy, however, a different, more complex and uneven picture of Europe's post-war political order emerges. The interests of the different military victors, occupation authorities and new domestic political elites interacted with political cultures and traditions that were reconstructed in the post-war context. These political cultures reflected above all the differing patterns of political identification in post-war Europe, as they re-shaped the fabric of national civil societies within the states of the continent, influencing the patterns of unity and diversity between them. When viewed from the perspective of legitimacy, the history of the immediate post-war years is about the influence that reproduced political cultures had on political development both within and between states. The outcomes of the political conflicts that emerged would have consequences for decades to follow.

It was north-western Europe where the strength of established notions of legitimacy and their relative survival during the war years enabled the early reconstruction of legitimate state authority; in these states the political contours of domestic post-war settlements were visible within five years of the end of the war. The longer term impact of war on the social and cultural fabrics of north-western European civil societies was less than that present in either central or south-eastern Europe, thus enabling the smoother reproduction of political continuities than elsewhere in the continent.[10] Consequently national states were reconstructed around democratic, consensual but very definitely bourgeois polities that drew on notions of legitimacy that emerged from the social transformations of the war years. In Switzerland this transformation could be said to have been at its smoothest in view of that country's relative containment from the upheavals of war and the anchoring of its political system in strongly localist, participatory structures that bound populations tightly to established patterns of government.[11] In similarly neutral Sweden, the indirect impact of war cemented the welfarist settlement constructed by the political alliance of Social Democrats and Agrarians during the 1930s, through generating a high degree of political and social consensus, required to maintain neutrality during the war years, which in turn provided the basis for a continuation of the construction of the welfare state in the post-war period.[12] Ireland had remained formally neutral and informally supportive of the United Kingdom. This had necessitated exceptional political measures and economic deprivation that stimulated the rise of the Left in the country's major cities. In the immediate post-war years the Left was quickly beaten back, while a political system based upon the hegemony of Fianna Fail, punctuated by occasional periods of diverse centre-Left coalitions, the first of which took power in

1948, was established.[13] In the United Kingdom the war strengthened the legitimacy of dominant national identities and established political institutions, which were seen to have proved themselves to be resilient in the face of war. Demands for social change were successfully absorbed by the Labour Party, propelling it to victory in 1945. While Labour was to remain stronger throughout the post-war period than it had been in the inter-war years, its victory did not mark a lasting break with previous forms of political affiliation. The Conservatives, dominant in the inter-war years, had reasserted themselves by the time of the general elections of 1950 and 1951, and ruled the country between 1951 and 1964.[14] Even in the states of formerly occupied north-western Europe, which unlike Britain, saw their party system change, the political orders that emerged by the late 1940s were marked by a considerable degree of restoration. In Denmark and Norway established political elites were able to absorb the appeal of the resistance to restore the political system after the end of German occupation.[15] In the Netherlands the reconstruction of the post-war political order was marked by a dynamic of restoration and renewal, as patterns of pre-war political identification within society rapidly re-emerged.[16] Belgium was similarly marked by a rapid restoration of pre-war political traditions, that were in turn forced to adapt to the more individualistic and material climate that had emerged from their supporters as a consequence of the war years.[17]

Elsewhere the nature of the state had been more contested. Post-war transitions were consequently more protracted, conflict-ridden and messier, ensuring that political instability, and in some cases open social conflict, often persisted into the 1950s, with some form of viable post-war political settlement only emerging at the end of the decade. While transitions in legitimacy in the rest of the continent were characterized by these common elements, they were far from uniform, either in nature or in outcome. The transitions in south-eastern Europe presented a particularly extreme manifestation of the impact of inter-war crises of legitimacy and war on post-war events and eventual outcomes. These generated social revolutionary pressures, which in some states produced social revolutionary outcomes, and in one state in particular in the region violent political polarization resulted in a civil war. In Yugoslavia the events of the war had both discredited the pre-war monarchy and the politics of ethnic exclusivity that had led to civil war following the first Yugoslavia's collapse after the German invasion in 1941. Tito's partisans had been able to mobilize support, particularly in parts of Bosnia and Croatia, but also Slovenia, on the basis that the Communists offered a clear alternative to both during the mid-1940s. While the creation of socialist dictatorship in Yugoslavia between 1944 and 1946 was a violent process, the new regime sought a viable settlement based on the co-operation of nationalities, institutionalized in the 1946 constitution, which rested on a formula of 'the brotherhood and unity' of peoples building a new socialist order.[18] The weakness of the inter-war state, dismembered in 1939, opened the door for a strategy of revolutionary legitimation in neighbouring Albania.[19] In Bulgaria, Communists and their supporters, backed by a partisan movement connected to that in neighbouring Yugoslavia moved in 1944 and 1945 to seize power and institute their own social revolution, and were only prevented from doing so by the presence of the Red Army and the desire of Moscow for the pursuit by Bulgarian Communists of a more moderate course.[20] Elsewhere in south-eastern Europe, political groupings seeking to reconstruct the state on revolutionary lines were able to gain a considerable degree of legitimacy from society for their vision of transformation, though they clashed with groups that sought a different form of political order, generating extreme political polarization. In such societies no agreed definitions of a legitimate political order emerged. In Romania, the withdrawal of the country from the war in August 1944 produced a revolutionary wave that the country's Communists were able to exploit. This generated considerable political polarization. The presence of the Red Army was crucial to ensuring that those who adhered to a revolutionary vision of the post-war state persevered.[21] Different visions of the nation and the post-war social order led to civil war in Greece, and the eventual violent defeat of those who supported social revolution.[22]

In view of the violent outcome of Greece's struggle for legitimacy, the defeat of its social revolution and the persistence of the weakness of legitimate state authority in Greece well into the post-war years, it belongs as much to a southern European variant of the transition in legitimacy as it does to a south-eastern European one. In Spain, the crisis of legitimate state authority had resulted in the explosion of political conflict a decade before that in Greece. While the victorious nationalists formally occupied power in 1939, the Franco regime was only able to consolidate its victory through politics of cultural isolation and repression by the late 1940s. Yet even this was insufficient to bring about a durable consolidation of the regime, based upon a partial legitimacy, which came about as a result of policies of economic liberalization and modernization launched at the end of the 1950s.[23] Another variant of the southern European pattern was provided by Portugal, where an inter-war crisis in legitimacy had been resolved through the creation of a Right-wing authoritarian regime after 1926. Geographically isolated from the rest of the continent, the upheaval of war had no immediate effect on the regime, though post-war transformation elsewhere brought a slow decay in the ideological cement that bound the regime to its social base.[24]

Thus the south-eastern European and southern European transitions in legitimacy represented extreme manifestations of the effect of the weakness of legitimate state authority on political transformation in a period of intense conflict. In between these and the more clear-cut north-western European transitions, lay those in central Europe. Across central Europe civil societies were characterized by majorities who supported forms of democratized and renewed conservative politics and minorities who supported various forms of Left-wing, revolutionary projects akin to those pursued in south-east Europe. In Hungary and Slovakia these revolutionary minorities were stronger than elsewhere in the region, given the relative weakness of the alternative Left-wing project of social democracy/socialism.[25] This was not true in Germany where the Communists, supported in the Soviet zone by the occupation authorities, faced the restoration of the local variant of social democracy with a broad base of support, that rested on continuities inherited from the pre-1933 period.[26] Nor was it the case in Austria where the Communists' marginal position in so far as its support base was concerned was clear from 1945, even though the presence of Soviet troops in the country's eastern provinces meant that a transition to a political order based on revolutionary strategies of legitimation was something feared by the anti-communist majority well into the 1950s.[27] While political outcomes in these states differed, with West Germany and Austria developing political orders that conformed to the north-western European pattern by the mid-1950s, as Hungary, Slovakia and East Germany joined the Soviet bloc, their transitions can nevertheless be grouped together. The dynamics of a struggle for legitimacy characterized by a clash between conservative majorities and a more radical political project – which

Figure 6.1 A large poster of Stalin hangs from the front of the Vienna Opera House in the autumn of 1945. In the foreground stand an American soldier, and a group of armed Soviet soldiers. Courtesy of Netherlands Institute for War Documentation, Amsterdam.

enjoyed varying degrees of support in each of the states – shaped the political cultures that underpinned the post-war order despite the differing political outcomes in the various states.

The states that bordered these countries all experienced variants of these Central European transitions. Finland's transition, like many in Central Europe, was characterized by a deep split between those who sought a reconstruction of the state based on revolutionary legitimacy and those concerned to protect Finland's autonomy from its Soviet neighbour. The polarization that characterized the early Cold War years bolstered Finland's anti-communist majority, providing the social base of a political system akin to its Scandinavian neighbours, underpinned internationally by guarantees of neutrality.[28] Poland's clash between different political visions was accompanied by violent civil conflict that, to some extent, made it as much like south-eastern European states such as Romania or Bulgaria.[29] In the Czech lands, Communists advancing a strategy of revolutionary legitimation found themselves in a position of power and with a substantial base of support as a result of an anti-fascist national consensus. This consensus, which non-Communist political parties bought into, gave the Communists political cover to lay the foundations of future social

Figure 6.2 President Beneš of Czechoslovakia watches a parade by Czech troops returned from exile, accompanied by Allied military dignitaries. Courtesy of Netherlands Institute for War Documentation, Amsterdam.

revolution. The anti-fascist consensus supported social revolutionary goals only to an extent, however, limiting the extent of the Communists' exercise of legitimate power and leading to growing political polarization, which in turn led to the creation of overt dictatorship. This particular transition can be characterized as the temporary acquisition, then erosion of legitimacy, that in turn led to dictatorship.[30]

The Italian and French cases were more complex still in that they combined aspects of the north-western, central and southern European transitions. As in southern Europe, social revolutionary pressure produced social polarization, which led to the defeat of post-war demands for radical change. Unlike in the rest of southern Europe, however, this defeat did not represent the creation of a dictatorship that sought the outright elimination of the Left but merely a set of political arrangements that rested on nominally democratic institutions, which contained the Left. However, hegemonic notions of legitimacy that were based on concepts of republican nationalism were shared by the Communists and other political actors alike. These hegemonic notions of legitimacy provided the cultural backdrop that allowed the Communists to behave in ways that bolstered the legitimacy of a political system that sought their containment. The experience of the collapse of Fascism, Italy's formal withdrawal from the war, and the subsequent German occupation of northern and central Italy produced a specific set of circumstances at war's end. In the north of the country, resistance provided the base for the hegemony of revolutionary strategies of legitimation that spread from the industrial centres of Lombardy and Piedmont through Central Italy. This was, however, contested by an alternative centre-Right, Christian Democratic grouping centred on the agrarian populations of the south and north-east. The outcome of political struggle remained unclear throughout the mid-1940s, and while the occupation of the state by the Christian Democrats was sealed by the 1948 elections, the construction of a form of legitimate state authority through which the Left was contained, based upon the Left's paradoxical acceptance of this containment and thus the integration of a previously potentially revolutionary constituency into the political system, was a slow, protracted and partial process, which continued throughout the 1950s.[31] In France, meanwhile, as in much of north-western Europe transition was underpinned by a project of the restoration of a 'renewed' nation and state after the humiliation of military capitulation in 1940. The meanings of national renewal were profoundly contested within French society, with actors on the Left advancing a revolutionary notion of national renewal that clashed with alternative, more conservative projects. This clash produced social polarization, and as in Italy, the exclusion and containment of the Communists. Though, just as in Italy, the hegemony of a notion of legitimacy that rested on a republican nationalism was bought into by both Left and Right, allowing the Left, to an extent, to participate in a political settlement, which paradoxically re-inforced its containment. Furthermore the projects of national renewal confronted, especially in so far as decolonization was concerned, the relative weakness of the French state, and social polarization produced political instability throughout the 1950s. The consolidation of a form of partial, legitimate state authority – which, as in Italy, excluded those who supported the radical Left – was only brought by the creation of the Fifth Republic after 1958.[32]

When transitions in legitimacy are added to our consideration of the dynamics of the construction of the post-war order in Europe a more complex picture of political change emerges than is suggested by a simple concentration on the realities of geopolitics or elite politics. Yet, behind the patterns of diversity that existed between different European states and regions, what are more striking when one examines these changes from the perspective of legitimacy are the patterns of unity within the transformation of political culture that lay behind these divergences. In order to explore these patterns of unity and to analyse the operation of legitimacy in concrete terms we wish to concentrate on four areas: first, the attempts of actors to seek degrees of democratic legitimation through the mechanism of election. Second, the use of retributive justice by new post-war governments in order to distance themselves from the regimes of fascist and occupation Europe. Third, the issues connected with military occupation and fourth, those connected with economic reconstruction.

With the end of the Second World War, Europe's political elites, of both Right and Left, committed themselves rhetorically to a nominally democratic system of government, emphasizing their wish to hold elections in which the people at least nominally chose their governments as soon as possible after the end of the war. Europe's new political actors differed about what they meant by a democratic system of political rule; in north-western Europe it meant a restoration of the kind of liberal democratic institutions that had existed before the onset of fascism, albeit in a modified form. This deep-seated commitment to a liberal interpretation of democracy based on competitive election was shared across Europe by political actors on the reconstructed centre-Right and by most of the continent's social democrats. Austria's Social Democrats, reconstructed as the Socialist Party (SPÖ) affirmed their commitment to 'a democratic country' even if there was 'no majority for socialism' within it.[33] Yet even at the level of the rhetoric of political elites it was clear in 1945 that democracy was a concept that was contested by different political actors, as for Europe's Communists it had a distinctly more radical content. For Mátyás Rákosi, secretary of Hungary's Communists (MKP), it meant as much a state which led to the 'full economic and political realization of the power of the working class' as one based on representative political institutions.[34] This tension between different concepts of democracy was already shaping differences in the attitudes of political leaders to elections during the first two years of post-war Europe. In Yugoslavia and Albania in late 1945, Bulgaria in October 1946, Romania in the following month, Poland in January and Hungary in August 1947, elections were more about ensuring that Communist parties achieved the outward semblance of democratic legitimacy than ensuring that the citizens of those countries had any meaningful choice of rulers.[35]

The very fact that such political actors used elections as legitimating mechanisms, even as they planned to create dictatorships, was testimony to the influence of a profound change in popular expectations regarding the proper relationship between rulers and the ruled brought about by the war. Notions of popular sovereignty were central to the political cultures of post-war Europe as a result of the general discrediting of Right-wing authoritarianism. In defeated Axis states this stemmed from a perception that the dreams of leaders for territory had led the populations to disaster. In eastern Austria in early 1945, as the political authority of the National Socialist regime collapsed in the face of the imminent arrival of the Red Army, the population blamed the regime in Berlin for the impending disaster they believed would overtake them.[36] Elsewhere the slow crisis of occupation regimes profoundly discredited collaborationist Right-wing authoritarian movements right across the continent.[37] Even in those states marked by extensive 'collaboration' such as Hungary, the memory of the wartime demonstration of the power of the state directed against its own citizens, especially its Jewish citizens, provoked a sense of both shame and unease – even among those who had held anti-semitic opinions – which stimulated in turn protests against actions of the state that were perceived as violent and arbitrary in the post-war years.[38] This led to a marked shift in popular perceptions of what constituted legitimate political authority. War experiences threw up demands for the placing of limits on state power, that state intervention be refocused on the immediate needs of communities and that it be justified through a notion of popular sovereignty that formally subordinated leaders to the ruled. In view of this shift those political movements or charismatic leader that either aimed to lead by consent or were able to present themselves as servants of the 'people' found themselves able to access legitimacy to a greater degree than those that did not. The marked illegitimacy of certain socialist leaders in the eastern half of the continent that was revealed by Khrushchev's denunciation of 'the cult of personality' in 1956 was testimony to a shift in these societies that occurred a decade earlier.[39] This shift in popular expectations of political leadership, in which charismatic leaders were forced to justify their rule with reference to popular wishes rather than ideological programmes, was accompanied by a popular demand that responsibility for government be shared by rulers and ruled. This particular shift created a climate which allowed free and competitive elections to be seen by populations as the norm; it underpinned the way in which fraudulent elections such as those held in Hungary in August 1947 came to symbolize for neighbouring populations, like those of Austria, the type of political system they did not wish to see created on their soil.[40] Even after the institutionalization of socialist dictatorship in Central and Eastern Europe, the refusal of populations to accept the legitimacy of the single-list elections was widespread. During Hungary's 1949 elections agitators were faced with opposition from people who demanded to know why they 'should vote when there is no choice, and no opposition to vote for'.[41]

Behind this apparent democratization of popular expectations of politics lay demands for the reconstruction of the state as a 'protector' focused on the immediate and largely local needs of populations in the immediate post-war context. This can be illustrated particularly with references to the political responses to crime waves in post-war central Europe. 'Liberated' eastern Austria was characterized by widespread violent crime between 1945 and 1947 and considerable fear among the largely rural population of the Soviet troops and displaced persons who were widely believed to be responsible. Village local authorities, in the absence of functioning police forces, organized their own irregular police forces from among the village residents to protect property and people against those they saw as unwelcome outsiders.[42] Denied the right to carry arms by the local occupation authorities and unable to face down armed and dangerous opponents, the attempts of village authorities to organize their own irregular police were quickly replaced by overwhelming demands on the part of the population that the provincial government increase the resources and powers of the gendarmerie and that the occupation authorities allow them to carry arms.[43] In western Hungary, in the context of a similar crime wave, the 'overly political' role of the newly reconstructed police was sharply criticized, as it had to confront popular demands that it pay more attention to conventional petty and violent crime instead.[44]

The shifts in legitimacy that underpinned popular insistence on a limited and accountable politics combined with demands for a protective state that met local needs had deeply ambiguous meanings when set against conventional understandings of Left and Right, restoration and renewal or notions of distrust of or support for state intervention. As Austrian Communists were quick to recognize, demands for more state provision of law and order played into the hands of gendarmerie officers who had backed both the National Socialist regime and the authoritarian *Ständestaat* that preceded it.[45] At the same time, however, the change in the tone of politics that the shifts in popular expectations of the state generated produced a political culture across most of Europe, that was more democratic than that which had existed prior to the war, even if it was more conservative than some of the more radical political actors wished it to be. Perhaps the most striking cultural expression of this shift, outside Germany at least, was the hegemony of a democratic, patriotic political discourse. In many cases this was closely allied to a 'myth' of the wartime resistance as the bearers of a homogeneous, national, anti-fascist sentiment. This was particularly marked in societies such as Yugoslavia, where a radically, democratic 'resistance'-based patriotism was deployed to legitimate social revolution.[46] In politically divided Italy, democratic patriotism based on the notion that the end of Fascism heralded national renewal equivalent to 'a new Risorgimento' was advanced, at least in the immediate post-war years, in a way which masked the real ideological differences between significant anti-Fascist political actors.[47] In many contexts, especially where Communist traditions were strong, this democratic patriotism was tied to a tradition of the 'popular front' which cast the Left as the representative of a progressive, national tradition.[48] Often, however, the attempts of Left-wing or resistance-based groupings to deploy a radical version of patriotism ran into trouble as even the democratized versions of national identity placed hidden limits on the radicalism of their vision of change. In Hungary, Communist attempts to legitimate their hegemony through the use of patriotic discourse were limited, among other things, by the actions of neighbouring states, particularly Czechoslovakia, which used anti-fascist discourse to justify attempts to expel Slovakia's Magyars; a step which sparked painful memories of the post-First World War Treaty of Trianon within Hungary itself, thus reviving more conservative discourses of patriotism.[49] In Austria, patriotic discourse placed more subtle limits on radical change in that they celebrated local and provincial traditions that stressed the preservation of the apparently timeless in a period of upheaval and uncertainty.[50] In post-war Belgium it emphasized the cultural continuity of the state, thus closing off the possibility of radical political change, and bolstering the restoration of pre-war political institutions.[51]

The same patterns of tradition and change were visible in the political affiliations of post-war Europeans, such as they were revealed by elections between 1945 and 1951. Perhaps the most striking feature of the free elections in Europe were the limits they revealed to the support for large-scale social change; the political map of central and north-western Europe was characterized above all by support for anti-socialist, Christian Democratic parties, even though they offered a thoroughly different kind of Right-wing politics to that which had been on offer in the inter-war years. The new centre-Right parties came from different starting points. Austria's Peoples' Party (ÖVP) established itself on the basis of the social networks left by the inter-war Christian Socials, the dominant party of the years between the wars and the one responsible for the end of political pluralism in 1934. Hungary's Smallholders were based on the pro-land reform, yet nevertheless Right-wing opposition to the dominant conservative oligarchy of the inter-war years, while other organizations such as West Germany's Christian Democratic parties (CDU/CSU), Italy's *Democrazia Cristiana* (DC), or France's *Mouvement Républicain Populaire* (MRP) emerged from inter-war traditions of political Catholicism, though they were all substantially new parties. All of these parties drew substantially on Catholic political activism and benefited considerably from the importance of religion in shaping the cultural identities of many of their middle-class and rural supporters. In some cases, particularly that of DC, they were able to expand their base of support through the political polarization that resulted from the existence of a powerful Communist opponent; the DC increased its vote from 35.21 per cent in elections to Italy's constituent assembly in 1946 to 48.51 in the elections of 1948, in such a climate.[52] Others, like the MRP, however, failed to benefit in similar circumstances and were instead squeezed by the rise of other Right-wing formations.[53] What was perhaps more important was that these Christian democratic parties were able to reflect the anti-socialist majorities in most of the central and north-western European states on the one hand, while they were able on the other to combine conservative appeal with the demands among their support base for a more muted, democratic form of politics than that which had been advanced by Right-wing formations in the inter-war years. They were also able to offer a vision of the state, which was both distinctively anti-socialist, yet captured the desire for greater intervention in the economic and social spheres, particularly that which would protect the interests of white-collar employees, and the agrarian population, though it also ensured that these parties were sufficiently open to those sections of the industrial working class to whom religious values were important.[54]

While post-war elections revealed the relative ascendancy of a new kind of centre-Right politics that addressed the anti-socialism of most of the continent's rural and middle-class majority, the labour movement remained relatively isolated. Industrial working-class communities retained distinctive traditions, mentalities and cultures, but their political representatives, outside post-war Scandinavia, and to a lesser extent Austria, were unable to build the kind of cross-class political alliances that would enable them to play a part in democratic politics, at least as anything more than a powerful minority. This is not to say that the war had undermined powerful traditions of working-class protest.[55] The persistence of the strike and a range of more informal forms of on-the-job protest as weapons in the workplace, suggested powerful continuities in work culture with the pre-war years, despite the material disruption such communities experienced as a consequence of war.[56] Furthermore there was deep anger in many working-class communities at miserable living conditions in the immediate post-war years. Organized hunger marches in working-class eastern Austrian towns to protest at restrictions in rations or price rises marked them out from their less proletarian counterparts[57] and similar phenomena were experienced in industrial Hungary.[58] Yet the position of the working class as a minority across much of Europe would determine the political fortunes of the labour movement during the immediate post-war years.

In terms of the political representation of the labour movement, the most important trend to be revealed was the nature of support for communism and its limits. With the exception of the Czech regions of Czechoslovakia, where the Communists were able to build on the experience of resistance to German occupation, popular post-war anti-fascism and the prestige of the Soviet Union to win 38 per cent in Czechoslovakia's 1946 elections, Communist parties were in a minority everywhere. The prestige of their role in the resistance and the relative weakness of social democratic/socialist parties in the post-war climate allowed them to make significant breakthroughs in France where their vote reached a post-war peak of 28.59 per cent in November 1946, and in Italy with 18.93 per cent in the same year. In Hungary, where they polled 16.95 per cent in November 1945, they were aided by the relative unpopularity of local Social Democrats among the working class and the popular memory of the short-lived Soviet republic in 1919. In much of central and eastern Europe and to a lesser extent in Italy, they attempted to turn to the poorer sections of the rural population as supporters of radical land reform to win support but, outside south-eastern Europe, only with distinctly mixed results. Within the political system of the immediate post-war years they represented a strong polarizing force in both halves of Europe. While fear of them among the majority of the population played a key role in shaping political systems organized around the political Right in France, Italy and in the western zones of Germany and it helped cement consensus politics in Austria, in Soviet-occupied Eastern Europe Communist parties attempted to mobilize the working class and rural poor around a rhetoric of class struggle. The dialectic of the mobilization of a subordinate minority against the majority and the polarization that followed in the wake of mobilization generated a pattern of social conflict within central and eastern societies, which later became internationalized in the climate of the Cold War.[59]

In many European states, however, social democracy, or socialism, remained dominant on the Left. This was at its most marked in Scandinavia, where patterns of social-democratic dominance in co-operation with agrarian parties had developed in the 1930s and persisted into the 1950s.[60] In Austria, the SPÖ were able to depend on patterns of political affiliation among the urban working class that had grown in opposition to Right-wing federal governments and the brief dictatorship prior to 1938 so as to marginalize the Communists, who were in turn compromised by the behaviour of Soviet occupation authorities in the east of the country.[61] The revival of pre-war political cleavages helped the SPD quickly to surpass the Communists as the main party on the German Left, not only in the Western zones but prior to its enforced union in eastern Germany with the KPD in 1946, in the Soviet zone as well.[62] Europe's social democrats, outside Scandinavia, however, were weakened in their attempts to become equal competitors for power by two different processes. The first of these was their failure in the immediate post-war years to broaden their appeal to middle-class and rural social groups. In much of north-western continental Europe this left social democrats with slightly less than a third of the vote through the late 1940s. The second was that they suffered from the polarization of European politics between Communists and anti-Communists that characterized and to some extent drove Europe's slide into the Cold War, generating a markedly anti-socialist climate in the continent by the end of the decade, which hindered social democrats in seeking new sources of support. The one exception to this rule was Austria, where the SPÖ joined the ÖVP in a grand coalition, gaining support from their centre-Right coalition partners for social reforms in exchange for maintaining a solid anti-Communist front and securing working-class consent for the painful economic measures necessary to integrate Austria into the Western economic sphere.[63]

The last most important trend that emerged from early post-war elections was the failure of the resistance to generate a lasting presence in post-war politics as an independent voice for itself. In the Netherlands, Belgium, Denmark and Norway it all but disappeared in the immediate post-war period as established patterns of political affiliation quickly reasserted themselves. The resistance 'myth', however, remained an enduring legacy of wartime activism, embedding itself in political culture.[64] In Italy, while all the major parties of the immediate post-war period, particularly the Communists, sought to draw on the legacy of the resistance for their legitimacy, the spirit of resistance was briefly represented in politics by the *Partito d'Azione*, led by the first post-war Prime Minister, Ferrucio Parri. Yet by the 1946 elections, crippled by internal division, it had been consigned – with only 1.5 per cent of the votes cast – to the margins of the political system.[65] The partial and somewhat ambiguous exception to the rule of the disappearance of the resistance from post-war politics was that of Gaullism in France. De Gaulle's ability to capture legitimacy as a result of the collapse of Vichy and of German occupation and through liberation, left him with considerable resources to act politically into the post-war period.[66] De Gaulle's political movement, launched following his resignation from the presidency in January 1946, grew rapidly in the climate of political polarization that followed the exclusion of the Communists from the government in May 1947, taking 22.29 per cent in the 1951 elections, achieved by votes gained from other Right-wing parties.[67]

Though the resistance failed to enter the political arena as a significant actor in its own right during the post-war period, states across the continent aimed to place distance between themselves and the fascist past, through the pursuit of politics of retribution. This was in part to contain the wave of 'wild retribution' pursued against sections of the populations at the moment of 'liberation', who were perceived to have transgressed the accepted norms of community during the period of occupation. In much of Europe 'wild retribution' was a sporadic affair; in the rural eastern Austrian district of Neusiedl am See, popular demands for retribution were primarily directed against the small number of individuals who were felt to have infringed community norms during the Nazi takeover in March 1938, or who were regarded as having been especially zealous in their attempts to implement orders to evacuate villages in the face of the Soviet advance during the first months of 1945.[68] Where the extent of conflict had been greater, 'wild retribution' was especially widespread. In Italy as many as 12,000 people were estimated to have been killed by partisans as part of this wave of retribution at the end of the war.[69] In those parts of central Europe, such as the former Protectorate of Bohemia and Moravia and western Poland, where the occupation authorities had sought to re-draw the ethnic map, 'wild retribution' took the form of widespread ethnic retribution against local Germans. The forced expulsion of 20,000 by the local authorities in the town of Brno was an extreme manifestation of what was termed 'wild expulsion'.[70]

The retributive climate that accompanied liberation produced a wave of state-sponsored 'cleansing' right across Europe that was sponsored by both new states and occupation authorities alike. In both occupied Germany and Austria the widespread internment of National Socialist functionaries – around 90,000 in the British zone of Germany alone – was as much about securing political authority and eliminating opposition as it was about judicial retribution per se.[71] Public administrations were purged of those implicated in supporting wartime regimes.[72] Measures against those believed to have committed 'crimes' during the period of war and occupation were often radical, as states introduced a range of illiberal measures to deal with those found guilty of such infractions; the death penalty was reintroduced in a number of countries where it had been long since abolished, notably in Denmark and Norway, for the most serious offences, while courts were not reluctant to inflict prison sentences on those found guilty, which would have been seen as overly draconian by the standards of the pre-war years.[73] In Czechoslovakia, retributive legislation provided courts with draconian powers that resulted in widespread recourse to the death penalty.[74]

When one moves beyond the desire that united European states in pursuing policies of judicial retribution – namely the attempt to divide their rule from the regimes that had preceded them and to secure legitimacy by defining themselves against the standard of 'criminal' wartime regimes – a picture emerges that reflected patterns of political diversity in wartime Europe. Communist parties, in particular, were among the most radical and determined to use processes of judicial retribution both to eliminate the traces of a 'fascist' past, and lay the foundations of a 'new' society. Consequently in the states where the Communist parties had most influence, in central and eastern Europe, the patterns of judicial retribution tended to go the furthest, including mass ethnic retribution against the German population. Furthermore, they merged with purges against political opponents of Communists in the police and civil services of the states of the region who stood in the way of attempts by the Communists to consolidate their rule. What is more,

Figure 6.3 Norwegians accused of collaboration with the German Occupiers are placed on trial. Courtesy of PA Photos.

they were used deliberately and consciously as part of an attempt to legitimate the dominant political position of Communist parties by stressing their anti-fascist identity and occasionally casting their programme of radical social transformation as a continuance of the process of post-war 'cleansing'.[75] Radical policies of retribution, both judicial and extra-judicial, employed in the interests of creating a new society were also implemented by the authoritarian Right-wing regimes of southern Europe, which mirrored and often exceeded, the radicalism of Communist regimes. In post-Civil War Spain violence was systematically deployed, motivated by an ideology that stressed the need to 'cleanse' the country of elements that had supported the Republic.[76] Similar notions motivated post-civil war violence in Greece.[77] Elsewhere the intentions of new political elites were more moderate and reflected the desire of leaders both to satisfy popular demands for retribution but to do so in ways that would guarantee the stability of the state and ensure a swift return to normality. This was the intention behind judicial retribution in France, though this aim was achieved with only limited success.[78] In the Netherlands the implementation of judicial retribution was motivated by the need of the restored state to control the widespread process of 'wild retribution' that spread throughout the country during the first half of 1945.[79] In Belgium state measures were motivated by the need to draw a line under the popular demands for retribution, in order to enable some form of return to political and economic normality.[80]

While, in most of Europe retribution was in part driven by 'a wave of public rage'[81] that spread through European societies during the first half of 1945, this 'wave' very quickly lost momentum, as the radicalism of many aspects of judicial retribution came to clash with the localism, materialism, and scepticism towards ideological politics that characterized the moral economies of European citizens. The limits to which a judicial anti-fascism could be a real legitimating force in post-war Europe, given popular attitudes and expectations, were at their most clear in central and eastern Europe, when rulers attempted to extend the scope of retribution beyond the prosecution of those who were seen to have breached commonly shared norms. This lay behind the failure of the attempts of Czechoslovakia's Communists to extend retribution in order to win legitimacy for their anti-capitalist vision of the country's future.[82] When Hungary's Communist-dominated police sought to extend the scope of internment and retribution as part of a drive to criminalize the entire inter-war regime, such steps provoked protest. In the town of Sopron members of the Smallholders' party openly compared the local internment camp, set up for alleged 'fascists', to those run in 1919 by the Soviet Republic and then in 1944 by the Gestapo.[83] Outside the highly charged political atmosphere of central and eastern Europe, where measures of judicial retribution were especially widespread they also ran up against resistance from local populations. In eastern Austria, local populations and even local authorities made up of the democratic parties opposed the internment of former National Socialists on the grounds that many were skilled craftsmen and local smallholders who were essential to the reconstruction effort in their communities.[84] The unpopularity of internment fuelled complaints in the region that only the 'little Nazis' were being punished, while those responsible for 'real' crimes went free.[85]

The limits of post-war anti-fascism were most disturbingly visible in the popular attitudes to survivors and victims of National Socialist policies of racist extermination. For Jewish survivors of Nazi extermination camps, finding public space to voice their experiences in the climate of Europe in the immediate post-war period was difficult. The dominant reaction to the knowledge of extermination seems to have been a deep-seated, enforced silence about its reality among the vast majority of Europeans. There was little appetite for any widespread 'reckoning with the past' among a population obsessed by their own physical and material security.[86] Among large sections of the population across the continent, anti-semitic attitudes persisted, which manifested themselves in isolated acts of violence against returnees, which were most marked in the tense atmosphere of central Europe in the post-war period.[87] In Kunmadaras in Hungary, as in a variety of other locations in the country, as well as in Slovakia and Poland, anti-semitism manifested itself in a limited number of open pogroms.[88] It was not only anti-semitism that stubbornly persisted into the early post-war period, but racist attitudes towards members of other groups who had been targeted by Nazi racial policy. Survivors from among Burgenland's Roma faced repressive police policies well into the 1960s, motivated and driven by popular and official hostility towards them, while both provincial and the Austrian federal authorities failed to recognize fully that they had been targets of policies of racial extermination well into the post-war period.[89]

While popular demands for a return to a sense of 'normality' placed clear limits on the politics of anti-fascism, they also drew clear boundaries around the legitimacy of occupying armies and the powers that lay behind them. This is not to say that all the victorious powers were held in equal esteem in post-war Europe, as some, particularly the United States, could help to legitimize certain post-war regimes, while others, most notably the Soviet Union, could delegitimize them. Nor were the various victorious powers viewed in the same ways in every European state. Their contribution to struggles around legitimacy was determined by a number of factors including the behaviour of occupying armies at the moment of 'liberation', but also by the perceptions of the states they represented within European societies, as well as their interaction with domestic political forces. Generally, however, their presence affected the balance of forces in politically segmented European societies.

The impact of the Red Army and the Soviet Union on the post-war struggle for legitimacy was, with the partial example of Czechoslovakia, a largely negative one. Across much of south-eastern and central Europe, the behaviour of invading Red Army troops towards civilian populations left a deep imprint on popular memory, even where such memories could not be openly expressed. Across large swathes of eastern Germany, Romania, Slovakia, Hungary and Austria, large-scale mass violence against civilian populations accompanied Soviet advance, which included, most traumatically, the mass rape of a substantial section of the female population.[90] Working-class Hungarians spoke of 'the period of fear' that followed the arrival of the Red Army in Budapest as troops raped, plundered, and arbitrarily detained large numbers of people.[91] In Austria, Germany and Hungary, the behaviour of the insurgent Red Army soldiers confirmed many of the stereotypes of the Russians as a 'barbaric' eastern other that had been carried in Nazi and fascist propaganda during the later period of the war. The conservative mayor of the eastern Austrian village of Frauenkirchen, writing some years after 'liberation', compared the first three months following the arrival of the Russians to 'the Turkish period' of the sixteenth and seventeenth centuries.[92] While in the former Soviet zone of Austria these became parts of a public memory of 'the years of occupation' between 1945 and 1955, behind the 'iron curtain' these remained part of a private memory that was hardly, if ever, recounted in the public sphere.[93]

The de-legitimating influence of the Red Army was exacerbated by the retributive policies pursued by the Soviet occupation authorities towards the populations of those states that had fought on the side of Germany. The rounding up and deportation as prisoners-of-war of nearly one in five of Transylvania's ethnic German population and the similar internment of large numbers of urban Hungarian males of working age in the months that followed the 'liberation' contributed to popular opposition not only to the Red Army itself, but to their domestic Communist allies.[94] The ways in which Soviet occupation authorities exacted reparations through dismantling industrial plant and carrying it off east provoked fury among local working-class populations across the eastern half of Germany, Austria and Hungary as they saw the basis of their livelihoods taken away from them.[95] The pursuit of such politics seriously impeded the advance of Communist parties across the region as they were frequently associated with the unpopular actions of the Red Army and the Soviet occupation authorities. They undoubtedly eroded support even among the working class for the KPD and, after 1946, the SED in the Soviet zone of Germany.[96] In Austria, Karl Renner, who served as the country's provisional Federal Chancellor prior to the first post-war elections in November 1945, correctly noted in a discussion with their leader that the perception of the Communists as 'the party of the Russians' would prove fatal for their election prospects.[97] During the first half of 1945 the hostility towards them that the behaviour of the Red Army generated, prompted Hungary's Communist leadership to write panic-stricken letters to Moscow.[98] This popular hostility forced Hungary's Communists to place distance between themselves and the Red Army and seek legitimacy through the espousal of a Left-wing version of Magyar nationalism.[99]

The continued presence of troops was seen everywhere as incompatible with the desire for a return to some semblance of political and social normality by European citizens. Not all of the victorious post-war armies were as unpopular on the territories they sought to administer as was the Red Army. In Austria on the border between the British and Soviet zones, the population found British occupation far more benign than they did Soviet occupation.[100] Yet everywhere foreign troops were seen as outsiders and the friction this could lead to generated unpopularity and frequent complaints. American troops were seen as particularly different, in part due to popular racism that was directed against African-American troops.[101] This friction was also generated by their obvious wealth relative to the troops of other countries and to local populations. In Austria the anti-communist trade union leader, Franz Olah remembered that 'the French looked really poor, similar to the Russians, or at least not much better. The same could be said of the English – the only rich ones were the Americans.'[102] Though their troops may have been unpopular, the United States enjoyed enormous prestige in many European societies, in part as a consequence of the country's wealth when Europe itself was gripped by severe hardship. This also reflected the marked popularity during the late 1940s of American popular culture among young Europeans.[103] This gave the United States considerable cultural leeway during the late 1940s when it bolstered dominant political forces in many countries throughout western Europe against their Communist opponents. The combination of the anti-socialism of majorities of European citizens, the political polarization between Communists and their more conservative opponents and the promise of US aid for societies was a potent one; a fact that was demonstrated by the 1948 election campaign in Italy, when the promise of aid was deployed by the United States in order to boost successfully the election chances of *Democrazia Cristiana* against the Left-wing alliance of Socialists and Communists.[104]

Promises of aid could be used to bolster legitimacy in part because of the parlous economic state in which Europe emerged from the war. The pressures of military conflict, which had included aerial bombardment, combined with the strains generated by several years of the widespread mobilization of economic resources in the interests of the war effort, left the continent's new rulers with a legacy of devastation. While in some parts of north-western Europe the impact of war damage and disruption to sources of supplies was relatively less than in Germany and much of central Europe,[105] right across the continent damage and material hardship were intense. Governments of various political compositions were forced to demand sacrifices in the interests of reconstruction in view of the parlous economic situation. This was as true in Hungary where the Communist Party called on workers not to strike and instead to accept severe economic hardship in the interests of reconstruction[106] as it was in Austria, where the country's second post-war Federal Chancellor Leopold Figl, told his country's citizens in December 1945 that 'we have nothing. I can only ask you to believe in this Austria.'[107]

The rhetoric of reconstruction emphasized the importance of construction and production to placing national economies back on their feet. Hungary's Communists stressed 'the battle for coal' as a central plank of the struggle to repair production, while it called on workers to 'turn their faces to the railways' in order to rebuild the shattered transport infrastructure.[108] Many were successfully mobilized behind such demands because of their expectations of a better material future that reconstruction would bring.[109] Behind such expectations lay a demand for as rapid a return to some form of economic normality as possible and in this the arena of consumption was more important to post-war citizens than production per se. This was a product of a backlash against the pervasiveness of black markets and barter that had become ubiquitous across much of continental Europe from 1942 onwards, as well as the goods shortages and hidden inflation that underpinned them.[110] Across much of Central Europe, 'liberation' was accompanied by a worsening in the material situation of households, as inflation and black-market activity spiralled, production collapsed, and rations were cut back.[111] As a consequence the economic concerns of populations tended to be centred on issues of consumption and demands that the supply of food in particular be improved. Behind the strike waves that hit Hungarian industry during the second half of 1945 lay a perception among industrial workers taking part that the state was not doing enough to defend them against the effects of food shortages and hyper-inflation that was then spiralling out of control.[112] In Austria hunger marches reflected a recentring of working-class protest around consumption, as the residents of industrial towns articulated discontent that was far more widely felt throughout local society.[113]

The deep-seated discontent that surrounded issues of consumption prompted some political actors, particularly Communists, to campaign against 'black market-eers' and 'speculators'.[114] It also prompted considerable concern with both price stability and the value of money. In Hungary, the introduction of a new currency, the Forint, and the role it played in ending the period of hyper-inflation that followed the end of the war, generated a degree of real economic stability, which allowed living standards to rise, albeit at the cost of rising unemployment.[115] In Austria it underpinned considerable popular support, even in working-class areas, for the 1947 'Law for the defence of the Schilling', which had provoked the Communists to walk out of the government. Though the controlled price rises that followed it, which were renewed through a series of Wages and Prices Agreements, provoked some discontent as the living standards of those living from fixed incomes fell, this was mitigated by a popular feeling that unrealistic wage demands would lead to higher prices and a return of the black market.[116] Similar concern with returning to a semblance of normality in the field of consumption and fear of inflation accompanied and underpinned the introduction of the Deutschmark in the western zones of Germany in June 1948.[117]

Working-class demands for greater social justice had not disappeared, as the ability of Communists in Hungary to mobilize workers against speculators and unpopular managers, or their counterparts in Austria to rally some workers against price rises in October 1950, showed.[118] Yet, by the end of the 1940s, at least in central Europe, a broad economic consensus had emerged, to which states were forced to adapt their policies. Populations demanded an end to the privations of the war years and preferred policies that concentrated on household welfare and economic stability, especially price stability. The development of this somewhat privatized, materialist consensus set the stage for a number of changes over the following decade. It underpinned the predominance of material, over ideological demands that characterized the politics of the 1950s west of the 'iron curtain'; the phenomenon identified by Burgenland's governor in 1953. Secondly, it provided an environment west of the 'iron curtain' that would be receptive to the mass consumerism that spread to even working-class households during the late 1950s.[119] Thirdly, east of the 'iron curtain' it created an environment in which socialist regimes were rejected by populations during the 1950s, on the basis that their rule was experienced in part as a continuation of the material privations of the war years. It would later create an environment that would allow regimes to recover some legitimacy by promising and securing for their populations a surrogate 'socialist consumerism'.[120]

The implications of these shifts in popular expectations of states only became clear a decade after the end of the 1940s, even though these shifts had their roots in the everyday European experience of war and of reconstruction. This was because many of these shifts were overtaken by conflicts over economic futures that were determined by the political cleavages within and between European societies. While Europeans remained at heart united about what they wanted – a higher standard of living and greater material comfort – a central theme in conflicts over legitimacy during the late 1940s was disputes over how to achieve it. Movements advancing revolutionary strategies of legitimation sought to base economic reconstruction on workerist, socialist visions of industrial productivism and wholesale social transformation.[121] With the advent of Marshall Aid after 1947 those supporting a liberal democratic strategy of legitimation that rested either on the hegemony of social democracy or centre-Right politics, were able to offer an alternative vision of a future of plenty. They also were thus able to offer a better future that underpinned a rhetoric of sacrifice deployed by political leaders; in other words a future of plenty would be bought by sacrifice today.[122] While the choices of which of these political visions would be adopted were determined by the complex interplay between international actors, political elites and the patterns of political affiliation that were woven into the fabric of national civil societies, the shift in the expectations of European citizens of politics and the state cut across lines of class, political affiliation and even across state borders. These expectations demanded a politics that centred on the immediate needs of local communities and provided them with a state that primarily built its legitimate authority through offering those communities protective measures that guaranteed their physical and material security. Yet, overwhelmed by the political polarization that accompanied the onset of the Cold War, the significance of the shifts in legitimacy was not visible as the political institutions of the post-war order were consolidated on both sides of the continent.

Though the precise nature and implications of the shifts in legitimacy may not have been immediately apparent to contemporaries or even to political leaders, they are nevertheless crucial to grasping the character and dynamic of post-war transitions. Transitions in legitimacy involved the reproduction of continuities in political cleavages within European society under circumstances of new post-war social expectations. These popular expectations rested on demands that political power be shared between rulers and ruled, that the state should focus its action on securing key demands of households and communities for security, both in the conventional sense of law and order and in the economic sense of material security. Furthermore, in the economic realm, popular expectations of the state demanded that politics pay close attention to the sphere of consumption, avoiding the occurrence of shortages of goods, black markets or of inflation. Such shifts suggested that if new political elites were to attain a degree of legitimacy for themselves then they were forced to develop a muted, more democratic and more privatized kind of politics than that which had existed in the inter-war years. Furthermore it required pragmatism about the means by which goals were to be attained. This pragmatism was most manifest in Western Europe in the ways in which political elites managed the role of the nation-state. While post-war political orders rested on the cultural hegemony of a democratic patriotism, the policies that national governments needed to pursue to build their legitimacy rested on the recognition of the limits of national sovereignty. Thus, in Western Europe, co-operation with the foreign and security policies of the United States guaranteed access to economic aid, while the development of transnational economic spaces guaranteed firstly by bodies such as the European Coal and Steel Community and then, after 1957, the European Economic Community, were manifestations of the ways in which the politics of post-war legitimacy affected the international dimensions of the post-war settlement.

The reproduction of continuities in political affiliation ensured that politics in the second half of the 1940s was characterized by a dynamic of restoration and renewal. A thoroughly modernized Right emerged in much of western and central Europe, yet majorities in most of Europe's states remained decisively anti-socialist. Visible class divisions persisted and the survival of working-class cultures ensured that the labour movement would play a crucial role in post-war European politics. Yet, its minority position in most states, outside Scandinavia, meant that it was either marginalized or only able to take power through building dictatorship. The patterns of polarization between Left and Right that tore apart political orders in inter-war Europe took new forms in the more muted, democratic climate of post-war Europe, becoming internationalized with the onset of the Cold War.

The patterns of transitions in legitimacy that characterized the immediate post-war years shaped the development of post-war orders on both sides of the 'iron curtain' in the four decades down to 1989. In much of Western Europe they enabled the consolidation of individualist, materialist democracies that provided a fertile environment for the burgeoning middle-class consumerism of the miracle years of the later 1950s, when the post-war boom transformed European economies. The clear success of this post-war political settlement laid the foundations for its export as an institutional model to southern Europe during the 1970s, and eventually central and eastern Europe at the end of the 1980s – even after the constellation of institutional, international and cultural factors that underpinned its successful consolidation in the 1950s had disappeared. In the eastern half of the continent, after the crises of the mid-1950s, socialist states reinforced their authority by accommodating the materialist sentiments of the populations they ruled. Beneath the surface of politics in central and eastern Europe's dictatorships, the political cleavages that had been prominent during the years of transition that followed the Second World War remained, to re-emerge and structure politics across the continent after 1989.

Notes

1. Burgenländisches Landesarchiv (Burgenland Provincial Archive, hereafter BgLA) Archiv der Landesregierung seit 1945, Sicherheitsdirektion für Burgenland (Archive of the post-1945 provincial government, Papers of the Burgenland Security Directorate, hereafter A/VIII) A/VIII-14/II-3; Brief, d.Hptm.u.Ld. Parteiobermann Dr Lorenz Karall, Wien, den 25.11.1953.
2. I have used 'social democracy' as a synonym for the post-war non-Communist Left, which referred to itself as often as 'socialist' as it did 'social democratic'.
3. The inter-war Social Democrats were reconstructed as the *Sozialistische Partei Österreichs* (Socialist Party of Austria, or SPÖ), while the Christian Socials re-emerged as the *Österreichische Volkspartei* (Austrian Peoples' Party, or ÖVP).
4. 'Karall, Lorenz Dr' in G. Schlag (ed.) *Burgenland: Geschichte, Kultur und Wirtschaft in Biographen. XX. Jahrhundert* (Eisenstadt, 1991), pp. 142–3; R. Widder 'Volkspartei im Burgenland' in R. Kriechbaumer and F. Schausberger (eds) *Volkspartei – Anspruch und Realität: Zur Geschichte der ÖVP seit 1945* (Vienna, Cologne and Weimar, 1995), pp. 489–526.
5. For the 1945 elections in one western Hungarian town see 'Döntő fölénnyel győzött a Kisgazda Párt', *Soproni Újság* (5 November, 1945), 1–3; for the 1947 elections see *Soproni Újság* (2 September, 1947), 1; for church processions as a focus of popular protest in the region see Győr-Moson-Sopron Megyei Győri Levéltár (Győr City Branch of the Győr-Moson-Sopron County Archive, hereafter GyMSMGyL.) Magyar Dolgozók Pártja Győr-Moson-Sopron Megyei Bizottság iratai (Papers of the Győr-Moson-Sopron County Committee of the Hungarian Workers' Party, hereafter X fond. 402)/2/Agitprop/32ö.e.; Jelentés. Győr, 1953. április 6-án.
6. For the material roots of popular discontent in 1950s Hungary, see M. Pittaway 'Retreat from Collective Protest: Household, Gender, Work and Popular Opposition in Stalinist Hungary' in J. Kok (ed.) *Rebellious Families: Household Strategies and Collective Action in the Nineteenth and Twentieth Centuries* (New York and Oxford, 2002), pp. 199–229.

7. T. Judt *Postwar: A History of Europe since 1945*, (London, 2005), pp. 13–164; J.E. Cronin *The World the Cold War Made: Order, Chaos and the Return of History* (New York and London, 1996), especially Chapter 2; W.I. Hitchcock *The Struggle for Europe: A History of the Continent since 1945* (London, 2003); D. Reynolds (ed.) *The Origins of the Cold War in Europe: International Perspectives* (New Haven and London, 1994); M.P. Leffler and D.S. Painter (eds) *Origins of the Cold War: An International History* (New York and London, 2nd edn, 2005).

8. For excellent attempts to do just this see the essays in R. Bessel and D. Schumann (eds) *Life After Death: Approaches to a Cultural and Social History of Europe during the 1940s and 1950s* (Washington DC and Cambridge, 2003); see also P. Lagrou *The Legacy of Nazi Occupation: Patriotic Memory and National Recovery in Western Europe, 1945–1965* (Cambridge and New York, 2000).

9. For a stimulating attempt to explore the potential of this approach for north- and central-western Europe see M. Conway 'The Rise and Fall of Europe's Democratic Age, 1945–1973', *Contemporary European History*, XIII (2004), 67–88.

10. This point is well made in relation to Belgium, France and the Netherlands, see P. Lagrou, *The Legacy of Nazi Occupation*, pp. 1–18.

11. J. Steinberg *Why Switzerland?* (Cambridge and New York, 2nd edn 1996), pp. 65–72.

12. N. Elvander 'State Intervention and Economic Freedom' in E. Allart et al. (eds) *Nordic Democracy: Ideas, Issues and Institutions in Denmark, Finland, Iceland, Norway and Sweden* (Copenhagen, 1981), pp. 280–2; J. Fulcher 'Sweden' in S. Berger and D. Broughton (eds) *The Force of Labour: the Western European Labour Movement and the Working Class in the Twentieth Century* (Oxford and New York, 1995), pp. 7–38; K. Samuelsson, *From Great Power to Welfare State: 300 Years of Swedish Social Development* (London, 1968), pp. 241–8.

13. H. Patterson *Ireland since 1939* (Oxford and New York, 2002), pp. 51–115.

14. K.O. Morgan *The People's Peace: British History, 1945–1990* (Oxford and New York, 1990), pp. 3–70.

15. H.F. Dahl 'Behind the Fronts: Norway', *Journal of Contemporary History*, V (1970), 47–9.

16. P. Romijn 'Niederlande – "Synthese", Säuberung und Integration' in U. Herbert and A. Schildt (eds) *Kriegsende in Europa; vom Beginn des deutschen Machtzerfalls bis zur Stabilisierung der Nachkriegsordnung 1944–1948* (Essen, 1998), pp. 223–4.

17. N. Wouters 'New order and good government: municipal administration in Belgium (1938–1946)', *Contemporary European History* XIII (2004), 405–7; M. Conway 'Belgium's Mid-Twentieth Century Crisis: Crisis of a Nation-State?' *Revue belge d'histoire contemporaine* XXXV (2005), 573–96.

18. C.S. Lilly *Power and Persuasion: Ideology and Rhetoric in Communist Yugoslavia 1944–1953* (Boulder CO and Oxford, 2001); A.B. Wachtel *Making a Nation, Breaking a Nation: Literature and Cultural Politics in Yugoslavia* (Stanford CA, 1998).

19. M. Vickers *Albania: A Modern History* (London, 1999).

20. V. Dimitrov 'Revolutions Released: Stalin, the Bulgarian Communist Party, and the Establishment of the Cominform', in F. Gori and S. Pons (eds) *The Soviet Union and Europe in the Cold War, 1945–1953* (Basingstoke, 1996), pp. 272–89.

21. K. Hitchins *Rumania 1866–1947* (New York and Oxford, 1994); G. Hunya (ed.) *România 1944–1990: Gazdaság- és Politikatörténete* (Budapest, 1990); T. Kunze *Nicolae Ceauşescu: o biografie*, trans. Alexandru Teodorescu (Bucharest, 2002), pp. 68–111; A.J. Rieber 'The Crack in the Plaster: Crisis in Romania and the Origins of the Cold War', *The Journal of Modern History*, LXXVI (2004), 62–106.

22. M. Mazower *Inside Hitler's Greece: The Experience of Occupation, 1941–44* (New Haven and London, 1993); M. Mazower (ed.) *After the War Was Over: Reconstructing the Family, Nation and State in Greece, 1943–1960* (Princeton and London, 2000); J.S. Koliopoulos *Plundered Loyalties: World War II and Civil War in Greek West Macedonia* (New York, 1999).

23. M. Richards *A Time of Silence: Civil War and the Culture of Repression in Franco's Spain, 1936–1945* (Cambridge and New York, 1998); M. Richards '"Terror and Progress": Industrialization, Modernity and the Making of Francoism' in H. Graham and J. Labanyi (eds) *Spanish Cultural Studies: An Introduction* (Oxford and New York, 1995), pp. 173–82; A. Cennarro 'Elite, Party, Church: Pillars of the Francoist "New State" in Aragon, 1936–1945', *European History Quarterly*, XXVIII (1998), 461–86.

24. A. Costa Pinto *Salazar's Dictatorship and European Fascism: Problems of Interpretation*, (Boulder CO, 1995), pp. 147–208.

25. For a history of post-war Czechoslovakia that treats the Slovak and Czech parts of the state as distinctive entities, see M. Myant *Socialism and Democracy in Czechoslovakia, 1945–1948* (Cambridge and New York, 1981); for Hungary, see M. Pittaway 'The Politics of Legitimacy and Hungary's Postwar Transition', *Contemporary European History* XIII (2004), 453–75.

26. J. Echternkamp *Nach dem Krieg. Alltagsnot, Neuorientierung und die Last der Vergangenheit 1945–1949* (Zurich, 2003), pp. 111–32; G. Pritchard, *The Making of the GDR 1945–53: From Antifascism to Stalinism* (Manchester and New York, 2000).

27. On the Communists in post-war eastern Austria, see H. Chmelar 'Partei ohne Chance. Die KPÖ im Burgenland 1945/46' in J. Seedoch (ed.) *Beiträge zur Landeskunde der burgenländisch-westungarischen Raumes. Festschrift für Harald Prickler zum 60. Geburtstag* (Eisenstadt, 1994), pp. 50–68.

28. O. Jussila, S. Hentilä and J. Nevakivi *From Grand Duchy to Modern State: A Political History of Finland since 1809*, translated by D. and E.-K. Arter, (London, 1999), pp. 217–51.

29. J. Coutovidis and J. Reynolds *Poland 1939–1947* (Leicester, 1987).

30. B.F. Abrams *The Struggle for the Soul of the Nation: Czech Culture and the Rise of Communism* (Lanham MD, 2004); B. Frommer *National Cleansing: Retribution against Nazi Collaborators in Postwar Czechoslovakia* (Cambridge and New York, 2004).

31. P. Ginsborg *A History of Contemporary Italy, 1943–1988* (Harmondsworth, 1990), pp. 39–185; F. Hausmann *Kleine Geschichte Italiens von 1945 bis Berlusconi* (Berlin, 2002), pp. 11–43.

32. R. Gildea, *France since 1945* (Oxford and New York, 2002), pp. 35–64; A. Shennan, *Rethinking France: Plans for Renewal 1940–1946*, (Oxford, 1989); R. Vinen *Bourgeois Politics in France, 1945–1951* (Cambridge and New York, 1995).

33. See F. Weber 'Die Angst der Parteiführung vorm Klassenkampf. Die SPÖ 1945–1950' in P. Pelinka and G. Steger (eds) *Auf dem Weg zur Staatspartei. Zur Geschichte und Politik der SPÖ seit 1945* (Vienna, 1988), pp. 16–17.

34. Quoted in M. Pittaway 'The Politics of Legitimacy and Hungary's Postwar Transition', 461.

35. See the overview of fraudulent post-war elections in M. Pittaway *Eastern Europe, 1939–2000* (London, 2004), pp. 47–8.

36. Niederösterreichisches Landesarchiv St Pölten (Archives of the Province of Lower Austria, hereafter NÖLA), Gau Niederdonau, Ia-10/B.nm.208/Karton 63 Lageberichte 1945; Der Landrat des Kreises Eisenstadt, Zl.Präs65-1945. Betrifft: Lagebericht für den Monat Jänner 1945.

37. See P. Romijn 'Niederlande – 'Synthese', Säuberung und Integration'; N. Wouters 'New Order and Good Government: Municipal Administration in Belgium'; D. Peschanski 'Legitimacy/Legitimation/Delegitimation: France in the Dark Years, a textbook case', *Contemporary European History* XIII (2004), 409–23; H.-F. Dahl *Quisling: A Study in Treachery*, trans. A.-M. Stanton-Ife (Cambridge and New York, 1999).

38. See the language which Hungary's local non-Communist (in this case social democratic) press used to protest at the expulsion of local ethnic Germans – 'Akiket elvittek, és akik itt maradtak', *Mosonmagyaróvári Bárátság* (2 June, 1946), p. 2.

39. M. Pittaway 'Industrial Workers, Socialist Industrialization and the State in Hungary, 1948–1958' (PhD. thesis, University of Liverpool, 1998), pp. 325–53.

40. BgLA A/VIII-14/I-2; Bezirkshauptmannschaft Oberpullendorf. Zahl: Pr.-244/19. Oberpullendorf, am 30 Sept.1947. Lagebericht für September 1947.

41. GyMSMGy.L.X. fond402/PTO/20ö.e.; Győr, 1949 óprilis 26. Jelentés.
42. BgLA A/VIII-11/VI; Gemeindeamt Deutsch-Jahrndorf. Deutsch-Jahrndorf, am 12. Juli 1960. Zl:207/1960. Betr.: Ereignisse 1945–1956, Bericht.
43. BgLA A/VIII-14/V-1; Landesgendarmeriekommando für das Burgenland. Situationsbericht für die Zeit vom 1. bis 30. Juni 1946. Eisenstadt, am 1. Juli 1946.
44. For such complaints in the western Hungarian town of Sopron, see 'Komoly munka folyik a városházán', *Soproni Újság* (14 October, 1945), p. 4.
45. In some places, like the eastern Austrian village of Frauenkirchen, this led to violence between local Communists and the gendarmerie, see BgLA Bezirkshauptmannchaft Neusiedl am See (Office of District Commissioner Neusiedl am See) Verschiedenes XI–1945; Gendarmerieabteilungskommando Eisenstadt Nr.1, E. Nr.224. Frauenkirchen, Posten, Uberfall auf desselben. An das Landesgendarmeriekommando f.d. Brgld. Neusiedl a. See, 21.Okt. 1945.
46. D. Roksandic 'Shifting References: Celebrations of Uprisings in Croatia, 1945–1991', *East European Politics and Societies* IX (1999), 256–71.
47. See D. Sassoon 'Italy after Fascism: the Predicament of Dominant Narratives' in R. Bessel and D. Schumann (eds) *Life After Death*, pp. 259–90.
48. For Hungary, see M. Mevius, *Agents of Moscow: The Hungarian Communist Party and the Origins of Socialist Patriotism 1941–1953* (Oxford, 2005).
49. See F. Radó 'Két magyar fiu kálvárias utja a szlovak deportálás elől-Sopronig', *Soproni Újság* (25 February, 1947), 2.
50. For a good example of this see *Burgenländische Freiheit* (27 October 1946), 1.
51. M. Conway 'Belgium's Mid-Twentieth Century Crisis', 576–9.
52. See the figures in G. Fábian and I. László Kovács *Parlamenti Választások az Európai Unió Országaiban (1945–2002)* (Budapest, 2004), p. 372.
53. F. Gazdag 'A Mouvement Républicane Populaire (1944–1958): Ideológia és gyakorlat a francia MRP politikájaban' in J. Gergely (ed.) *A Keresztény-Demokrácia Nyugat-Európában 1944–1958* (Budapest, 1980), pp. 153–211.
54. See W.C. Miller, F. Plasser and P.A. Ulram 'Wähler und Mitglieder der ÖVP, 1945–1994' in R. Kriechbaumer and F. Schausberger (eds) *Volkspartei – Anspruch und Realität*, pp. 163–4; J. Horváth 'A Democrazia Cristiana' in J. Gergely (ed.) *A Keresztény-Demokrácia Nyugat-Európában*, pp. 104–5; W. Becker 'Die CDU im demokratischen Neubeginn 1945/46: Motive der Gründung und parteipolitischer Standort' in G. Rüther (ed.) *Geschichte der christlich-demokratischen und christlich-sozialen Bewegungen in Deutschland* Vol. 1 (Bonn, 1984), pp. 333–60.
55. This is to disagree with those who argue that the pressures of war smashed the traditions of protest of the industrial working class. For this position, see M. Conway 'The Rise and Fall of Europe's Democratic Age, 1945–1973', pp. 79–80; F. Weber 'Die Angst der Parteiführung vorm Klassenkampf', pp.11; K.-D. Mulley 'Der Österreichische Gewerkschaftsbund 1945–1959'

in W. Maderthaner (ed.) *Auf dem Weg zur Macht. Integration in den Staat, Sozialpartnerschaft und Regierungspartei* (Vienna, 1992), p. 79.

56. This is powerfully suggested by much of the work on the social history of work in central and eastern Europe, see M. Pittaway 'The Reproduction of Hierarchy: Skill, Working-Class Culture and the State in Early Socialist Hungary', *The Journal of Modern History* LXXIV (2002), 737–69; P. Heumos 'Aspekte des Sozialen Millieus der Industriearbeiterschaft in der Tscheslowakei vom Ende des Zweiten Weltkriegs bis zur Reformbewegung der Sechziger Jahre', *Bohemia* XLII (2001) 323–62; H. Stadtland *Herrschaft nach Plan und Macht der Gewohnheit: Sozialgeschichte der Gewerkschaften in der SBZ/DDR 1945– 1953* (Essen, 2001).

57. BgLA Bezirkshauptmannschaft Mattersburg (District Commissioner, Mattersburg, hereafter BH Mattersburg) XI-1948-1950-Situationsberichten; Gendarmerieposten Neudörfl.

58. Politikatörténeti és Szakszervezeti Levéltár (Archive of Political History and of Trade Unions, hereafter PtSzL) SZKL Szaktanács/16d./1946; Felsőgalla-Ujtelep Bányamunkások Szakszervezetétol a MÁK Kózponti Igazagtóságnak, Felsogalla-Újtelep, 1946.III.5.

59. For Romania, see A.J. Rieber 'The Crack in the Plaster'; for Hungary, see M. Pittaway 'The Politics of Legitimacy'.

60. S. Rokkan 'The Growth and Structuring of Mass Politics' in E. Allart et al. (eds) *Nordic Democracy*, pp. 53–79.

61. F. Weber "Die Angst der Parteiführung vorm Klassenkampf'; K.-D. Mulley 'Der Österreichische Gewerkschaftsbund.'

62. J. Echternkamp *Nach dem Krieg*, pp. 115–20.

63. On the social and political underpinning of the grand coalition, see E. Hanisch *Der Lange Schatten des Staates. Österreichische Gesellschaftsgeschichte im 20. Jahrhundert* (Vienna, 1994), pp. 402–20.

64. For example, P. Romijn 'Niederlande 'Synthese', Säuberung und Integration.'

65. P. Ginsborg *A History of Contemporary Italy*, p. 99.

66. D. Peschanski 'Legitimacy/Legitimation/Delegitimation'.

67. P.-M. de La Gorce *Naissance de la France Moderne* Vol. 1 *L'Après Guerre* (Paris, 1978), pp. 381–407.

68. BgLA BH Neusiedl am See, XI-N-A-Zeugnisse von Registrieten des Bezirkes, 1938–1948.

69. H. Woller *Die Abrechnung mit den Faschismus in Italien 1945 bis 1948* (Munich, 1996), p. 280.

70. E. Glassheim 'National Mythologies and Ethnic Cleansing: The Expulsion of Czechoslovak Germans in 1945' *Central European History* 33 (2000), 475–7.

71. L. Niethammer 'Alliierte Internierungslager in Deutschland nach 1945. Vergleich und offene Fragen' in C. Jansen (ed.) *Von der Aufgabe der Freiheit. Politische Verantwortung und bürgerliche Gesellschaft im 19 und 20 Jahrhundert* (Berlin,

1995), pp. 469–92; R. Knight 'Denazification and Intergration in the Austrian Province of Carinthia', *The Journal of Modern History*, LXXIX (2007) especially 592–603.

72. D. Peschanski 'Legitimacy/Legitimation/Delegitimation', 422.
73. H.F. Dahl 'Dealing with the Past in Scandinavia: Legal purges and popular memories of Nazism and World War II in Denmark and Norway after 1945' in J. Elster (ed.) *Retribution and Reparation in the Transition to Democracy* (Cambridge and New York, 2005), pp. 9ff.
74. B. Frommer 'Retribution against Nazi Collaborators in Post-War Czechoslovakia' (PhD. Thesis, Harvard University, 1999), p. 2.
75. For central and eastern Europe, see the brief overview in M. Pittaway *Eastern Europe*, pp. 39–43; B. Frommer 'Retribution against Nazi Collaborators in Post-War Czechoslovakia'; I. Deák 'Political Justice in Austria and Hungary after World War II', Paper presented at the Mellon Seminar on Transitional Justice, Columbia University, May 1999.
76. M. Richards, *A Time of Silence*, pp. 26–46.
77. See the essays in M. Mazower (ed.) *After the War Was Over*.
78. D. Peschanski 'Legitimacy/Legitimation/Delegitimation', 422.
79. P. Romijn 'Niederlande – "Synthese", Säuberung und Integration', pp. 220–1.
80. M. Conway 'Justice in Post-war Belgium: Popular Pressures and Political Realities' in I. Deak, J. Gross and T. Judt (eds) *The Politics of Retribution in Europe* (Princeton, 2000), pp. 133–56.
81. H.F. Dahl 'Dealing with the Past in Scandinavia', pp. 1ff.; J. Elster *Closing the Books: Transitional Justice in Historical Perspective* (Cambridge and New York, 2004), Chapter 8.
82. B. Frommer 'Retribution as Legitimation: The Uses of Political Justice in Postwar Czechoslovakia' *Contemporary European History* 13 (2004), 477–92.
83. 'A soproni internáló-tábor szörnyűségei a kőzigazgatási bizottság előtt', *Soproni Újság* (17 November, 1945), pp. 1–2.
84. BgLA BH Neusiedl am See XI-125/45; Stadtgemeinde Neusiedl am See. Zl.667. Neusiedl am See, am 9. Mai 1946.
85. BgLA BH Neusiedl am See XI-125/45; Bezirkshauptmannschaft Neusiedl a.See. Zahl:XI-125/1. Neusiedl am See, 14.2.1946.
86. P. Lagrou 'Victims of Genocide and National Memory: Belgium, France and the Netherlands, 1945–1965' *Past and Present* No. 154 (1997), 181–222; M. Brenner *After the Holocaust: Rebuilding Jewish Lives in Postwar Germany* translated by Barbara Harshav (Princeton, 1997); K.H. Adler, *Jews and Gender in Liberation France* (Cambridge and New York, 2003).
87. H.P. Wassermann, *Naziland Österreich!? Studien zu Antisemitismus, Nation und Nationalsozialismus in öffentlichen Meinungsbild*, (Innsbruck, 2002), pp. 11–79.

88. For events in Kunmadaras, see P. Apor, 'A népi demokrácia építése. Kunmadaras 1946', *Századok* CXXXII (1998), 601–32.
89. G. Baumgartner, and F. Freund *Die Burgenland Roma, 1945–2000* (Eisenstadt, 2004), pp. 56–85.
90. For this see N. Naimark *The Russians in Germany, 1945–1949* (Harvard, 1997), pp. 69–140; A. Pető 'Memory and the Narrative of Rape in Budapest and Vienna in 1945' in R. Bessel and D. Schumann (eds) *Life After Death*, pp. 129–48.
91. 1956-os Intézet Oral History Archivium (1956 Institute Oral History Archive, hereafter OHA), 181 – Péterffy Miklós, p. 57.
92. BgLA A/VIII-11/V; Gross- und Marktgemeinde Frauenkirchen. Zl. 190/1/1960. Frauenkirchen, am 4. Jänner 1961. Bericht über die Ereignisse von 1945 bis 1956.
93. This point is made forcefully in A. Pető 'Memory and the Narrative of Rape in Budapest and Vienna in 1945'.
94. For Transylvania see P. Biddiscombe 'Prodding the Russian Bear: Pro-German Resistance in Romania, 1944–5' *European History Quarterly* XXIII (1993), 210–1; for Hungary, see M. Pittaway 'The Politics of Legitimacy and Hungary's Postwar Transition', 11.
95. For eastern Germany, see N. Naimark *The Russians in Germany*, pp. 166–70; for Austria, see O. Klambauer *Der Kalte Krieg in Österreich. Vom Dritten Mann zum Fall des Eisernen Vorhangs* (Vienna, 2000), pp. 24–30; for Hungary, see M. Pittaway 'Workers in Hungary' in E. Breuning, J. Lewis and G. Pritchard (eds) *Power and the People. A Social History of Central European Politics, 1945–56* (Manchester and New York, 2005), pp. 57–75.
96. N. Naimark *The Russians in Germany*, pp. 251–317.
97. E. Fischer *Das Ende einer Illusion: Errinerungen 1945–1955* (Vienna, 1973), p. 82.
98. L. Izsák and M. Kun (eds) *Moszkvának Jelentjük... Titkos dokumentumok 1944–1948*, (Budapest, 1994).
99. M. Pittaway 'The Politics of Legitimacy and Hungary's Postwar Transition', 461–2.
100. BgLA A/VIII-14/II-1; Bezirkshauptmannschaft Oberpullendorf. Oberpullendorf, am 30. Oktober 1947. Zahl: Pr.-244/22. Lagebericht für den Monat Oktober 1947.
101. Re. Belgium, see the contemporary reports in 'Rapport aux parents, épouses et fiancées' *Le Peuple* (18 September 1945), 1 and 'La grève des cafés', *Vers l'Avenir* (24 Aug. 1945), 1.
102. Quoted in O. Klambauer *Der Kalte Krieg in Österreich*, p. 22.
103. U.G. Poiger *Jazz, Rock and Rebels: Cold War Politics and American Culture in a Divided Germany* (Berkeley, London and Los Angeles, 2000);

R. Wagnleitner *Coca-Colonization and the Cold War: The Cultural Mission of the United States in Austria after the Second World War* (Chapel Hill NC and London, 1994).

104. P. Ginsborg, *A History of Contemporary Italy*, pp. 115–18.
105. For Germany, see J. Echternkamp *Nach dem Krieg*, pp. 15–73; for Hungary, see M. Pittaway 'The Politics of Legitimacy and Hungary's Postwar Transition', 457–61.
106. I. Kovács, 'A Nagyüzemi kommunista pártszervezet munkájáról és zeladatairól', *Pártmunka* (15 August 1945), p. 108.
107. Quoted in E. Hanisch *Der Lange Schatten des Staats*, p. 408.
108. M. Pittaway '"The Unlucky Worker Who Waits for the Building of the Country Goes Hungry": Workers, Politics and Reconstruction in Hungary, 1945–6' (mss., 1995).
109. E. Severini, *Munkaverseny és a Magyar Munkás Lelkisége: MáVAG és a Csepeli WM Müvek*, (Budapest, 1946).
110. J. Echternkamp *Nach dem Krieg*; for Austria, see the documents in NÖLA Ia–10; for Hungary, see M. Pittaway 'The Politics of Legitimacy'.
111. For the desperate situation in eastern Austria in 1945 and 1946, see R. Sandgruber 'Der Lebenstandard in der ersten Nachkriegszeit' in S. Karner (ed.) *Das Burgenland im Jahr 1945* (Eisenstadt, 1985), pp. 199–217.
112. M. Pittaway 'The Politics of Legitimacy and Hungary's Postwar Transition', 469–70.
113. BgLA BH Mattersburg XI-1945-1946-1947-Situationsberichten; Bezirkshauptmannschaft Mattersburg. Situationsbericht für Juni 1947.
114. For Hungary, see M. Pittaway 'The Politics of Legitimacy and Hungary's Postwar Transition', 470–2; for Czechoslovakia, see Public Records Office (PRO) FO 371/71264; 'Czechoslovakia: Weekly Information Summary, 20 February–3 March 1948'.
115. M. Pittaway 'The Politics of Legitimacy and Hungary's Postwar Transition'.
116. For a fairly representative account of the kinds of attitudes to economic circumstances, see BgLA A/VIII-14/II-2; Bezirkshauptmannschaft Oberpullendorf. Zahl: Präs.106/7-1949. Oberpullendorf, am 29.11.1949. Situationsbericht für den Monat November 1949.
117. J. Echternkamp *Nach dem Krieg*, p. 102.
118. On Hungary, see M. Pittaway 'The Politics of Legitimacy'; for Austria, see J. Lewis 'Austria 1950: Strikes, "Putsch" and their Political Context', *European History Quarterly* XXX (2000), 533–52.
119. M. Wildt *Auf kleinen Wohlstand: Eine Komsumgeschichte der fünfziger Jahre* (Frankfurt am Main, 1996).
120. These themes are explored in M. Pittaway *Eastern Europe*, pp. 109–31; see also S.E. Reid and D. Crowley (eds) *Style and Socialism: Modernity and Material Culture in Post-war Eastern Europe* (Oxford and New York, 2000).

121. Some of these visions and how they failed are analysed in M. Pittaway 'Retreat from Collective Protest', pp. 199–229.
122. For a stimulating analysis of how this worked in the Austrian case, see K.-D. Mulley 'Wo ist das Proletariat?' in Gerhard Jagschitz and K.-D. Mulley (eds) *Die 'Wilden' Fünfziger Jahre: Gesellschaft, Formen und Gefühle eines Jahrzehnts in Österreich* (St Pölten and Vienna, 1985), pp. 20–8.

Bibliography

Abrams, B.F., *The Struggle for the Soul of the Nation: Czech Culture and the Rise of Communism* (Lanham MD, 2004).

Added, S., 'Jacques Copeau and Popular Theatre in Vichy France', in G. Berghaus (ed.) *Fascism and Theatre: comparative studies on the aesthetics and politics of performance in Europe, 1925–1945* (Providence and Oxford, 1996).

Adler, K.H., *Jews and Gender in Liberation France* (Cambridge and New York, 2003).

Allum, P.A., *Politics and Society in Post-war Naples* (Cambridge, 1973).

Aly, G., *'Final Solution'. Nazi Population Policy and the Murder of the European Jews* (London, 1999).

Aly, G., *Hitler's Volksstaat. Raub, Rassenkrieg und nationaler Sozialismus* (Frankfurt a/M., 2005).

Anderson, B., *Imagined Communities. Reflections on the Origin and Spread of Nationalism,* revised edition, (London and New York, 1991).

Anderson, M., *Practicing Democracy. Elections and Political Culture in Imperial Germany* (Princeton, 2000).

Apor, P., 'A népi demokrácia építése. Kunmadaras 1946', *Századok* CXXXII (1998).

Arendt, H., *Über die Revolution* 4th edition (Munich, 2000).

Aron, R., *The Dawn of Universal History* (New York, 2002).

Aschenbrenner, S., 'The Civil War from the Perspective of a Messenian Village' in L. Bærentzen, J. Iatrides and O. Smith (eds) *Studies in the History of the Greek Civil War 1945–1949* (Copenhagen, 1987).

Ayçoberry, P., *The Social History of the Third Reich, 1933–1945* (New York, 1999).

Bähr, J., and Banken, R., (eds) *Das Europa des „Dritten Reichs" Recht, Wirtschaft, Besatzung* (Frankfurt a/M., 2005).

Balfour, S., *Dictatorship, Workers, and the City: Labour in Greater Barcelona since 1936* (Oxford, 1989).

Barker, R., *Legitimating Identities: The Self-Representation of Rulers and Subjects* (Cambridge, 2001).

Barnes, T., 'The Secret Cold War: The CIA and American Foreign Policy in Europe 1946–1956', *The Historical Journal* XXIV (1981) and XXV (1982).

Barnouw, D., 'Dutch exiles in London' in M. Conway and J. Gotovitch (eds) *Europe in Exile. European Exile Communities in Britain 1940–45* (New York and Oxford, 2001).

Baumgartner, G., and Freund, F., *Die Burgenland Roma, 1945–2000*, (Eisenstadt, 2004).

Becker, W., 'Die CDU im demokratischen Neubeginn 1945/46: Motive der Gründung und parteipolitischer Standort' in G. Rüther (ed.) *Geschichte der christlich-demokratischen und christlich-sozialen Bewegungen in Deutschland*, Vol.1 (Bonn, 1984).

Beetham, D., *The Legitimation of Power* (Basingstoke, 1991).

Beetham, D., 'The idea of democratic audit in comparative perspective', *Parliamentary Affairs* LII (1999).

Behan, T., *The Long-Awaited Moment. The Working Class and the Italian Communist Party in Milan, 1943–1948* (New York, 1997).

Ben-Ghiat, R., 'Envisioning Modernity. Desire and Discipline in the Italian Fascist Film', *Critical Inquiry* XXIII (1996).

Ben-Ghiat, R., *Fascist Modernities. Italy, 1922–1945,* 2nd edition (London, 2004).

Berger, P., 'The Austrian Economy, 1918–1938' in J. Komlos (ed.) *Economic Development in the Habsburg Monarchy and in the Successor States* (New York, 1990).

Berkhoff, K., *Harvest of Despair. Life and Death in Ukraine under Nazi Rule* (Cambridge MA, 2004).

Bessel, R., and Schumann, D., (eds) *Life after Death. Approaches to a Cultural and Social History of Europe during the 1940s and 1950s* (Washington DC, 2003).

Best, W., *Die deutsche Aufsichtsverwaltungen in Frankreich, Belgien, die Niederlande, Dänemark und im Protektorat Böhmen und Mähren* (Paris, 1941).

Biddiscombe, P., 'Prodding the Russian Bear: Pro-German Resistance in Romania, 1944–5', *European History Quarterly* XXIII (1993).

Bokovoy, M., 'Croatia' in K. Passmore (ed.) *Women, Gender and Fascism in Europe, 1919–45* (Manchester, 2003).

Bosworth, R.J.B., *The Italian Dictatorship: Problems and Perspectives in the Interpretation of Mussolini and Fascism* (London, 1998).

Bourricaud, F., 'Legitimacy and Legitimation', *Current Sociology* XXXV (1987).

Boyd, C., *Historia Patria: Politics, History and National Identity in Spain, 1875–1975* (Princeton, 1997).

Böll, H., *The Train was on Time* (republished Evanston IL, 1994).

Braddick, M.J., and Walter, J., 'Introduction. Grids of Power: Order, Hierarchy and Submission in Early Modern Society' in M.J. Braddick and J. Walter (eds) *Negotiating Power in Early Modern Society. Order, Hierarchy and Submission in Britain and Ireland* (Cambridge, 2001).

Brandes, D., *Die Tschechen unter deutschem Protektorat. Part 1 Besatzungspoltik, Kollaboration und Widerstand im Protektorat Böhmen und Mähren bis Heydrichs Tod (1939–1942)* (Munich, 1969).

Brenner, M., *After the Holocaust: Rebuilding Jewish Lives in Postwar Germany* (Princeton, 1997).

Bresadola, G., 'The Legitimising Strategies of the Nazi Administration in Northern Italy: Propaganda in the *Adriatisches Küstenland*', *Contemporary European History* XIII (2004).

Brown, M.P., 'The Possibility of Local Autonomy' *Urban Geography* XIII (1993).

Browning, C. (with a contribution by Matthäus, J.) *The Origins of the Final Solution. The Evolution of Nazi Jewish Policy 1939–1942* (London, 2005).

Buchanan, T., and Conway, M., (eds) Special Issue on 'Democracy in Twentieth-Century Europe', *European History Quarterly* XXXII (2002).

Burleigh, M., and Wippermann, W., *The Racial State: Germany 1933–1945* (Cambridge, 1991).

Burrin, P., *La France à l'heure allemande, 1940–1944* (Paris, 1995).

Caldwell, L., 'Reproducers of the Nation: Women and the Family in Fascist Policy,' in D. Forgacs (ed.) *Rethinking Italian Fascism. Capitalism, Populism and Culture* (London, 1986).

Camarero-Núñez, T., *Mi nombre nuevo 'Magnificat': Mª del Pilar Lamamié de Clairac y Alonso* (Madrid, 1960).

Carabott, P., and Sfikas, T., (eds) *The Greek Civil War. Essays on a Conflict of Exceptionalism and Silences* (Aldershot and Burlington VT, 2004).

Carter, E., *Dietrich's Ghosts. The Sublime and the Beautiful in Third Reich Film* (London, 2004).

Casanova, J., *Anarquismo y revolución en la sociedad rural aragonesa 1936–1938* (Madrid, 1985).

Cennarro, A., 'Elite, Party, Church: Pillars of the Francoist "New State" in Aragon, 1936–1945', *European History Quarterly* XXVIII (1998).

Chiari, B., 'Has there been a People's War? The History of the Second World War in Belarus, 60 years after the surrender of the Third Reich' in B. De Wever, H. van Goethem and N. Wouters (eds) *Local Government in Occupied Europe (1939–1945)* (Gent, 2005).

Chmelar, H., 'Partei ohne Chance. Die KPÖ im Burgenland 1945/46' in J. Seedoch (ed.) *Beiträge zur Landeskunde der burgenländisch-westungarischen Raumes. Festschrift für Harald Prickler zum 60. Geburtstag* (Eisenstadt, 1994).

Christensen, C.B., Lund, J., Olesen, N.W., and Soerensen, J., *Danmark besat. Krig og hverdag 1940–45* (Copenhagen, 2005).

Ciano, Count G., *The Ciano Diaries, 1939–1943*, edited by H. Gibson, reprint (Safety Harbor FL, 2001).

Clark, I., *Legitimacy in International Society* (Oxford, 2005).

Clément, J.-L., *Monseigneur Saliège, archevêque de Toulouse, 1929–1956* (Paris, 1994).

Clogg, R., *Parties and Elections in Greece. The Search for Legitimacy* (London, 1987).

Close, D., (ed.) *The Greek Civil War 1943–1950. Studies of Polarization* (London, 1993).

Conway, M., *Collaboration in Belgium: Léon Degrelle and the Rexist Movement 1940–1944* (New Haven and London, 1993).

Conway, M., *Catholic Politics in Europe 1918–45* (London and New York, 1997).

Conway, M., 'Justice in post-war Belgium: Popular Pressures and Political Realities' in I. Deak, J. Gross and T. Judt (eds) *The Politics of Retribution in Europe* (Princeton, 2000).

Conway, M., 'Legacies of Exile: The Exile Governments in London during the Second World War and the Politics of Post-War Europe' in M. Conway and J. Gotovitch (eds) *Europe in Exile. European Exile Communities in Britain 1940–45* (New York and Oxford, 2001).

Conway, M., 'The Age of Christian Democracy: The Frontiers of Success and Failure', in T. Kselman and J. Buttigieg (eds) *European Christian Democracy. Historical Legacies and Comparative Perspectives* (Notre Dame, 2003).

Conway, M., 'Introduction', *Contemporary European History* XIII (2004).

Conway, M., 'The Greek Civil War: Greek Exceptionalism or Mirror of a European Civil War?' in P. Carabott and T. Sfikas (eds) *The Greek Civil War. Essays on a Conflict of Exceptionalism and Silences* (Aldershot and Burlington VT, 2004).

Conway, M., 'The Rise and Fall of Western Europe's Democratic Age 1945–73', *Contemporary European History* XIII (2004).

Conway, M., 'Belgium's Mid-Twentieth Century Crisis: Crisis of a Nation-State?', *Revue belge d'histoire contemporaine* XXXV (2005).

Cooter, R., Harrison, M., and Sturdy, S., (eds) *War, Medicine and Modernity* (Stroud, 1998).

Corner, P., 'Women in Fascist Italy. Changing Family Roles in the Transition from an Agricultural to an Industrial Society', *European History Quarterly* XXIII (1993).

Coutovidis, J., and Reynolds, J., *Poland 1939–1947* (Leicester, 1987).

Crampton, R.J., *Eastern Europe in the Twentieth Century- and After* 2nd edition (London and New York, 2004).

Cronin, J.E., *The World the Cold War Made: Order, Chaos and the Return of History* (New York and London, 1996).

Cyrulnic, B., *Un merveilleux malheur* (Paris, 2002).

Dahl, H.F., 'Behind the Fronts: Norway', *Journal of Contemporary History* V (1970).

Dahl, H.F., *Quisling. A Study in Treachery* (Cambridge, 1999).

Dahl, H.F., 'Dealing with the Past in Scandinavia: Legal purges and popular memories of Nazism and World War II in Denmark and Norway after 1945' in J. Elster (ed.) *Retribution and Reparation in the Transition to Democracy* (Cambridge and New York, 2005).

Davies, N., *God's Playground* Vol. 2 (Oxford, 1981).

De Grand, A., *Fascist Italy and Nazi Germany. The 'Fascist' Style of Rule* (London and New York, 1995).

De Grand, A., 'Mussolini's Follies: Fascism in its Imperial and Racist Phase, 1935–1940', *Contemporary European History* XIII (2004).

De Grazia, V., *How Fascism Ruled Women: Italy 1922–1945* (Berkeley, 1992).

De Grazia, V., *The Culture of Consent. Mass organization of Leisure in Fascist Italy* (Cambridge, 1981).

De Jong, L., *Het Koninkrijk der Nederlanden in de Tweede Wereldoorlog*, Vols. 1 and 4 (The Hague, 1969 and 1972).

De Jonghe, A., 'La lutte Himmler-Reeder pour la nomination d'un HSSPF à Bruxelles', *Cahiers d'histoire de la seconde guerre mondiale* III (1974), IV (1976), V (1978), VII (1982) and VIII (1984).

Deak, I., Gross, J., and Judt, T., (eds) *The Politics of Retribution in Europe: World War II and its Aftermath* (Princeton, 2000).

Dehli, M., *Fredrikstad under krig og okkupasjon* (Fredrikstad, 1981).

De Rooy, P., 'Een zoekende tijd. De ongemakkelijke democratie, 1913–1949' in R. Aerts et. al. (eds) *Land van kleine gebaren. Een politieke geschiedenis van Nederland, 1780–1990* (Nijmegen, 1999).

Di Febo, G., *Ritos de guerra y de victoria en la España franquista* (Bilbao, 2002).

Díaz, L., *La radio en España, 1923–97* (Madrid, 1997).

Dimitrov, V., 'Revolutions Released: Stalin, the Bulgarian Communist Party, and the Establishment of the Cominform', in F. Gori and S. Pons (eds) *The Soviet Union and Europe in the Cold War, 1945–1953* (Basingstoke, 1996).

Drapac, V., *War and Religion. Catholics in the Churches of Occupied Paris* (Washington DC, 1998).

Duquesne, J., *Les catholiques français sous l'occupation* (Paris, 1966).

Durand, J.-D., 'L'épiscopat italien devant l'occupation allemande, 1943–1945' in J. Sainclivier and C. Bougeard (eds) *La Résistance et les Français* (Rennes, 1995).

Durand, Y., 'Les notables' in J.-P. Azéma and F. Bédarida (eds) *Vichy et les Français* (Paris, 1992).

Durand, Y., and Vivier, R., *Libération des pays de Loire. Blésois, Orléanais, Touraine* (Paris, 1974).

Echternkamp, J., *Nach dem Krieg. Alltagsnot, Neuorientierung und die Last der Vergangenheit 1945–1949* (Zurich, 2003).

Eisterer, K., and Steininger, R., (eds) *Die Option. Südtirol zwischen Faschismus und Nationalsozialismus* (Innsbruck, 1989).

Eley, G., *Forging Democracy. The History of the Left in Europe, 1850–2000* (Oxford and New York, 2002).

Ellwood, D., *Italy 1943–1945* (Leicester, 1985).

Ellwood, D., 'Italy, Europe and the Cold War: The Politics and Economics of Limited Sovereignty' in C. Duggan and C. Wagstaff (eds) *Italy in the Cold War: Politics, Culture and Society, 1948–58* (Oxford, 1995).

Elster, J., *Closing the Books: Transitional Justice in Historical Perspective*, (Cambridge and New York, 2004).

Elvander, N., 'State Intervention and Economic Freedom' in E. Allart et al. (eds) *Nordic Democracy: Ideas, Issues and Institutions in Denmark, Finland, Iceland, Norway and Sweden* (Copenhagen, 1981).

Eriksen, A., 'The Paper Clip War. The Mythology of the Norwegian resistance' in *La résistance et les européens du Nord* (Brussels, 1994).

Faber, J., *Naar wijder horizon* (Utrecht, 1935).

Fábian, G., and Kovács, I.L., *Parlamenti Választások az Európai Unió Országaiban (1945–2002)* (Budapest, 2004).

Falasca-Zamponi, S., *Fascist Spectacle. The Aesthetics of Power in Mussolini's Italy* (Berkeley, 1997).

Farmer, S., *Martyred Village: Commemorating the 1944 Massacre at Oradour-sur-Glane* (Berkeley, 1999).

Farmer, S., 'The Communist Resistance in the Haute Vienne', *French Historical Studies* XIV (1985).

Fasseur, C., *Wilhelmina. Krijgshaftig in een vormeloze jas* (Amsterdam, 2001).

Fischer, E., *Das Ende einer Illusion: Errinerungen 1945–1955* (Vienna, 1973).

Fischer-Galati, S., (ed.) *Man, State, and Society in East European History* (New York, 1970).

Fishman, S., *We Will Wait. Wives of French Prisoners of War, 1940–1945* (New Haven and London, 1991).

Fittko, L., *Escape through the Pyrenees*, trans. D. Koblick (Evanston IL, 2000).

Flonneau, J-M, 'L'évolution de l'opinion publique de 1940 à 1944' in J.-P. Azéma and F. Bédarida (eds) *Vichy et les Français* (Paris, 1992).

Fouilloux, É., *Les chrétiens français entre crise et libération 1937–1947* (Paris, 1997).

Fraenkel, E., *The Dual State* (New York, 1941).

Frank, A., *The Diary of a Young Girl,* eds O.H. Frank and M. Pressler (London, 2001).

Friedländer, S., *Das dritte Reich und die Juden, Die Jahre der Verfolgung 1933–1939* (Munich, 1998).

Frommer, B., 'Retribution against Nazi Collaborators in Post-War Czechoslovakia' (PhD. Thesis, Harvard University, 1999).

Frommer, B., 'Retribution as Legitimation: The Uses of Political Justice in Postwar Czechoslovakia', *Contemporary European History* XIII (2004).

Frommer, B., *National Cleansing. Retribution against Nazi collaborators in postwar Czechoslovakia* (Cambridge, 2005).

Fulbrook, M., *Anatomy of a Dictatorship. Inside the GDR 1949–1989* (Oxford, 1995).

Fulcher, J., 'Sweden' in S. Berger and D. Broughton (eds) *The Force of Labour: the Western European Labour Movement and the Working Class in the Twentieth Century* (Oxford and New York, 1995).

Furet, F., *Le passé d'une illusion. Essai sur l'idée communiste au XXe siècle* (Paris, 1995).

Fusi, J., *Franco. A Biography* (London, 1987).

Gazdag, F., 'A Mouvement Républicane Populaire (1944–1958): Ideológia és gyakorlat a francia MRP politikájaban' in J. Gergely (ed.) *A Keresztény-Demokrácia Nyugat-Európában 1944–1958* (Budapest, 1980).

Gellately, R., *Backing Hitler: Consent and Coercion in Nazi Germany* (Oxford, 2001).

Gellner, E., *Nations and Nationalism* (Ithaca NY, 1983).

Gentile, E., *The Sacralization of Politics in Fascist Italy* (Cambridge MA, 1996).

Gentile, E., 'The Theatre of Politics in Fascist Italy', in G. Berghaus (ed.) *Fascism and Theatre: Comparative Studies on the Aesthetics and Politics of Performance in Europe, 1925–1945* (Providence and Oxford, 1996).

Gérard-Libois, J., and Gotovitch, J., *L'an '40: la Belgique occupée* (Brussels, 1971).

Gildea, R., *The Past in French History* (London and New Haven, 1994).

Gildea, R., *France since 1945* (Oxford and New York, 2002).

Gildea, R., *Marianne in Chains. In Search of the German Occupation, 1940–1945* (London, 2002).

Gildea, R., 'Resistance, Reprisals and Community in Occupied France', *Transactions of the Royal Historical Society* Sixth Series XIII (2003).

Gildea, R., 'Mediators or Time-servers? Local Officials and Notables in the Loire Valley, 1940–1945', in B. De Wever, H. van Goethem and N. Wouters (eds) *Local Government in Occupied Europe (1939–1945)* (Gent, 2005).

Ginsborg, P., *A History of Contemporary Italy, 1943–1988* (Harmondsworth, 1990).

Glassheim, E., 'National Mythologies and Ethnic Cleansing: The Expulsion of Czechoslovak Germans in 1945', *Central European History* XXXIII (2000).

Goldhagen, D.J., *Hitler's Willing Executioners. Ordinary Germans and the Holocaust* (New York, 1996).

Golsan, R.J., 'Henry de Montherlant. Itinerary of an Ambivalent Fascist', in R.J. Golsan (ed.) *Fascism, Aesthetics and Culture* (Hanover NH and London, 1992).

Goubet, M., 'La Haute Garonne' in P. Buton and J.-M. Guillon (eds) *Les pouvoirs en France à la Libération* (Paris, 1994).

Graham, H., 'Popular Culture in the "Years of Hunger"' in H. Graham and J. Labanyi (eds) *Spanish Cultural Studies. An Introduction* (Oxford, 1995).

Graham, H., 'Spain 1936. Resistance and revolution: the flaws in the Front' in T. Kirk and A. McElligott (eds) *Opposing Fascism. Community, Authority and Resistance in Europe* (Cambridge, 1999).

Gramsci, A., *Selections from Prison Notebooks* (London, 1971).

Griffin, R., (ed.) *Fascism* (Oxford, 1995).

Gross, J., *Polish Society under German Occupation. The General Government 1939–44* (Princeton, 1979).

Gross, J., *Neighbors: The Destruction of the Jewish Community in Jedwabne* (Princeton, 2001).

Groult, B. and F., *Journal à quatre mains* (Paris, 1994).

Grugel, J., and Rees, T., *Franco's Spain* (London, 1997).

Grunberger, R., *A Social History of the Third Reich* (Harmondsworth, 1991).

Guillon, J., 'La résistance au village' in J. Sainclivier and C. Bougeard (eds) *La Résistance et les Français* (Rennes, 1995).

Gumz, J., '*Wehrmacht* Perceptions of Mass Violence in Croatia, 1941–2', *Historical Journal* XLIV (2001).

Gundle, S., *Between Hollywood and Moscow. The Italian Communists and the Challenge of Mass Culture 1943–1991* (Durham NC and London, 2000).

Haffner, S., *Geschichte eines Deutschen. Die Erinnerungen 1914–1933* (Stuttgart and Munich, 2000).

Hake, S., *Popular Cinema of the Third Reich* (Austin, 2001).

Hanisch, E., *Der Lange Schatten des Staates. Österreichische Gesellschafts-geschichte im 20. Jahrhundert* (Vienna, 1994).

Hausmann, F., *Kleine Geschichte Italiens von 1945 bis Berlusconi* (Berlin, 2002).

Hay, J., *Popular Film Culture in Fascist Italy: the Passing of the Rex* (Bloomington IN, 1987).

Herf, J., *The Jewish Enemy. Nazi Ideology and Propaganda during World War II and the Holocaust* (Cambridge MA, 2006).

Heumos, P., 'Aspekte des Sozialen Millieus der Industriearbeiterschaft in der Tscheslowakei vom Ende des Zweiten Weltkriegs bis zur Reformbewegung der Sechziger Jahre', *Bohemia* XLII (2001).

Hiden, J., and Farquharson, J., *Explaining Hitler's Germany,* 2nd edition (London, 1989).

Hirschfeld, G., *Fremdherrschaft und Kollaboration. Die Niederlande unter deutscher Besatzung 1940–1945* (Stuttgart, 1984).

Hitchcock, W.I., *The Struggle for Europe: A History of the Continent since 1945* (London, 2003).

Hitchins, K., *Rumania 1866–1947* (New York and Oxford, 1994).

Hitler, A., *Mein Kampf,* ed. D.C. Watt (London, 1969).

Hobsbawm, E., *Age of Extremes. The Short Twentieth Century 1914–1991* (London, 1995).

Hobsbawm, E., *Bandits* (London, 1969).

Holguín, S., *Creating Spaniards: Culture and National Identity in Republican Spain* (Madison, 2002).

Hondros, J., *Occupation and Resistance. The Greek Agony 1941–1944* (New York, 1983).

Horváth, J., 'A Democrazia Cristiana' in J. Gergely (ed.) *A Keresztény-Demokrácia Nyugat-Európában 1944–1958* (Budapest, 1980).

Houwink ten Cate, J., and Otto, G., (eds) *Das organisierte Chaos. 'Ämterdarwin-ismus' und 'Gesinnungsethik' Determinanten nationalsozialistsicher Besatzungs-herrschaft* (Berlin, 1999).

Hudson, M.C., *Arab Politics: The Search for Legitimacy* (New Haven and London, 1977).

Huizinga, J.H., *Nederlands geestesmark* (Leiden 1935).

Hunya, G., (ed.) *Románia 1944–1990: Gazdaság- és Politikatörténete* (Budapest, 1990).

Hurstfield, J.G., *America and the French Nation 1939–1945* (Chapel Hill and London, 1986).

Iatrides, J., (ed.) *Greece in the 1940s. A Nation in Crisis* (Hanover NH, 1981).

Iklé, F.C., *Every War Must End,* 2nd edition (New York, 2005).

Irons, J., 'Staging Reconciliation: Popular Theatre and Political Utopia in France in 1937', *Contemporary European History* XIV (2005).

Iverson, G., 'Norway', in T. Soila (ed.) *Nordic National Cinemas* (London and New York, 1998).

Izsák, L., and Kun, M., (eds) *Moszkvának Jelentjük…: Titkos dokumentumok 1944–1948* (Budapest, 1994).

Jackson, J., *France. The Dark Years 1940–1944* (Oxford, 2001).

Jankowski, P., *Communism and Collaboration: Simon Sabiani and Politics in Marseille, 1919–1944* (New Haven and London, 1989).

Jarausch, K., 'Care and Coercion: the GDR as Welfare Dictatorship' in K. Jarausch (ed.) *Dictatorship as Experience. Towards a Socio-Cultural History of the GDR* (New York and Oxford, 1999).

Joas, H., *War and Modernity* (Oxford, 2003).

Joly, L., 'Les débuts de l'Action Française (1899–1914) ou l'élaboration d'un nationalisme antisémite', *Revue historique* 308 (2006).

Judt, T., 'Introduction' in T. Judt (ed.) *Resistance and Revolution in Mediterranean Europe 1939–1948* (London and New York, 1989).

Judt, T., *Postwar: A History of Europe since 1945* (London, 2005).

Jussila, O., Hentilä, S., and Nevakivi, J., *From Grand Duchy to Modern State: A Political History of Finland since 1809* (London, 1999).

Kalyvas, S., *The Logic of Violence in Civil War* (Cambridge, 2006).

Kanstrup, J., and Ousager, S., (eds) *Kommunal opgaveløsning 1842–1970* (Odense, 1990).

Karakasidou, A., *Fields of Wheat, Hills of Blood. Passages to Nationhood in Greek Macedonia 1870–1990* (Chicago and London, 1997).

Kedward, H.R., *Resistance in Vichy France* (Oxford, 1978).

Kedward, H.R., 'The Vichy of the other Philippe' in G. Hirschfeld and P. Marsh (eds) *Collaboration in France: Politics and Culture during the Nazi Occupation 1940–1944* (Oxford, 1989).

Kedward, H.R., *In Search of the Maquis: Rural Resistance in Southern France, 1942–1944* (Oxford, 1993).

Kedward, H.R., 'Introduction: Ici commence la France libre' in H.R. Kedward and N. Wood (eds) *The Liberation of France. Image and Event* (Oxford, 1995).

Kershaw, I., *Popular Opinion and Political Dissent in the Third Reich. Bavaria 1933–1945* (Oxford, 1983).

Kershaw, I., *The Hitler Myth. Image and Reality in the Third Reich* (Oxford, 1987).

Kershaw, I., '"Working towards the Führer": reflections on the nature of the Hitler Dictatorship' in I. Kershaw and M. Lewin (eds) *Stalinism and Nazism. Dictatorships in Comparison* (Cambridge, 1997).

Kershaw, I., *Hitler 1936–1945 Nemesis* (London, 2000).

Kershaw, I., 'War and Political Violence in Twentieth-Century Europe', *Contemporary European History* XIV (2005).

Kertzer, D., *Ritual, Politics and Power* (New Haven and London, 1988).

Keynes, J.M., *Economic Consequences of the Peace* (New York, 1920).

King, J., *Budweisers into Czechs and Germans: a Local History of Bohemian Politics, 1848–1948* (Princeton, 2002).

Kjeldstadli, K., *Et splittet samfunn 1905–1935. Norgeshistorie*. Vol. 10 (Oslo, 1994).

Klambauer, O., *Der Kalte Krieg in Österreich. Vom Dritten Mann zum Fall des Eisernen Vorhangs* (Vienna, 2000).

Knight, R., 'Denazification and Intergration in the Austrian Province of Carinthia', *The Journal of Modern History* LXXIX (2007).

Knox, M., 'Fascist Regime and Territorial Expansion: Italy and Germany', reprinted in A.A. Kallis (ed.) *The Fascism Reader* (London, 2003).

Koliopoulos, J.S., *Plundered Loyalties: World War II and Civil War in Greek West Macedonia* (New York, 1999).

Konrád, G., *Geluk* (Amsterdam, 2002).

Koonz, C., *Mothers in the Fatherland. Women, the Family and Nazi Politics* (London, 1986).

Koonz, C., *The Nazi Conscience* (Cambridge MA, 2003).

Koreman, M., *The Expectation of Justice. France 1944–46* (Durham NC and London, 1999).

Kossmann, E., *The Low Countries 1780–1940* (Oxford, 1978).

Kreimeier, K., *Die Ufa-story. Geschichte eines Filmkonzerns* (Munich, 1992).

Kroener, B.R., Müller, R.-D., and Umbreit, H., *Das deutsche Reich und der zweite Weltkrieg* Vol. 5: *Organisation und Mobilisierung des deutschen Machtbereichs* Part One: *Kriegsverwaltung, Wirtschaft und Personelle Ressourcen 1939–1941* (Stuttgart, 1988).

Kunze, T., *Nicolae Ceauşescu: o biografie* (Bucharest, 2002).

La Gorce, P.-M. de, *Naissance de la France Moderne* Vol. 1, *L'Après Guerre* (Paris, 1978).

Laborie, P., *L'opinion française sous Vichy* (Paris, 1990).

Laborie, P., 'Vichy et ses représentations dans l'imaginaire social' in J.-P. Azéma and F. Bédarida (eds) *Vichy et les Français* (Paris, 1992).

Laborie, P., '1940–1944: Double-Think in France' in S. Fishman *et al.* (eds) *France at War: Vichy and the Historians* (Oxford and New York, 2000).

Lagrou, P., 'Victims of Genocide and National Memory: Belgium, France and the Netherlands, 1945–1965', *Past and Present,* No. 154 (1997).

Lagrou, P., *The Legacy of Nazi Occupation: Patriotic Memory and National Recovery in Western Europe, 1945–1965* (Cambridge and New York, 2000).

Lammers, C.J., 'Levels of Collaboration. A Comparative Study of German Occupation Regimes during the Second World War', *The Netherlands Journal of Social Sciences* XXXIII (1995).

Lampe, J.R., *Yugoslavia as History. Twice there was a Country* (Cambridge, 1996).

Landy, M., 'Culture and Politics in the Work of Antonio Gramsci', *boundary 2,* XIV (1986).

Larsen, S.U., 'Kommunalforordningen', in H.F. Dahl *et al.* (eds) *Norsk Krigsleksikon* (Oslo 1995).

Le Maner, Y., 'Town Councils of the Nord and Pas-de-Calais region: local power, French power, German power', in T. Kirk and A. McElligott (eds) *Opposing Fascism. Community, Authority and Resistance in Europe* (Cambridge, 1999).

Lecornu, B., *Un Préfet sous l'Occupation allemande* (Paris, 1997).

Leffler, M.P., and Painter, D.S., (eds) *Origins of the Cold War: An International History,* 2nd edition (New York and London, 2005).

Leval, G., *Collectives in the Spanish Revolution* (London, 1975).

Lévy, C., and Veillon, D., 'Propagande et modelage des esprits' in J.-P. Azéma and F. Bédarida (eds) *Vichy et les Français* (Paris, 1992).

Lewis, A., 'A Turbulent Priest? The Forbin-Janson Affair (1824–1839)', *French History* XIX (2005).

Lewis, J., 'Austria 1950: Strikes, "Putsch" and their Political Context', *European History Quarterly* XXX (2000).

Lilly, C.S., *Power and Persuasion: Ideology and Rhetoric in Communist Yugoslavia 1944–1953* (Boulder CO and Oxford, 2001).

Lindenberger, T., (ed.) *Herrschaft und Eigensinn in der Diktatur* (Cologne, 1999).

Linz, J., 'The Breakdown of Democratic Regimes. Crisis, Breakdown and Reequilibriation' in J. Linz and A. Stepan (eds) *The Breakdown of Democratic Regimes* (Baltimore and London, 1978).

Linz, J., and Shain, Y., *Between States. Interim Governments and Democratic Transitions* (Cambridge, 1995).

Linz, J., and Stepan, A., (eds) *The Breakdown of Democratic Regimes* (Baltimore and London, 1978).

Lloyd, C., 'Divided Loyalties: Singing in the Occupation,' in H. Dauncey and S. Cannon (eds) *Popular Music in France from Chanson to Techno* (Aldershot, 2003).

Lorentzen, S., 'Norsk lokalforvaltning under førerprincippet. Okkupasjonstidens kommunale nyordning 1940–1945', in S.U. Larsen, (ed.) *Fra idé til dom. Noen trekk fra utviklingen av Nasjonal Samling* (1976).

Lowry, S., 'Heinz Rühmann – The Archetypal German', in T. Bergfelder, E. Carter and D. Göktürk (eds) *The German Cinema Book* (London, 2002).

Lucas, C., *The Structure of the Terror: the Example of Javogues and the Loire* (Oxford, 1973).

Lukes, I., *Czechoslovakia Between Stalin and Hitler: The Diplomacy of Edvard Beneš in the 1930s* (New York, 1996).

Lun, M., *NS-Herrschaft in Südtirol. Die Operationszone Alpenvorland 1943–1945* (Innsbruck, 2004).

Maerten, F., 'Résistance et société en Hainaut belge. Histoire d'une brève rencontre' in R. Vandenbussche (ed.) *L'engagement dans la Résistance (France du Nord – Belgique)* (Lille, 2003).

Maier, C., 'Two Post-war Eras and the Conditions for Stability in Twentieth-Century Western Europe' *American Historical Review* LXXXVI (1981).

Malcolm, N., *Bosnia. A Short History* (London, 1994).

Mann, M., *Fascists* (Cambridge, 2004).

Mann, M., *The Sources of Social Power* Vol. 2 (Cambridge, 1993).

Mannheim, K., *Man and Society in an Age of Reconstruction* (London, 1940).

Mason, T., *Nazism, Fascism and the Working Class* (Cambridge, 1995).

Mastny, V., *The Czechs under Nazi Rule. The Failure of National Resistance 1939– 1942* (New York, 1971).

Matesis, P., *The Daughter* (London, 2002).

Matless, D., *Landscape and Englishness* (London, 1998).

Mazower, M., *Inside Hitler's Greece. The Experience of Occupation 1941–44* (New Haven and London, 1993).

Mazower, M., *Dark Continent: Europe's Twentieth Century* (London, 1998).

Mazower, M., 'Structures of authority in the Greek resistance, 1941–1944', in T. Kirk and A. McGelligott, (eds) *Opposing Fascism. Community, Authority and Resistance in Europe* (Cambridge, 1999).

Mazower, M., (ed.) *After the War Was Over: Reconstructing the Family, Nation and State in Greece, 1943–1960* (Princeton and London, 2000).

Mazower, M., 'Violence and the State in the Twentieth Century', *American Historical Review* CVII (2002).

McDougall, A., *Youth Politics in East Germany. The Free German Youth Movement 1946–1968* (Oxford, 2004).

Meershoek, G., *Dienaren van het gezag: de Amsterdamse politie tijdens de bezetting* (Amsterdam, 1999).

Mencherini, R., *Guerre froide, grèves rouges* (Paris, 1998).

Metzger, T., *Escape from Predicament. Neo-Confucianism and China's Evolving Political Culture* (New York, 1977).

Mevius, M., *Agents of Moscow: The Hungarian Communist Party and the Origins of Socialist Patriotism 1941–1953* (Oxford, 2005).

Mikolajczyk, S., *The Rape of Poland. Pattern of Soviet Aggression* (New York and Toronto, 1948).

Millar, G., *Maquis* (London, 1945).

Miller, W.C., Plasser, F., and Ulram, P.A., 'Wähler und Mitglieder der ÖVP, 1945–1994' in R. Kriechbaumer and F. Schausberger (eds) *Volkspartei – Anspruch und Realität: Zur Geschichte der ÖVP seit 1945* (Vienna, 1995).

Mitchell, M., 'Materialism and Secularism: CDU Politicians and National Socialism, 1945–1949', *Journal of Modern History* LXVII (1995).

Moeller, R., *German Peasants and Agrarian Politics, 1914–1924. The Rhineland and Westphalia* (Chapel Hill, 1986).

Mommsen, W., 'Max Weber's Theory of Legitimacy Today' in W. Mommsen *The Political and Social Theory of Max Weber* (Oxford, 1989).

Moore, B., (ed.) *Resistance in Western Europe* (Oxford, 2000).

Moreno Gómez, F., *Córdoba en la posguerra: la represión y la guerrilla, 1939–50* (Córdoba, 1987).

Morgan, K.O., *The People's Peace: British History, 1945–1990* (Oxford and New York, 1990).

Muel-Dreyfus, F., *Vichy and the Eternal Feminine. A Contribution to a Political Sociology of Gender,* trans. K.A. Johnson (Durham NC and London, 2001).

Müller, K., 'Vaterländische und nazistische Fest- und Weihespiele in Österreich', in H. Haider-Pregler and B. Reiterer (eds) *Verspielte Zeit. Österreichisches Theater der dreissiger Jahre* (Vienna, 1997).

Mulley, K-D., 'Wo ist das Proletariat?' in G. Jagschitz and K-D. Mulley (eds) *Die 'Wilden' Fünfziger Jahre: Gesellschaft, Formen und Gefühle eines Jahrzehnts in Österreich* (St Pölten and Vienna, 1985).

Mulley, K-D., 'Der Österreichische Gewerkschaftsbund 1945–1959' in W. Maderthaner (ed.) *Auf dem Weg zur Macht. Integration in den Staat, Sozialpartnerschaft und Regierungspartei* (Vienna, 1992).

Myant, M., *Socialism and Democracy in Czechoslovakia, 1945–1948* (Cambridge and New York, 1981).

Naimark, N., *The Russians in Germany, 1945–1949* (Harvard, 1997).

Nash, M., 'Pronatalism and Motherhood in Franco's Spain' in G. Bock and P. Thane (eds) *Maternity and Gender Policies: Women and the Rise of the European Welfare States, 1880s–1950s* (London, 1994).

Niethammer, L., 'Alliierte Internierungslager in Deutschland nach 1945. Vergleich und offene Fragen' in C. Jansen (ed.) *Von der Aufgabe der Freiheit. Politische Verantwortung und bürgerliche Gesellschaft im 19. und 20. Jahrhundert* (Berlin, 1995).

Nøkleby, B., *Nyordning. Norge i Krig* Vol. 2 (Oslo, 1985).

Oestergaard, U., *Peasants and Danes: The Danish National Identity and Political Culture. Comparative Studies of Society and History* 34 (Copenhagen 1992).

Osmond, J., *Rural Protest in the Weimar Republic. The Free Peasantry in the Rhineland and Bavaria* (Basingstoke and London, 1993).

Otero Urtaza, E., *Las misiones pedagógicas: una experiencia de educación popular* (Coruña, 1982).

Page, E., *Localism and Centralism in Europe: The Political and Legal Bases of Local Self-Government* (Oxford, 1991).

Passerini, L., *Fascism in Popular Memory. The Cultural Experience of the Turin Working Class* (Cambridge, 1987).

Patterson, H., *Ireland since 1939* (Oxford and New York, 2002).

Pavone, C., *Una guerra civile: saggio storico sulla moralità nella resistenza* (Turin, 1991).

Paxton, R., *The Anatomy of Fascism* (London, 2004).

Perez de Olaguer, A., *'Piedras Vivas': biografía del Capellán Requeté José Mª Lamamié de Clairac y Alonso* (San Sebastián, 1939).

Perlmutter, A., *The Military and Politics in Modern Times: On Professionals, Praetorians, and Revolutionary Soldiers* (New Haven, 1977).

Peschanski, D., 'Legitimacy/Legitimation/Delegitimation: France in the Dark Years, a textbook case', *Contemporary European History* XIII (2004).

Pétain, P., *Actes et écrits* edited by. J. Isorni (Paris, 1974).

Pető, A., 'Memory and the Narrative of Rape in Budapest and Vienna in 1945' in R. Bessel and D. Schumann (eds) *Life after Death. Approaches to a Cultural and Social History of Europe during the 1940s and 1950s* (Washington DC, 2003).

Peukert, D., *Inside Nazi Germany. Conformity, Opposition and Racism in Everyday Life* (London, 1987).

Pinto, A.C., *Salazar's Dictatorship and European Fascism: Problems of Interpretation* (Boulder CO, 1995).

Pipes, R., *A Concise History of the Russian Revolution,* 2nd edition (New York, 1996).

Pittaway, M., 'Industrial Workers, Socialist Industrialization and the State in Hungary, 1948–1958' (PhD. thesis, University of Liverpool, 1998).

Pittaway, M., 'The Reproduction of Hierarchy: Skill, Working-Class Culture and the State in Early Socialist Hungary', *The Journal of Modern History* LXXIV (2002).

Pittaway, M., 'Retreat from Collective Protest: Household, Gender, Work and Popular Opposition in Stalinist Hungary' in J. Kok (ed.) *Rebellious Families: Household Strategies and Collective Action in the Nineteenth and Twentieth Centuries* (New York and Oxford, 2002).

Pittaway, M., *Eastern Europe 1939–2000* (London, 2004).

Pittaway, M., 'The Politics of Legitimacy and Hungary's Postwar Transition', *Contemporary European History* XIII (2004).

Pittaway, M., 'Workers in Hungary' in E. Breuning, J. Lewis and G. Pritchard (eds) *Power and the People. A Social History of Central European Politics, 1945–56* (Manchester and New York, 2005).

Poiger, U.G., *Jazz, Rock and Rebels: Cold War Politics and American Culture in a Divided Germany* (Berkeley, London and Los Angeles, 2000).

Poulsen, H., 'Denmark at War? The Occupation as History' in S. Ekman and N. Edling (eds) *War Experience, Self Image and National Identity: The Second World War as Myth and History* (Södertälje, 1997).

Preston, P., *Franco* (London, 1993).

Pritchard, G., *The Making of the GDR 1945–53: From Antifascism to Stalinism* (Manchester and New York, 2000).

Procès du Maréchal Pétain, Le (Paris, 1945).

Prost, A., (ed.) *La Résistance: une histoire sociale* (Paris, 1997).

Prost, A., 'Representations of War in the Cultural History of France' in J. Winter and H. McPhail (eds) *Republican Identities in War and Peace* (Oxford and New York, 2002).

Quine, M.S., *Population Policies in Twentieth-Century Europe: Fascist Dictatorships and Liberal Democracies* (London, 1996).

Quine, M.S., *Italy's Social Revolution: Charity and Welfare from Liberalism to Fascism* (Basingstoke, 2002).

Raguer, H., *La pólvora y el incienso: La Iglesia y la Guerra Civil española, 1936–1939* (Barcelona, 2001).

Reid, S.E., and Crowley, D. (eds) *Style and Socialism: Modernity and Material Culture in Post-war Eastern Europe* (Oxford and New York, 2000).

Reynebeau, M., 'L'homme sans qualités' in *Les années trente en Belgique* (Brussels, 1994).

Reynolds, D., (ed.) *The Origins of the Cold War in Europe: International Perspectives* (New Haven and London, 1994).

Reynolds S., *France between the Wars: Gender and Politics* (London and New York, 1996).

Richards, M., *A Time of Silence: Civil War and the Culture of Repression in Franco's Spain, 1936–1945* (Cambridge, 1998).

Richards, M., '"Terror and Progress": Industrialization, Modernity and the Making of Francoism' in H. Graham and J. Labanyi (eds) *Spanish Cultural Studies: An Introduction* (Oxford, 1995).

Rieber, A.J., 'The Crack in the Plaster: Crisis in Romania and the Origins of the Cold War', *The Journal of Modern History* LXXVI (2004).

Rigby, T.H., and Feher, F., (eds) *Political Legitimation in Communist States* (London, 1982).

Rigby, T.H., 'Political Legitimacy, Weber and Communist Mono-Organisational Systems' in T.H. Rigby and F. Feher (eds) *Political Legitimation in Communist States* (London and Basingstoke, 1982).

Roberts, M.L., *Civilization Without Sexes: Reconstructing Gender in Postwar France, 1917–1927* (Chicago, 1994).

Rokkan, S., 'The Growth and Structuring of Mass Politics', in E. Allart et al. (eds) *Nordic Democracy: Ideas, Issues and Institutions in Denmark, Finland, Iceland, Norway and Sweden* (Copenhagen, 1981).

Roksandic, D., 'Shifting References: Celebrations of Uprisings in Croatia, 1945–1991', *East European Politics and Societies* IX (1999).

Romein, J., and Romein-Verschoor, A., *Erflaters van onze Beschaving* (Amsterdam, 1939).

Romijn, P., 'Did Soldiers become Governors? Liberators, Resistance, and the Reconstruction of Local Government in the Liberated Netherlands, 1944–1945' in C. Brower (ed.) *World War II in Europe. The Final Year* (New York, 1998).

Romijn, P., 'Niederlande – "Synthese", Säuberung und Integration' in U. Herbert and A. Schildt (eds) *Kriegsende in Europa; vom Beginn des deutschen Machtzerfalls bis zur Stabilisierung der Nachkriegsordnung 1944–1948* (Essen, 1998).

Romijn, P., 'Ambitions and Dilemmas of Local Authorities in the German-occupied Netherlands, 1940–1945', in B. de Wever, H. van Goethem and N. Wouters (eds) *Local Government in Occupied Europe (1939–1945)* (Gent, 2005).

Romijn, P., *Burgemeesters in oorlogstijd. Besturen onder Duitse bezetting* (Amsterdam, 2006).

Ross, C., *Constructing Socialism at the Grass-Roots. The Transformation of East Germany, 1945–65* (Basingstoke, 2000).

Ross, C., *The East German Dictatorship. Problems and Perspectives in the Interpretation of the GDR* (London, 2002).

Rothschild, J., *East Central Europe between the Two World Wars* (Seattle, 1974).

Rousso, H., *Le syndrome de Vichy* (Paris, 1987).

Sabetti, F., *The Search for Good Government. Understanding the Paradox of Italian Democracy* (Montreal, 2000).

Sabrow, M., 'Dictatorship as Discourse. Cultural Perspectives on SED Legitimacy' in K. Jarausch (ed.) *Dictatorship as Experience. Towards a Socio-Cultural History of the GDR* (New York and Oxford, 1999).

Sainclivier, J., *La résistance en Ille-et-Vilaine, 1940–1944* (Rennes, 1993).

Samuelsson, K., *From Great Power to Welfare State: 300 Years of Swedish Social Development* (London, 1968).

Sandgruber, R., 'Der Lebenstandard in der ersten Nachkriegszeit' in S. Karner (ed.) *Das Burgenland im Jahr 1945* (Eisenstadt, 1985).

Sarti, R., *Long Live the Strong. A History of Rural Society in the Apennine Mountains* (Amherst MA., 1985).

Sassoon, D., 'Italy after Fascism: the Predicament of Dominant Narratives' in R. Bessel and D. Schumann (eds) *Life after Death. Approaches to a Cultural and Social History of Europe during the 1940s and 1950s* (Washington DC, 2003).

Saz Campos, I., *Fascismo y franquismo* (Valencia, 2004).

Schama, S., *Landscape and Memory* (London, 1995).

Schelsky, H., *Die skeptische Generation: Eine Soziologie der deutschen Jugend* (Düsseldorf, 1957).

Schlag, G., (ed.) *Burgenland: Geschichte, Kultur und Wirtschaft in Biographen. XX. Jahrhundert* (Eisenstadt, 1991).

Schwarzenbach, A., 'Royal Photographs: Emotions for the People', *Contemporary European History* XIII (2004).

Semelin, J., *Sans armes face à Hitler* (Paris, 1998).

Serrano, S., *Maquis: historia de la guerrilla antifranquista* (Madrid, 2001).

Severini, E., *Munkaverseny és a Magyar Munkás Lelkisége: MÁVAG és a Csepeli WM Müvek* (Budapest, 1946).

Shennan, A., *Rethinking France: Plans for Renewal 1940–1946* (Oxford, 1989).

Skinner, Q., *The Foundations of Modern Political Thought,* Vol. 1 (Cambridge, 1978).

Snyder, T., 'The Causes of Ukrainian-Polish Ethnic Cleansing 1943', *Past and Present* No. 179 (May 2003).

Soila, T., (ed.) *Nordic National Cinemas* (London and New York, 1998).

Spiker, M., *Hollywood unterm Hakenkreuz. Der amerikanische Spielfilm im Dritten Reich* (Trier, 1999).

Spitzer, A., 'The elections of 1824 and 1827 in the department of the Doubs', *French History* III (1989).

Stadtland, H., *Herrschaft nach Plan und Macht der Gewohnheit: Sozialgeschichte der Gewerkschaften in der SBZ/DDR 1945–1953* (Essen, 2001).

Stahr, G., *Volksgemeinschaft vor der Leinwand? Der nationalsozialistische Film und sein Publikum* (Berlin, 2001).

Stalin, J., *History of the Communist Party of the Soviet Union (Bolsheviks): Short Course* (New York, 1939).

Steigmann-Gall, R., *The Holy Reich. Nazi Conceptions of Christianity 1919–1945* (Cambridge, 2003).

Steinberg, J., *Why Switzerland?* 2nd edn (Cambridge, 1996).

Stengers, J., *Les racines de la Belgique* Vol. 1 (Brussels, 2000).

Sternhell, Z., *La droite révolutionnaire 1885–1914. Les origines françaises du fascisme* 2nd edn (Paris, 2000).

Taylor, L., *Between Resistance and Collaboration. Popular Protest in Northern France, 1940–45* (Basingstoke and New York, 2000).

Taylor, R., *The Word in Stone. The Role of Architecture in the National Socialist Ideology* (Berkeley and London, 1974).

Teichova, A., 'The Protectorate of Bohemia and Moravia (1939–1945): the economic dimension', in M. Teich (ed.) *Bohemia in History* (Cambridge, 1998).

Teissier du Cros, J., *Divided Loyalties: A Scotswoman in Occupied France* (republished Edinburgh, 1992).

Te Velde, H., *Gemeenschapszin en Plichtsbesef. Liberalisme en Nationalisme in Nederland, 1870–1918* (The Hague, 1992).

Tismaneanu, V., *Stalinism for All Seasons. A Political History of Romanian Communism* (Berkeley, 2003).

Todorov, T., *A French Tragedy: Scenes of Civil War, Summer 1944* (Hanover NH, 1996).

Tomasevich, J., *The Chetniks* (Stanford, 1975).

Tomasevich, J., *War and Revolution in Yugoslavia, 1941–1945. Occupation and Collaboration* (Stanford, 2001).

Tooze, J.A., *The Wages of Destruction: The Making and Breaking of the Nazi Economy* (London, 2006).

Toranska, T., *Oni. Stalin's Polish Puppets* (London, 1987).

d'Udekem d'Acoz, M.-P., *Pour le Roi et la Patrie. La noblesse belge dans la Résistance* (Brussels, 2002).

Umbreit, H., *Der Militärbefehlshaber in Frankreich 1940–1944* (Boppard am Rhein, 1968).

Van Bolhuis, J.J., (ed.) *Onderdrukking en Verzet. Nederland in Oorlogstijd* Vol. 1 (Amsterdam and Arnhem, 1950).

Vande Winkel, R., and Welch, D., (eds) *Cinema and the Swastika* (Houndmills, 2007).

Van der Zee, N., *Om erger te voorkomen* (Amsterdam, 1997).

Van Gelderen, J., Geyl, P., Kraemer, H., Sassen, F., and Van Schelven, A.A., *Nederland Erfdeel en Taak* (Amsterdam, 1940).

Van Yperseele, L., *Le Roi Albert. Histoire d'un mythe* (Ottignies, 1995).

Verhoeyen, E., *La Belgique occupée* (Brussels, 1994).

Vickers, M., *Albania: A Modern History* (London, 1999).

Vidal Castaño, J.A., *La memoria reprimida: historias orales del maquis* (Valencia, 2004).

Vincent, M., 'The Martyrs and the Saints: Masculinity and the Construction of the Francoist Crusade', *History Workshop Journal* XLVII (1999).

Vincent, M., 'The Keys of the Kingdom: Religious Violence in the Spanish Civil War, July-August 1936' in C. Ealham and M. Richards (eds) *The Splintering of Spain: New Historical Perspectives on the Spanish Civil War* (Cambridge, 2004).

Vinen, R., *Bourgeois Politics in France, 1945–1951* (Cambridge and New York, 1995).

Virgili, F., *Shorn Women. Gender and Punishment in Liberation France* (Oxford, 2002).

Vrints, A., 'Patronen van polarisatie. Homicide in België tijdens de Tweede Wereldoorlog', *Cahiers d'Histoire du Temps Présent – Bijdragen tot de Eigentijdse Geschiedenis* XV (2005).

Wachtel, A.B., *Making a Nation, Breaking a Nation: Literature and Cultural Politics in Yugoslavia* (Stanford, 1998).

Wagnleitner, R., *Coca-Colonization and the Cold War: The Cultural Mission of the United States in Austria after the Second World War* (Chapel Hill, 1994).

Wall, I., *French Communism in the Era of Stalin. The Quest for Unity and Integration, 1945–1962* (Westport, 1983).

Warner, G., 'Allies, Government and Resistance: The Belgian Political Crisis of November 1944', *Transactions of the Royal Historical Society* Fifth Series XXVIII (1978).

Wassermann, H.P., *Naziland Österreich!? Studien zu Antisemitismus, Nation und Nationalsozialismus in öffentlichen Meinungsbild* (Innsbruck, 2002).

Watts, J., *Henry VI and the Politics of Kingship* (Cambridge, 1996).

Weber, E., *Peasants into Frenchmen: The Modernization of Rural France* (London, 1977).

Weber, F., 'Die Angst der Parteiführung vorm Klassenkampf. Die SPÖ 1945–1950' in P. Pelinka and G. Steger (eds) *Auf dem Weg zur Staatspartei. Zur Geschichte und Politik der SPÖ seit 1945* (Vienna, 1988).

Weber, M., *The Theory of Social and Economic Organization* (New York, 1964).

Weber, M., *Economy and Society*, edited by G. Roth and C. Wittich (New York, 1968).

Weir, S. and Beetham, D., *Political Power and Democratic Control in Britain* (London, 1999).

Welch, D., *The Third Reich. Politics and Propaganda* (London and New York, 1993).

Welzer, H., *Täter. Wie aus ganz normalen Menschen Massenmörder werden* (Frankfurt a/M., 2005).

Widder, R., 'Volkspartei im Burgenland' in R. Kriechbaumer and F. Schausberger (eds) *Volkspartei – Anspruch und Realität: Zur Geschichte der ÖVP seit 1945* (Vienna, Cologne and Weimar, 1995).

Widdig, B., *Culture and Inflation in Weimar Germany* (Berkeley, 2001).

Wildt, M., *Auf kleinen Wohlstand: Eine Komsumgeschichte der fünfziger Jahre* (Frankfurt a/M., 1996).

Willson, P., 'Women in Fascist Italy' in R. Bessel (ed.) *Fascist Italy and Nazi Germany. Comparisons and Contrasts* (Cambridge, 1996).

Willson, P., *Peasant Women and Politics in Fascist Italy. The* Massaie Rurali (London and New York, 2002).

Winter, J., *Sites of Memory, Sites of Mourning: The Great War in European Cultural History* (Cambridge, 1995).

Winter, J., and Sivan, E., (eds) *War and Remembrance in the Twentieth Century* (Cambridge, 1999).

Wirsching, A., 'Political violence in France and Italy after 1918', *Journal of Modern European History* I (2003).

Wolff, R.J., and Hoensch, J.K., (eds) *Catholics, the State and the European Radical Right 1919–1945* (Boulder CO, 1987).

Woller, H., *Die Abrechnung mit den Faschismus in Italien 1945 bis 1948* (Munich, 1996).

Woller, H., *Rom, 28. Oktober 1922. Die faschistische Herausforderung* (Munich, 1999).

Wouters, N., *Oorlogsburgemeesters 40/44. Lokaal bestuur en collaboratie in België* (Tielt, 2004).

Wouters, N., 'New Order and Good Government: Municipal Administration in Belgium (1938–46)', *Contemporary European History* XIII (2004).

Wouters, N., 'Localisation in the age of centralisation: local government in Belgium and Nord-Pas-de-Calais (1940–1944)', in B. De Wever, H. van Goethem and N. Wouters (eds) *Local Government in Occupied Europe (1939–1945)* (Gent, 2005).

Wouters, N., *De Führerstaat: Overheid en collaboratie in België (1940–1944)* (Tielt, 2006).

Wylie, L., *Village in the Vaucluse,* 3rd edition (Cambridge MA and London, 1974).

Zimmerer, J., 'The Birth of *Ostland* Out of the Spirit of Colonialism: A Postcolonial Perspective on the Nazi Policy of Conquest and Extermination', *Patterns of Prejudice*, IXL (2005).

Index